THE SWORD AND THE GRAIL

THE SWORD
AND THE GRAIL

ANDREW SINCLAIR

Birlinn

This edition published in 2005 by
Birlinn Limited
West Newington House
10 Newington Road
EH9 1QS

www.birlinn.co.uk

First published in 1992 by
Crown Publishers Inc., New York,

ISBN10: 1 84158 396 0
ISBN13: 978 1 84158 396 9

British Library Cataloguing-in-Publication Data
A catalogue record for this book is available from the British Library

Typeset by Hewer Text, Edinburgh
Printed and bound by Nørhaven Paperback, Viborg

Dedicated to NIVEN SINCLAIR *without whose support
and research this book would not have been written*

Contents

I

A Quest

A SWORD AND a Grail in the shape of a chalice are carved on a stone in Rosslyn Chapel near Edinburgh in Scotland. The sword points to an early landfall and discovery of North America nearly a century before Columbus reached the West Indies. The steps of the Temple of Solomon incised into the base of the Grail initiate an investigation into the fate of the Knights Templars, who were officially dissolved early in the fourteenth century, but who have continued to exist to this day. They were reported to be the seekers and keepers of the Holy Grail – so Wolfram von Eschenbach wrote in his *Parzifal* – and of the Stone of Scone or Destiny and the Shroud of Turin. Some of them were known to have escaped to Scotland from France with their fleet and their treasure. Their symbols and associated rites evolved into the practices of the Masons of the world.

This story is history. But it is also a personal story, for the name written on a stone with a sword is Sir William de St Clair of that branch of the Sinclairs who have lived at Rosslyn Castle from the time of the Norman Conquest to the present day. All these stories start on that stone.

While staying in Rosslyn Castle at the beginning of this quest, I went to the chapel and asked if there was any connection with the Templars. The Curator was reluctant to say much, because the Templars had been condemned as heretics and their Grand Master had been burned at the stake, while Rosslyn Chapel is presently a part of the Scottish Episcopal Church. Although there are still five branches of the Order of the Temple of Solomon in existence in Scotland, Freemasons have always held an ambiguous position within the Christian Church. I was shown, however, a mounted knight with a lance carved on a boss by a chapel window: behind him, an angel bearing a cross. Later I was brought to a carved Templar Seal of two hands opening a curtain to reveal the device of the Lamb of God with the Cross, and also of Pegasus, the winged horse of the Greek gods and a Templar symbol. Still later I was to see a carving of a group carrying the 'Mandylion' or Christ's head on a banner, thought to be the Veil of St Veronica or the folded Shroud of Turin.

But on this first visit, I was merely shown marks scratched on the wall-stones by the masons who had built the chapel in the fifteenth century. The eight-pointed crosses were said to be crosses of rededication, because of a legend that an apprentice had built an ornate pillar in the chapel while his Master Mason was absent on a pilgrimage in Rome. He was said to have been killed by a blow on his head from his Master, enraged at the excellence of his pupil's work. I also found an obscure oblong slab abandoned in a dark corner. It was small enough to be the tombstone of a dwarf. I could not see it clearly. Crouching down in the gloom, I could just make out the design of a sword carved upon it, also some octagonal tracery at its head as the outline of a rose window. This discovery is the cornerstone of this book.

A month later, a rubbing was made of the stone by an expert, using flower and vegetable dyes, petunias and marigolds from Rosslyn churchyard, also woad and red cabbage, rhubarb and beeswax. The stone revealed clues to some mysteries, but suggested many more. The small tombstone was the first that had been recently discovered with the Grail carved upon its length. Inside the communion cup was an eight-pointed cypher of the Templars, which referred to the Holy Light within Christ's blood in the shape of an 'engrailed' octagon with a rose at its centre. It bore the name of the dead man, carved in Lombard lettering, WILLHM DE SINNCLER. The very name of the chapel was said to derive from the Old Scottish ROS-LIN or Rosy Stream or Fall, again suggesting the blood of Christ. The St Clair knights of the Middle Ages had fought with the 'Engrailed Cross' on their shields; these were also carved on the chapel walls. The base of the Grail or chalice formed the pattern of the steps to the Temple of Solomon.

Moreover, the corrupted spelling of the name of the man who had been buried under the stone was included within the steps of the base of the Grail. The last two letters of his name, E R, had been turned up at a right angle in the set-square of the Templars and the Master Masons. E R usually signified in the Middle Ages ET RELIQUA in Latin, meaning AND HIS REMAINS or RELICS. The battle sword that ran down the other side of the stem of the cup had a hilt that curved down at either end, characteristic of knights' swords in the first part of the fourteenth century, when Lombard lettering was inscribed on tombstones. While the communion cup of the Grail signified the grave of a Scottish Master of the Temple, the stone dated from the early fourteenth century, when the Templars had been dissolved and their leaders had been tortured and burned alive in France.

The knights and masons of the period were mostly illiterate, and names were rarely spelt consistently in the Middle Ages. The tombstone was certainly that of a William de St Clair of Rosslyn. It had been removed from the original Collegiate Church of St Matthew, situated in the graveyard below the present chapel – only two of its buttresses survive. Although the name of William was common in the St Clair family at the time, the dating of the sword hilt and the lettering pointed to one particular Sir William de St Clair, who fought with Robert the Bruce at Bannockburn and died in 1328, while taking Bruce's heart in a silver casket to be buried at Jerusalem. Surrounded by the Moorish cavalry in Spain, he and Sir James Douglas and two other Scottish knights had flung the casket into the enemy ranks and had charged the whole Muslim army and had been slaughtered. Their courage had so earned the respect of their foes that the Heart of Bruce and the relics of the four knights were returned to the sole Scottish survivor, Sir William Keith, who took them back to their native land. The Heart of Bruce was buried at Melrose Abbey, and the heart of Douglas at his family chapel, while the bones of William de St Clair were apparently buried at Rosslyn. It is intriguing that the remains of the Templars were often interred in the position of the skull over crossed leg-bones, an important symbol in their ritual and later Masonic ceremonies. If William de St Clair, as a Master of the Temple, was buried in this fashion, the small size of his tombstone was explained.

At the east end of the chapel under the arches luxuriant with stone vegetables and leaves and fruits, steps led down to a crypt, probably the site of the eleventh-century chapel and castle of Rosslyn. On the walls were scratched architectural designs to aid the masons who had built this extraordinary chapel. One of these designs demonstrated how the cross-section of the building conformed to the sacred geometry of the encircled octagon and crossed triangles, which were used by the Templars in their construction of their churches and castles. Prince Henry St Clair, the First Earl of Orkney, was held to be buried beneath the crypt. He was the possessor of Orkney and the Shetland Isles, and he owed allegiance to Norway as well as to Scotland. Under the name of Prince Zichmni, he was also held to be the hero of the *Zeno Narrative* and *Map*, an account of two Venetian brothers, Nicolò and Antonio Zen, who worked as sea captains for a northern prince; Antonio took him in 1398 on a colonizing expedition to North America. As the dominant city-state of the eastern Mediterranean, Venice had long had connections with the Crusaders and the Military Orders. After the Templars had lost the Holy Land and had been dissolved, their quest to found a new empire of the West across the Atlantic was as likely as the Teutonic Knights' crusades to found an empire in the East on the German marches. Prince Henry St Clair's father, indeed, had died fighting for that German Order.

If the St Clairs had also been involved in an early discovery of North America, the branch that derived from Rosslyn was as remarkable as Sir Walter Scott believed. He lived at Lasswade down from the town and glen of Roslin – a variant spelling – and he made famous twenty of the St Clair knights, buried in their full armour in the vaults beneath the chapel, closed for nearly three and a half centuries after the last one was interred there on the day of Cromwell's victory at the Battle of Dunbar. In *The Lay of the Last Minstrel*, Scott wrote of the lovely Rosabelle, who would sail across the stormy Firth of Forth at night to go to a ball at the St Clair castle. She sank, but a wondrous fire blazed over the two castles of the glen of the Esk river at Rosslyn and Hawthornden. And in the chapel, the twenty St Clair knights buried in the hidden vaults below were said still to glow at times of tragedy:

> Seem'd all on fire that chapel proud,
>   Where Roslin's chiefs uncoffin'd lie
> Each Baron, for a sable shroud,
>   Sheathed in his iron panoply.

Scott also confirmed the fact that the Templars, if not explicitly the Templar St Clairs, continued to fight for Scotland after the suppression of their Order in France. In his poem on the Battle of Halidon Hill, which took place three years after the death of Sir William de St Clair of the tombstone in Rosslyn Chapel, he had a Scottish Templar knight, Adam de Vipont, speak to King Edward III of England.

Edward III: Vipont, thy crossed Shield shows ill in warfare
          Against a Christian King.
Vipont: That Christian King is warring upon Scotland.
          I was a Scotsman ere I was a Templar,
          Sworn to my country ere I knew my Order.

The present Rosslyn Chapel itself was built by the third St Clair Earl of Orkney, who was also called William. From his time in the fifteenth century, if not since the Battle of Bannockburn, the St Clairs of Rosslyn became the hereditary Grand Master Masons of Scotland. He brought craftsmen from all over Europe to construct his building to the glory of God. It was his personal design. The chapel was unique in all the world in its symbolism and profusion of styles. Nordic and Celtic influences as well as Templar and Masonic iconography decorated this one wing of an intended cruciform church that was never completed. The famous Apprentice Pillar within the chapel was as pagan and Masonic as it was Christian. At its base, eight octagonal serpents with their tails in their mouths surrounded an apparent stone tree-trunk, which supported the roof. This was clearly Yggdrasil, the tree of Norse myth that held up the heavens from the earth, which itself was kept together by a serpent or dragon twining its body nine times round the circumference of the world. It also referred to the Tree of Life, as well as to the Tree of Knowledge of Good and Evil in the Garden of Eden, for the serpent with its tail in its mouth was not only Lucifer but also part of the secret wisdom of the Cathars and the Templars. The Apprentice Pillar derived from Nordic myth in spite of the four strands of stone that twisted as ivy about it, probably a posy to the Four Gospels.

There was further symbolism on the Apprentice Pillar. By Rabbinic and Arabic legend, King Solomon built his Temple by means of the Shamir, a worm or serpent of wisdom whose touch split and shaped stone. For Deuteronomy in the Old Testament had stated that the Temple should be built without the use of tools made of iron. It was the secret of the Shamir that the martyr Hiram, the architect of the Temple, refused to surrender in Masonic tradition, and that remained one of the Grand Secrets for Freemasons in higher degrees. Furthermore, eight worms or serpents or Shamirs were grouped in a rough octagon round the base of the Apprentice Pillar. These comprised the number of points and the shape of the Cross of the Knights of the Order of the Temple of Solomon, who knew of the Shamir when they built their own reconstruction of the Temple on its original site in Jerusalem, before its tradition and its symbolism were brought to Scotland by the designer and the masons of the chapel at Rosslyn.

A similar accretion of Christianity overlaid the carvings in the rest of the chapel. The representation of a man with a wound in his forehead was always associated with the legendary Apprentice who carved the pillar and was killed by his Master Mason. In fact, he was held to be Hiram, the martyred builder of the Temple of Solomon. The legend of the murdered Apprentice was only a Christian cover story for an apocryphal saint and founder of the Order of the Temple of Solomon and of all Masonry with its symbols of the sword and the trowel, the compasses and the maul. Earl Magnus of Orkney was also martyred with a blow to the head, but his death was a re-enactment of the murder of Hiram. He, too, was known to the Templar St Clairs, who took Orkney and had their Norse predecessor beatified.

To see Rosslyn Chapel is to see Christ on the Cross overlaid on pagan beliefs. There are dozens of carvings of the wild face of the Green Man peering from the stone foliage on the arches. For that is the wonder of this curious chapel. On every pillar, from each architrave and boss, all the plants of the earth multiply and replenish the innumerable carvings. I might have been watching the third day of creation in stone, the day before the God of Genesis made man in His own image. Each one of these lush and defined fruits and herbs and leaves had its symbolic meaning in medieval herbal and arcane lore. Nobody has even begun to unravel all the meanings. They merely prove that the architect and designer of Rosslyn Chapel, the hereditary Master Mason of Scotland, William St Clair, the Earl of Orkney, was privy to the gnostic and cabbalistic knowledge of the Templars and the herbalists and their followers.

It is no accident that Rosslyn has become the core chapel to all the Masons of the earth, and that the secrets of its carvings and its symbols are still to be revealed. Even while I was staying at Rosslyn Castle, the present Nova Scotia chapter of the Canadian Knights Templars had their Investiture Ceremony in the chapel. What had brought them all the way there from the place that Prince Henry St Clair was meant to have visited nearly six centuries ago? I had discovered the first of the mysteries, a sword on a stone with a Grail. I had not understood what I was seeing. But I will try to use its blade to force the lock of the barred door. What happened to the Templars and their treasure after their suppression? What were their secret rituals? Were these passed on to the Masons? What is the meaning of the Grail on the St Clair tombstone? Why is Rosslyn particularly a Chapel of the Holy Grail, its dedication to that mystic quest written in stone within its walls? Did the Venetians and Prince Henry St Clair try to colonize North America nearly a century before Columbus? And who were the Zen family who took them there?

2

Venice and the Zens

THE ZEN FAMILY, called Zenone or Zeno in Italian and Geno or Genus in Latin, was one of the older families of Venice. The Zens had been Tribunes for the New Rome of Byzantium, later called Constantinople, and they came from Padua to Venice when the building of the city on its lagoon was begun early in the eighth century. They were involved in the election of the First Doge. Most Europeans in the Middle Ages, whether they were Celts or Norsemen or Saxons or Lombards, thought of themselves as Christians and still as Romans in some distant way. The Zen family traced its origins back to two saints, Zeno of Vicenza and Marco Zeno, martyred by Diocletian, as well as to two Byzantine emperors, Zeno and Leo. The name was as old as classical philosophy. It was the Greek Zeno of Alexandria who had set the paradox of Achilles never catching up with the tortoise. In their desire to assert a Roman heritage, the Zen family claimed to derive from the Fannius *gens*, which traced its ancestry back to Aeneas, whom Virgil declared to be the founder of Rome with his band of refugees from Troy.

Through their growing city of Venice, the Zens had long had connections with the Vikings and the Normans and the Crusaders, after their first incursions into the Mediterranean. In 911, the Vikings had taken Normandy, leaving a St Clair as a border baron against an attack from Paris. They had become Normans and then

had conquered England. Nine of the St Clair family had fought at
the Battle of Hastings. Then the Normans had swept down past
Spain and established kingdoms in the Sicilies, along with principalities in the Near East. Normans and Franks were the spearhead of
the Crusaders, although a Norwegian King Sigurd appeared in 1107
with Norse ships at the siege of Sidon. A Venetian squadron saved
that Viking fleet from defeat by a Muslim flotilla from Tyre. In
1152, another Norse crusade under Rognvald, then Earl of Orkney,
gathered at Grossay for the voyage to the Holy Land. At the time,
Venice was competing with Genoa and Pisa and Marseilles for the
carrying trade of soldiers and pilgrims to the Levant. Its first
successful intervention was on the First Crusade, when Haifa
was taken with the assistance of a Venetian fleet. Thereafter, Venice
played an increasing role in Levantine trade and war, always
demanding a third or half of the spoils and privileged trading
concessions.

The Venetians co-operated with the Military Orders. The nine
knights who officially founded the Order of the Temple of
Solomon in 1118 had been companions of Godfrey de Bouillon
on the First Crusade, as had an early St Clair knight. De Bouillon
had refused the crown of the Kingdom of Jerusalem, but had
remained its strongest protector. He had taken the title of Defender
of the Holy Sepulchre and had founded a small order of monastic
knights to protect the Church of the Saviour Himself. His example
had been followed by Hugh de Payens, by Godfrey de St Omer, by
the Count of Provence, and by six other knights, who initiated a
Military Order to protect pilgrims visiting the Holy Land. Most of
these founding members derived from the Langue d'Oc and the
Court of Champagne. They were first assigned a part of the King's
own palace in Jerusalem near to the site of the Temple of Solomon.
Later they were given, beside the Muslim shrine of the Dome of the
Rock, the al-Aqsā mosque, which they rebuilt as a headquarters
with a cruciform church modelled on the Holy Sepulchre. They
were the actual guardians of the Temple of Solomon, which
pilgrims confused with the Dome of the Rock itself.

Six years after the official founding of the Templars, followed by that of the Knights of the Hospital of St John or the Hospitallers, the Venetians joined the Military Orders in the capture of Tyre. Until the Orders took to the waters and built their own flotillas, Venice and the other merchant cities of Italy and France were necessary to preserve the Kingdom of Jerusalem from attack by sea from Egypt. In 1204, on the Fourth Crusade, Venetian policy misled the Crusaders into the sack of a maritime rival, Byzantium or Constantinople. So harsh were the terms of the Venetians for transporting the Crusaders that they took over much of the Byzantine Empire, Greece and the Peloponnese and many islands, including Crete. A Venetian, Thomas Morosini, was even installed as Patriarch of Constantinople with authority over the great basilica of Sancta Sophia. This led to Venetian dominance of the eastern Mediterranean during the thirteenth and fourteenth centuries in spite of counter-attacks by Genoese and Muslim fleets.

Although the Zen family was one of the twenty-four Venetian families that were held to be 'long' or 'old,' it was not as powerful in the city as the Dandolos or the Grimanis. It also reached the height of its influence during the thirteenth and the fourteenth centuries. Its first significant member, Marino Zen, was Captain-General of the Sea and carried the warriors of the Fourth Crusade to Constantinople, which, as the chronicler Villehardouin wrote, had as many holy relics as there were in all the rest of Christendom. Marino Zen himself became the first Vice-Doge or Podestà of Constantinople; he wore the purple shoes and stockings of the Doge of Venice; and he built a wall and a fort to protect the Venetian quarter on the Golden Horn from the rest of the city. He was also responsible for transporting the military knights on to the Holy Land, which was their proper destination. It began a long association between the Zen family and the knightly orders, which was to last for more than three centuries.

In those early days of diplomacy, the Zen family continued to supply the state with many Captain-Generals of the Sea, admirals in the fleet, colonial administrators of the many Venetian island possessions and legates or ambassadors. One of its members, Reniero, became Doge after he defeated a Genoese admiral, whose coat of arms he adopted – four diagonal purple stripes on a silver field, which was later quartered with a lion. He was responsible for the first comprehensive Venetian maritime code. It was meant to protect private enterprise rather than curb it, but the owners of the ships were made more responsible: the *patronus* was supposed to act as captain on every trade voyage. When Reniero died in 1268, he left a vast fortune, some of which came from the spoils of Constantinople – now repossessed by the Greek emperors – spoils used to endow the family church of Crosichieri in Canareggio. During his time as Doge, the Piazza San Marco also took on its present form. The marbles and treasures of Constantinople were used to embellish it, particularly the four gilded bronze horses set above the façade of the basilica – along with many religious relics. Later, the Zen family was to endow the Zen baptismal chapel in San Marco, ornamented by radiant mosaics commemorating the voyage of St Mark himself to Egypt and the later return of his remains to Venice.

In the centuries to come, this trading wealth and these colonial connections led to the Zen family producing one cardinal, four bishops, three Dukes of Crete, six Dukes of Candia, twelve Procurators and dozens of ambassadors, especially to the Levant. The Venetian sea-borne empire made the Zens influential and rich, particularly as the carriers of the pilgrims and the Crusaders. Pietro Zen, called Dracone, became Captain-General of the Christian Confederation against the Turks, and put a dragon on the family shield, as Prince Henry St Clair was to do on his shield. They were the leading defenders of Venetian sea-power, not only against the Turks and the Mamelukes of Egypt, but against the fleets of the rival maritime cities, Genoa, Pisa and Marseilles, and also against the growing strength of the navies of the Military Orders. These had begun to build their bases on the sea, as the Templars did at Castle Pilgrim, in order to defend their banking and trading activities.

They had, after all, lost Jerusalem to the armies of the victorious Saladin and their role as guardians of pilgrims to the Holy Places. And so the Knights of the Red Cross had taken to the waves.

A hundred years after the founding of their Order, the Grand Master William de Chartres had made the Templars build Castle Pilgrim on the promontory of Athlit, south of Haifa. This huge fortress included a natural harbour and a shipyard within the walls. It would serve as a model for Prince Henry St Clair's later sea-palace at Kirkwall in the Orkneys. It could support 4,000 people from its enclosed orchards and fishponds, salt-mines and fresh-water springs. Its octagonal church was built on the model of the Church of the Holy Sepulchre and of the chapter houses of early English cathedrals, a near-circle based on the eight points of the Templar Cross. Its vast eastern wall facing the Holy Land was its chief defence, for so confident were the Templars in their new sea-power that they left their western, eastern and southern flanks open to attack up the cliffs from the Mediterranean. The fleet of the Fifth Crusade, bound for Damietta on the Nile, put in at Athlit to take aboard the forces of the Templars. The shipping supervisor in charge of the pilgrim trade was called the *Magister Passagii*. The Templars could be ordered by the Pope to provide up to twenty galleys in defence of coastal waters. They maintained commercial and passenger depots in all major Mediterranean ports and some Atlantic ones. The Close Rolls of King Henry III of England show them to have had the free export of wool in their own fleet between Bristol and La Rochelle in France. They gave up the horse for the rudder, and they became master mariners and navigators.

In the thirteenth century, they were a major Mediterranean force. Castle Pilgrim was to endure for 75 years as a centre for trade and banking in the Levant until the fall of Acre, when its garrison was to be evacuated to Cyprus with the treasure of the Order. Even with their sea-power, the Templars had found it difficult to maintain their remaining fortifications in the Holy Land. Their inland strongholds had been increasingly beset and made untenable.

By 1267, desperate letters were reaching the Master of the Temple in France, demanding a transfer of treasure to the Templars in the Holy Land to pay off crossbowmen and mercenary knights, recruited against Muslim assaults. 'And, for the love of God,' the letter ended, 'make peace between the Genoese and the Venetians, and hasten the departure of a new Crusade.'

No new Crusade appeared to save Acre and the last mainland Templar castles from falling at the end of the century to Baibars, the Sultan of Egypt, whose Mamelukes were known as 'Muslim Templars'. The Order withdrew to Cyprus and Venice, the Hospitallers to Rhodes and later to Malta, to continue the struggle against the infidels by sea. They were aided by the Venetians, who sometimes co-operated with Muslim powers rather than with their Italian maritime rivals, but who viewed the Military Orders as fellow Christian soldiers, even though the Templars were permeated with Arab influence and were known to have made treaties with the Islamic sect of the Assassins in order to preserve their properties in the Holy Land.

Since their inception, the Templars had long had connections with the Scottish nobility. Their founder, Hugh de Payens, had been married to the French Catherine de St Clair, and on his European recruiting drive, he had attracted members of that family in Scotland to join the Order as well as setting up the Templar headquarters at Balantrodoch, only six miles from the St Clair stronghold at Rosslyn. Crusaders from Scotland generally passed through Venice on their way to the Holy Land. They knew of the maritime skills and power of the Republic. Prince Henry St Clair himself would go on a crusade with King Peter I of Cyprus, who briefly captured Alexandria from the Muslims.

Carlo Zen, the son of Pietro Dracone, was then a leading Captain of Venice and responsible for transport on the voyage to Egypt. His later biographer told of his meeting with a Scottish Prince in the Holy Land and of his returning to defend Cyprus. He had spent his early manhood in Eastern trade and diplomacy. When war broke out between Venice and Genoa, he raised a fleet that plundered the

Genoese colonies of the Levant. The war went badly in home waters, and in 1380, a fleet from Genoa captured the south-western tip of the lagoons at Chioggia and blockaded the Venetians in their city. Their ships could not break out. Then Carlo Zen's fleet sailed back with its spoils from the East and blockaded the Genoese forces in their turn. He foiled all their attempts to escape, and after six months of siege and starvation, they capitulated. A decisive factor in the battle was the use of a new mounted ship's cannon, the *petriero*. It was made of welded rods held together by six or seven rings. It was a breech-loader and fired a small stone ball, which caused more fear than damage. Four of these cannon have recently been dredged from the docks in the Arsenal and are on display in the Museo Storico Navale. They were obsolete by the beginning of the fifteenth century, when cannon could be cast in iron or brass in one piece.

Carlo Zen had not only delivered Venice 'as Furius Camillus delivered Rome', but he had ended the Genoese threat in the Levant. He was given the name of the Lion, which he had painted on his shield. Trade and diplomacy in the eastern Mediterranean were now wholly controlled by the Venetians in concert with the Military Orders of Knights, who had taken over Rhodes and other islands and had exchanged their horses for fighting vessels. He nearly effected the escape of Emperor John of Constantinople from his captors, and he remained a power in the politics of the Levant. He was to be made Procurator and nearly elected Doge. He was one of the more influential men of his time in Venice, where both the Templars and the Teutonic Knights had now established headquarters. He was to save the later Emperor Manuel from Timur (or Tamburlaine) and his Mongols, but not from the young Suleiman and his Turks, in the same period that his brother was taking Prince Henry St Clair to seek a new empire in a New World.

Carlo Zen had two brothers, Nicolò and Antonio, both of whom served as naval officers and colonial officials. Nicolò's distinguished service of the state earned him the title of *Ser Dracone* or *Cavaliere*, which was also given to Carlo the Procurator. When Marco Barbaro, another Venetian patrician, wrote about sixty-four noble families of Venice, his entry under the Zen name recorded that Nicolò was called 'the rich man' and was the captain of a galley in the Chioggia battle against Genoa, won by his brother Carlo. In other accounts, he was named as one of three syndics elected in 1388 to command the colonial city of Treviso. In the four years before 1400, when he made his will, there was no mention of him in the Venetian Annals.

Treviso lay to the north-west of Venice on the way to the Brenner Pass over the Alps. It carried the rich overland trade to Germany and Lombardy and the Baltic States. It was a spearhead to the north. As Venice was the leading commercial power and business practitioner of the time, German merchants flocked through Treviso to learn the new Arabic numerals and double-entry book-keeping and mathematical methods of navigation, which the Venetians had acquired from the Levant. The Germans even set up a factory in Venice, the *Fondaco dei Tedeschi*, to facilitate their trade and their education in business.

Marco Barbaro further stated in his *Libro di nozze* that Nicolò then went on the exploration of the northern seas, followed by his brother Antonio. They wrote together 'the voyages among the islands under the Arctic Pole and the discoveries of 1390 – by order of Zicno [St Clair], King of Frislanda, he [Antonio] took himself to the continent of Estotilanda in Northern America. He dwelt fourteen years in Frislanda, four with his brother Nicolò, and ten alone.' Nicolò's death was wrongly reported during this period, but Antonio returned just before his own death in 1406 to Venice, where his surviving brother Carlo was Procurator. Apparently, he brought back some of the records and charts from his voyages, which his descendant, another Nicolò Zeno, saw as a child in the family palace in Canareggio. Partially destroyed, the evidence was published in Venice in 1558 as the *Zeno Narrative* and *Map*, which has caused controversy to this day. If it was based on authentic letters, as Barbaro suggested in his account of the

Zen family published 22 years earlier, then Venice and Antonio Zen should take the credit for a discovery and colonization of North America, nearly a century before Christopher Columbus from rival Genoa.

Before entering into the details of the *Zeno Narrative* and *Map*, there are enquiries to be made. Why did two important Venetian captains and administrators, brothers of one of the more powerful figures in the city, spend all those years absent in the northern seas? They could hardly be spared from the Mediterranean. There were only some 1,300 nobles who qualified as members of the Great Council at the end of the fourteenth century. From their ranks derived the naval commanders, administrators and ambassadors of the time. The nobles were few and valuable, one in a thousand of the population of Venice and her possessions. Genoa was still a maritime threat, as were the Muslim fleets of Egypt and Turkey. Qualified colonial governors and experienced diplomats were scarce. The tradition of the Zen family was in these professions and continued to be so. It seems improbable that Nicolò Zen could have been spared from Venetian service merely to explore the northern seas. Without orders from the Council, his brother Antonio would not have joined him in Orkney and the Shetland Isles, bringing out a Venetian ship that he had bought himself.

The likelihood is that there was a secret mission known to the state, which allowed two such distinguished brothers to go to the north and serve a Scottish Prince for so long. The appointment of Nicolò Zen to Treviso had already given him experience in northern commerce. The interest of Venice in developing trade and alliances in the North Atlantic is made more probable by the fact that Carlo Zen himself was sent as ambassador to France and England in 1396, while his surviving brother Antonio was preparing a Scottish fleet for a colonizing mission to the West. According to the *Zeno Narrative*, Nicolò Zen had already sailed on an expedition to Greenland, had begun a survey of its east coast and had reported back to Carlo Zen on a flourishing trade in salted fish and furs between the Norse colonies there and Iceland and the Shetlands and Scandinavia. He had also described the naval power of the Scottish Prince he was serving, and the St Clair conquest of Orkney and the Shetlands and some of the Faroe Islands. These conquests are matters of fact. One of the proofs of the truth of most of the *Zeno Narrative*, said to be based on the letters sent back by Nicolò and Antonio Zen to their brother Carlo from Orkney and the Shetlands, is the accurate description of obscure campaigns and wars in the islands, reports of which would usually never have reached Venice. The Zen family was being directed by the Venetian state in a drive for trade and influence in the North Atlantic.

There is also no doubt about the close connection of Venetian diplomacy and members of the Zen family with the Military Orders from the time of their founding in Jerusalem after the First Crusade until their last stand on Malta, where they remained a minor sea-power. With the destruction of the Templars after 1307, the Hospitallers took over many of their properties and functions: this was done at the Templar headquarters at San Georgio di Schiavoni. It is therefore not surprising to find a crowned figure dressed as a bearded Templar Knight, ruling over a colonial plantation, drawn onto an engraving by the Venetian printer Vavassatore from the world map of Casper Vopell of Cologne, printed in 1545. Vavas-satore published his version in Venice thirteen years later, the same year as the publication of the *Zeno Map*. What is significant is that the figure of the crowned knight is drawn roughly in Nova Scotia, called Baccalearum Regio after Mercator by Vopell, and Estotiland by Nicolò Zeno. It suggests some traditional family knowledge of the real reason for the northern mission of the first Nicolò Zen in 1390, later followed by his brother Antonio.

A figure of a crowned knight appears on no other early extant map of North America. It is unique to Vavassatore's engraving of Vopell's map. He would have known of Nicolò Zeno's map of the same year, as Zeno was considered the leading cartographer in Venice. It was a small city, where everybody in the same field saw one another. Some reason was given to Vavassatore to place the figure of the crowned knight where he did if Vopell had not already placed it there. And the long contact over many centuries of the Zen family with the Crusaders and the Templars provides a reason for the quest of the first Venetian explorers in the far north, serving a Scottish prince in search of a New Jerusalem to the west.

The Knights of the Sword, the Trowel and the Grail

To CHRISTIANS in Europe, Jerusalem was literally the centre of the circle of the world. In legend, the first man, Adam, was buried on Golgotha, where Jesus, the Son of God, would die on the Cross. To Jews, Jerusalem was also the centre of Israel and the world, and the centre of the holy city was the foundation stone of the Temple of Solomon, before which lay the Ark of the Covenant. The Christians had an alternative navel stone for the universe, the ὀμφαλός under the dome of the Church of the Holy Sepulchre, where the True Cross was sometimes kept. It was a pillar of marble two feet high, on which was set a vessel containing a stone, another source of inspiration for the Grail romances and the Gnostics and the alchemists, one of whom wrote: 'Make a round circle and you will have the Stone of the Philosopher.' The Grail Castle itself was based on the idea of the heavenly and perfect Jerusalem, an orb that was the heart of faith and existence. To the Crusaders, Jerusalem was both an actual and a visionary city, a walled place in Palestine and a Paradise in the Holy Land. The pilgrimage there was also the quest for the Grail Castle.

One of the influences on German descriptions of the Grail Castle was historical as well as oriental. In the medieval romance *The Young Titurel*, The Temple of the Grail stood on an onyx Mount of

Salvation. It was built in the round beneath a golden dome, on which jewelled constellations blazed above a mechanical gold sun and silver moon. In the early seventh century, the Persian King Chosroes II had built a similar palace on the holy mountain of Shîz, where there was a previous circular sanctuary of sacred fire in memory of the seer Zoroaster, whose Manichean beliefs influenced Gnostics and alchemists. The circular palace of precious metals and stones showed the heavens, which were rotated by teams of horses pulling ropes from sunken pits below. Mineral deposits from a crater lake made the mountain gleam as if onyx. This early planetarium was called the Throne of Arches, the Takt-i-Taqdis; twenty-two ornate arches surrounded the central round, the same number of lesser temples that encircled the main hall of the Grail Castle in *The Young Titurel*. Unfortunately, the Byzantine Emperor Heraclius defeated Chosroes and tore down the Takt and took back the True Cross, which Chosroes had removed there after his seizure of Jerusalem. This early crusade to recapture the True Cross was well-known in medieval Europe and served as material for the songs of the troubadours.

When a Christian army took Jerusalem in 1099, the fanaticism of its soldiers turned the First Crusade's completion of its quest into an indelible crime that still makes the Muslim world shudder. Jerusalem was the third holy city of Islam after Mecca and Medina, for in the Koran, Allah led the Prophet Muhammad there on a miraculous journey one night to the sites of the Al-Aqsā mosque and the Dome of the Rock, and then to Heaven, where he met Jesus and Moses. This encounter symbolized the continuity of the three religions of Judaism and Christianity and Islam under the great glittering Dome at Jerusalem. But when the Crusaders burst into the city, they ravaged it, killing most of its inhabitants. One Arab contemporary wrote that the population of the holy city was put to the sword, and the Franks spent a week massacring Muslims, mostly in the al-Aqsā mosque, where they had fled for sanctuary. Another Arab commentator wrote: 'The Jews had gathered in their synagogue and the Franks burned them alive. They also destroyed the monuments of the saints and the tomb of Abraham, may peace be upon him!' They expelled the oriental Christian priests, the Greeks and Copts and Syrians, from the Church of the Holy Sepulchre and tortured some of them to make them reveal where they had hidden the True Cross. So the earthly Jerusalem was cleansed by the Crusaders in an orgy of violence, hardly the acts of knights achieving at last the heavenly city of the Castle of the Grail.

The Crusaders also sacked the mosque of Umar, built in order to commemorate the second successor of the Prophet Muhammad. Ironically, Umar had saved the Church of the Holy Sepulchre when he had entered Jerusalem, riding on his white camel. Then the Greek Patriarch had taken him round the holy places of the Christian community. The time for Muslim prayer had arrived when Umar was in the Church of the Holy Sepulchre. Umar asked if he might unroll his prayer mat and worship, and the Patriarch agreed. But Umar said that if he prayed within the church, the Muslims would make it into a mosque on the grounds that Umar had prayed there. So he knelt and prayed outside, and a mosque in his name was built there and destroyed by the Crusaders. They still had to learn an accommodation with other religions, which was one of the many lessons their civilized Arab enemies would teach them.

The first of the Christian Military Orders founded by Godfrey de Bouillon of the yellow beard became the guardians of the Church of the Holy Sepulchre, sited at the place where Christ was believed to have risen from the dead. But they were rapidly superseded by the Knights Templars, who became the guardians of the Temple of Solomon, the original centre of Jerusalem and Israel and the world. Its presumed site was covered by the al-Aqsâ mosque, which the Templars changed into their Temple and church, based on that of the Holy Sepulchre. The neighbouring octagonal Dome of the Rock was thought by pilgrims to be the original Temple of Solomon and was shown on the seal of the Templar Grand Master. It was on the sacred rock itself that Hugh de Payens and his fellow knights swore the foundation oath of the Templars. The knights absorbed a great deal of contemporary Arab philosophy and science and building techniques, which had derived from classical Greek thought. They had many masons and builders in their Order, and they used the Temple and building tools in their symbolism and their designs and their ceremonies. They and many of the Masons afterwards were Neo-Platonists. They believed in One God, the Architect of the World, in whom the members of all religions, Christian and Muslim and Jew, might believe. This was central to their beliefs and led to later charges of heresy. The Templars were also the conduit from the Near East of hermetic and cabbalistic knowledge to the original Scottish Masons and so eventually to all Freemasons.

The Templars adopted from oriental mysticism the secret knowledge, the *gnosis*. Its sacred geometry was the octagon contained within the circle. The Dome of the Rock, which contained a holy stone, was built by Islamic architects as eight equal walls holding up a golden dome. The building was guarded by the Templars during the 90 years of the Christian Kingdom of Jerusalem in the twelfth century, and its shape influenced all Templar architecture and persuaded the Templars and visiting pilgrims that it resembled the original Temple of Solomon. Octagonal chapels are found in many Templar presbyteries, particularly at their centre in Portugal, Tomar. Eight regular walls were favoured in the design of chapter houses beside the Gothic cathedrals in the twelfth and thirteenth centuries. There is one at the ancient Scottish abbey of Inchcolm in the Firth of Forth. And the octagon within the circle was to be the plan for the rebuilding of Rosslyn Chapel by its creator, William St Clair, the Earl of Orkney – a scholar who was versed in the Templar and hermetic tradition.

The Templars were not only the bankers of the Kingdom of Jerusalem during its century of survival, but also its diplomats with the Muslim world. Only when unschooled Grand Masters preferred confrontation did the kingdom fall. One story told by the emir Usāmah Ibn Munqidh, a diplomat and writer from Damascus, showed how far the Templars had learned tolerance from their Muslim neighbours. When he visited Jerusalem, he wished to pray at the al-Aqsā mosque, which was now converted into a Christian church. The Templars placed a small chapel beside it at his disposal. When the emir began his prayers, a knight, newly come from Europe, turned him forcibly toward the east, saying, 'We pray that way'. The Templars took the newcomer away, but when the emir resumed his prayers towards Mecca, the knight repeated his outrage. This time he was ejected by the Templars, who apologised to the emir with the words, 'He is a foreigner. He has just arrived from Europe and has never seen anyone pray without turning to face east.' The emir ceased from his prayers, but forgave his Templar friends. Among the Crusaders, he explained, 'We find some people who have come to settle among us and who have cultivated the society of the Muslims. They are far superior to those who have freshly joined them in the territories they now occupy.'

Although dependent on the new recruits and income from their presbyteries in Europe, the Templars were a permanent standing army in the Holy Land, a few hundred knights holding the Holy City and a broken necklace of castles across Palestine. Their existence depended on playing off one Arab ruler or warlord against another. Any combination of all the Muslim states against them would have been their end. They were particularly influenced by the rival Muslim warrior Shi'ite and Ismaili sect of the Assassins, who held castles and lands in the mountains near the Caspian Sea and in Syria, and were supporters of the Fatimid caliphs of Egypt. Their founder and first Grand Master, Hassan Ibn al-Sabbah, was a poet and a scientist and the inventor of modern terrorism. He indoctrinated fanatical young men to go out and murder his enemies, usually at the cost of their own lives. From these suicide squads derived the word *fedayeen*, still used of Palestinian guerrillas. The Assassins found the Templars to be willing allies in the disintegration of the Sunni rulers of Syria and other Arab states, as well as converts to some of the secrets of their organisation and doctrines.

Marco Polo, who travelled through Persia on his way to China, brought back to Europe the legend of the Assassins. He wrote that, in a fortified valley between two mountains, the Sheikh or 'Old Man' of the Assassins had planted a beautiful garden that grew every fruit in the world. The garden was watered with streams of wine, milk and honey. As the Prophet Muhammad's paradise, on which it was modelled, it held gilded palaces, *houris*, dancers, musicians and singers. And it was seen only by those who were to be made Assassins. Young men who had been trained in arms at the Old Man's court were drugged, taken to the hidden garden, and initiated into its delights. They lived there in luxury for a few days, convinced that their leader had transported them to paradise. When they were suddenly drugged again and taken back to his court, they were eager to risk their lives for him in order to return. 'Away they went,' concluded Polo, 'and did all they were commanded. Thus it happened that no man ever escaped when the Sheikh of the Mountain desired his death.'

The medieval story of a castle and a paradise on earth akin to the Grail Castle of the Fisher King was true in that respect. There is little doubt that the Assassins were drug-takers, for their name was derived from the Arabic word *Hashshīshīn*, meaning 'users of hashish'. The tale of the garden paradise possibly had its origin in the hallucinations produced by the drug. But oriental legend had already created an Eden out of the fertile valley near the chief Assassin stronghold at Alamut, south of the Caspian Sea. Stories about the sect may have been confused with this tradition and with the legend of King Shedad, who tried to equal Allah's paradise by building his own.

Missionaries trained in the Grand Lodge of the Ismailis in Cairo preached a doctrine that negated most of orthodox Islamic beliefs. They held that Muslim law and scriptures contained an inner meaning that was known only to the imams. They taught that there were only seven prophets: Adam, Noah, Abraham, Moses, Jesus, Muhammad and the imam Ismail. In the order of creation, the prophets stood at the level of Universal Reason, second only to God. Last in the sevenfold chain of creation stood man. Though God Himself was unknowable, a man could work through these grades as far as Universal Reason, and a new aspect of the teaching would be revealed to him at each level. Because such views were heretical, every Ismaili initiate was required to conceal his beliefs in accordance with the Shia demand of secrecy and to conform, outwardly, with the state religion. In Ismaili writings, there was usually an obsessed wanderer like a Perceval in quest of a Grail. He sought truth through trial and suffering, until he was at last accepted into the faith by an imam, who revealed to him the true meaning of Muslim law and scriptures.

Such a quest was described by Hassan Ibn al-Sabbah in his own memoirs. He pursued spiritual power through political power and changed the role of the Ismaili initiate to the role of assassin. At the same time, he modified the grades of initiation. The only descriptions of these grades, and of the mysteries revealed to initiates, were written by European scholars, who saw the Ismaili hierarchy itself as a mere brain-washing system. According to their accounts, the teaching given at each level negated everything that had been taught before. The innermost secret of the Assassins was that Heaven and Hell were the same, all actions were indifferent, and there was no good or evil except the virtue of obeying the imam. Nothing is known of the Assassins' secrets, because their books of doctrine and ritual were burned by the Mongols in 1256 with their library at Alamut. Hassan emphasized the Shia doctrine of obedience to the imam and made changes in the Ismaili hierarchy. Persian tradition had it that below Hassan, the chief *da'i* or Grand Master, came the senior *da'is*, the ordinary *da'is*, the *rafiqs* or companions, the *lasiqs* or laymen, and the *fidais* (devotees) who committed the murders. The division of the Templars under their Grand Master into grand priors, priors, knights, esquires and lay brothers was closely to follow the hierarchy of the Assassins.

In his asceticism and singleness of purpose, Hassan was an ideal revolutionary leader and conspirator. He is said to have remained continuously within his nest in his fortress for more than thirty years, going out only twice and appearing twice more on his roof. His invisibility increased his power. From his seclusion, he strengthened the defences of Alamut, purged the ranks of his followers (even putting to death two of his own sons) and continued with his strategy of seizing hill positions as centres of local subversion. He elevated his authority to tyranny over life and soul. The will of the Old Man was the will of his imam, the caliph, and thus the will of God. By winning over garrisons and assassinating local governors, he occupied strongpoints and terrorized the Sunnis, Persians and Turks alike. The conspiracy of the determined few, as usual, was hardly opposed by the fearful many. On the model of Muhammad himself, who had fled to Medina to rally support and reconquer Mecca and all Arabia, Hassan hoped to take over the whole caliphate of Baghdad.

By the authority of his rank and by the use of drugs, Hassan trained *fidais* in such blind obedience that, as the Japanese suicide pilots of the Second World War, they welcomed death during an attempt at assassination. They preferred the dagger as a weapon, and the court or the mosque as a place of execution. They scorned the use of poison and backstairs intrigue, for their code was more that of soldiers than of harem murderers. Legend tells of one *fidai's* mother who rejoiced when she heard that her son had died in an attempt on a ruler's life, then put on mourning when he returned alive. Similar legends grew up around other loyal *fidais* who stabbed themselves or dashed out their brains on the rocks below the battlements to prove their obedience to the Old Man's command.

Rather like the Mafia of later times, the Assassins operated from their strongholds a protection racket under threat of death. Their techniques helped to undermine the Turkish empire and to fragment even more the fractured Arab world. Suspicion ran riot, and murder was a normal method of princely government. Thus the Crusaders, coming to the Holy Land, found only a divided enemy, disorganized by the Assassins. Hassan may not have intended to aid the Christian invaders; but he did help the Crusaders to entrench themselves in the Levant.

The founder of the Templars, Hugh de Payens, knew of the Assassins when he formed his organization. The Christian and

Muslim Military Orders were aware of each other in Syria before 1128, when the Templar Rule was written. Even the colours worn by the knights, red crosses on a white ground, were the same as those of the Assassin *rafiqs*, who wore red caps and belts and white tunics. Some claim that the Templars adopted the Assassin 'hues of innocence and blood, and of pure devotion and murder' only because the rival Knights Hospitallers wore black. However that may be, the function of the Templars was virtually the same as that of the Assassins – to serve as an independent power on the side of their religious faith.

When the Assassins murdered the Count of Tripoli, the Templars forced the Syrian branch to pay them a yearly tribute. And when the Shi'ite caliphate of the Fatimids finally fell in Egypt, the Assassins in Syria were in such despair that they offered to convert to Christianity. Yet, by now, the Templars did not want to lose their income. Thus they assassinated the Assassin envoys on their return from interviewing the King of Jerusalem. It was the end of co-operation between the two Warrior Orders of Christianity and Islam. Equally rash decisions by the Templar Grand Master in 1187 put an end to the Kingdom of Jerusalem. Three years before, the Andalusian traveller Ibn Jubayr had noted the complete under-standing and respect that Christians and Muslims had for each other's rights and commerce in Palestine. But this was doomed, for the great Kurdish general Saladin had succeeded in uniting the divided Muslim states in a *jihad* or holy war against the infidels, after the Franks had raided the trade routes in the Red Sea and the pilgrim caravans to Mecca. He sent a reconnaissance force of 7,000 cavalry under safe conduct, but these were attacked by the Templar and Hospitaller Knights, who were decimated. The survivors berated the King of Jerusalem for dealing with the Muslims, as they had done themselves for 90 years. They persuaded him to march out and fight Saladin's united army.

And at the Horns of Hittîn, the Christian army was trapped without water and cut to pieces. For once, Saladin gave up his usual policy of mercy to punish infidel perfidy. All his prisoners from the

Military Orders of knights were beheaded by Muslim equivalents, the Sufis. Yet in contrast to the Christian massacre of the citizens of Jerusalem during the First Crusade, Saladin spared the sacred place. The leader of the resistance, Balian of Ibelin, threatened to destroy the holy city, including the Dome of the Rock, unless the defenders were ransomed, and Saladin accepted the terms. He even put guards in the Christian places of worship and refused to rase the Church of the Holy Sepulchre in retaliation for the brutality of the Christians, when they had taken Jerusalem. The al-Aqsā mosque became an Islamic shrine again after its walls were sprinkled with rose-water.

The fall of Jerusalem put an end to the purpose of the Templar Order, for its knights were the guardians of the Temple of Solomon and the protectors of pilgrims to the Christian holy places, now in Muslim hands. Although they were to survive for another 120 years as a Military Order, the Templars had to find a new role. They fell back to the sea and built fortresses there, preparing for a new crusade to take back Jerusalem. Only the Third Crusade with King Richard I of England came near to achieving this second quest; but Saladin proved a match for the Lionheart himself. More and more, the Templars became merchants and bankers and administrators of their estates.

Their fate was foreshadowed by another crusade, now directed by Christian against Christian in France. The victims, the *cathari* or pure ones, were called heretics, as the Templars were to be in their turn. Since their foundation by Hugh de Payens, the Templars had been closely connected with the Court of Champagne and Provence and the Langue d'Oc. The writers of the medieval romances had made them the Knights of the Grail. The patrons of the culture of the south of France, certainly the richest and most civilised in Europe in the twelfth century, supported the Crusades and died while serving upon them. But the Kings of France coveted the independent principalities of the south, and the Popes distrusted the increasing power of the Cathar priests, called *perfecti*, who wanted to reform the faith.

Both the Cathars and the Templars were influenced by Sufi and

Manichean and Islamic doctrines as well as by early Christianity and the Cabbala. They believed the flesh was corrupt and life was an ascension to the spirit rather like the quest for the Grail. Lucifer or the Devil had brought about the creation of man. Plato was right in the *Gorgias* when he quoted Euripides: 'Who knows, if life be death, and if death be life?' Also right was the Grail king in *Diû Krône*. 'We only seem to be alive, in reality we are dead.' Through the mystical feast known as the *manisola* and the chaste kiss of reception into the faith called the *consolamentum*, the *perfecti* took their initiates into the path of the spirit. This religion was certainly more pure and personal than Catholicism at the time, for an individual was made responsible for his or her own soul by an ascetic way of life. Cathar influences are evident in the quest for the Grail and in the early crusading quest for the holy city of Jerusalem. It was a tragedy that the Albigensian Crusade was turned against a source of the previous crusades to the east.

The lands and cities of the Langue d'Oc were as thoroughly ravaged by poor and unemployed mercenary knights, as the Holy Land had initially been. And, predictably, the last castle of the Cathars to hold out at Montségur was held to be the Grail Castle, where spiritual food and life were available to the *perfecti*. A chalice used at the *manisola* was meant to have been smuggled out of Montségur before its fall and to be buried still – another real Grail – in the caves beneath the fortress. Although some of the Templars joined in the Albigensian Crusade, most of the Cathar knights who escaped the slaughter were received into the Military Order of the Temple of Solomon, which was itself permeated with oriental influences. But another King Philip of France would attack the Templars themselves for their wealth and power and heresies. The new kingdoms of Europe might approve of crusades to liberate the holy city of Jerusalem, but they would not tolerate a secret state within their state, however sacred its purpose might appear to be.

The impending fall of the Templars and the flight of some of the knights with their treasure and their fleet were to change the fortunes of the old Norse and Norman and Scottish family of the St Clairs. The disaster of the Order was the opportunity of the Lords of Rosslyn. They would ingest Templar resources and skills, lead the remaining knights in a battle to win the independence of their country, claim the Orkney and the Shetland Isles and even establish a colony in a New World across the western ocean.

4

The Blood of the Holy Light

WHEN ONE of the Møre family of Viking and Norman ancestry took on the name of St Clair, he took on the name of Holy Light. The name was spelt in Latin in the tenth century. It was Sanctus Clarus, which meant Sainted or Holy, then Clarity or Shining or Light. The Møre family controlled some of coastal Norway, the Orcadian Isles and Caithness in Scotland. The founder of its power was Earl Rognvald, who was celebrated in saga and folk memory. While one of his sons, Torf Einar, took over the Orcadian Isles and became the father of the formidable Thorfinn I, another of Rognvald's sons – Rolf the Ganger (Rollo to the French) – was outlawed by the King of Norway and took a marauding expedition down the North Sea to conquer most of Brittany and Normandy. On the Epte river, he concluded the Treaty of St Clair in 911 with King Charles the Simple, whose daughter he married after he was converted to Christianity. He refused to be a vassal and to kiss the King's foot. 'Not so, by God,' he said, and his Viking seaman who performed the act of homage toppled the seated King by raising the royal foot to his rude mouth.

A saint who had given his name to St Clair-sur-Epte was a Scotsman called Guillermus or William, a favourite Christian name of the later Lords of Rosslyn. He lived at the beginning of the seventh century in a cell near a well, the waters of which were held to cure eye diseases. Healing wells were always associated with Saint

Clair. This one was beheaded for condemning the sins of a local lady. The well still exists by the river Epte, surveyed by the statue of Saint Clair holding his head in the palms of his hands. His cult was widespread in Normandy, because of other Saint Clairs, who had evangelized France from the south. And across the Epte, the Møre cousins, who were left to guard the borders against a French attack from Paris, took the name of St Clair and built a castle with a round keep. Its ruins still dominate the lush cornfields that roll down to the little river that runs into the Seine.

Rolf made himself the First Duke of Normandy. By his second wife, Poppa, he had a son, William Longsword, the second Duke, who extended Norman control as far as the Channel Isles. He granted further lands to his St Clair cousins and hunting reserves near Cerisy. The Bruce family, which had also accompanied his father Rolf from the Orcadian Isles, was given grants in the Contentin. These two Norman neighbours were to play an important role in later Scottish history.

William Longsword's son Richard, the Third Duke of Normandy, had a son Mauger, who became the Count of Corbeil. His eldest son Richard became the Fourth Duke and had another son called Mauger, the first to take the title of the Count de St Clair. After serving as the Archbishop of Rouen, he was given the jurisdiction of the town of St Lô and the land to the north between the rivers Vire and Elle. He built a castle and a church in his domain, giving his foundations the name of St Clair and himself the title. The castle was to be destroyed in the Hundred Years' War, the church to be rebuilt in the nineteenth century, and the river Elle itself to disappear in cattle ponds. Another healing well still survives there in a stew of mud, neglect and nettles.

Walderne was the second son of the first Count de St Clair. With his two brothers, Hamon and Hubert, he opposed the rise of the Bastard William to the Dukedom of Normandy after the death of his father, Robert the Devil. Hamon and Walderne were killed at the battle of Val-es-Dunes, which gave a victory to the future William the Conqueror. Walderne was reputed to have married

Helena, a daughter of the Fifth Duke of Normandy, and thus to have been a cousin of the Conqueror. Certainly, the surviving brother, Hubert de St Clair, was received back into favour and joined other nephews and cousins in the expedition to conquer England. Nine knights bearing the name of St Clair fought at the Battle of Hastings, and one of them was recorded by Wace in his *Roman de Rou* as having charged with three other knights 'a body of the Angles who had fallen back on a rising ground, and overthrew many.' They were richly rewarded by the Conqueror and became his instruments in the rule of England.

Before the conquest, the Normans had many contacts with the ancient Saxon and Cerdic Royal House of Wessex and England. A Cerdic King Ine had founded the monastery at Glastonbury, later associated with the legend of King Arthur and the Knights of the Grail – the cup from the Last Supper that Joseph of Arimathea was meant to have carried there. The last of the Cerdic kings, Edward the Confessor, had a Norman mother and ran a court permeated with Norman influence. Indeed, Walderne's youngest son, William de St Clair, was attached as a youth to the English household of Margaret, the granddaughter of Edmund Ironsides, who was buried in Glastonbury. Her brother Edgar the Atheling had a more legitimate claim to the English Crown than either 'King' Harold Godwin, who died at the Battle of Hastings, or the Bastard Duke of Normandy, who was only the first cousin once removed of Edward the Confessor, although chosen by him as his successor.

Margaret, her brother Edgar and her attendant William de St Clair had to spend many years in Hungary as refugees from the turmoils of the struggles for the English succession. There Margaret learned the extreme piety of its devout Catholicism introduced by King Stephen. And when she was chosen by King Malcolm Canmore as his wife, she took with her to Scotland one of the precious relics of her adopted country, a piece of the True Cross, dark with age and enshrined in a silver and gold and jewelled reliquary, the Holy or Black Rood. Its guardian was her cup-bearer, William de St Clair, now known as 'the Seemly' because of his demeanour and appearance – 'well proportioned in all his members, of midle stature, faire of face, yellow hair'd'.

Her husband King Malcolm III had defeated and killed Macbeth, who had killed his father, King Duncan, in alliance with another cousin, Earl Thorfinn of Orkney, the holder of a further nine Scottish earldoms. Malcolm's first wife, Ingibjorg, had been Thorfinn's daughter and had given him three sons and a truce with the powerful Norse principality to the north. His second marriage, to Margaret Atheling, made him the protector of the rightful king of England with a claim on that throne through his children. By bringing the Holy Rood to Scotland, Margaret appeared to confirm the divine right of the wearers of the Scottish Crown, which was also derived from the Stone of Destiny, held to have been carried to the Kingdom from Jerusalem by way of Ireland.

In that mystical and devout age, the Holy Rood symbolised the possession of the Holy Blood of Christ, while the Stone of Destiny represented the keystone of the Temple of Solomon and the bloodline of the Kings of Judah. The cup-bearer of the Queen Margaret, William de St Clair, now became the keeper of these precious relics. In return, his family were given as their symbol on their shield the Engrailed Cross. The scalloping of the edges of the Cross in a series of cup shapes had three significances. Firstly, it represented the chalice or Grail of the Last Supper, which held the blood of Christ. Secondly, it called up the scallop-shells, which were worn by the pilgrims to St James's shrine at Santiago de Compostela in Spain, then the holiest place in Christendom until the capture of Jerusalem by the First Crusade. Thirdly, it showed an enclosure or engrailing of the True Cross, worn by its bearer as a Knight of the Grail and guardian of that precious relic.

Another mystical association was formed between Queen Margaret and her keeper of sacred pieces. Near Edinburgh by the North Esk river lay the lands of Roslin – not yet also known as Rosslyn. These lands guarded Edinburgh from any attack from the south, and near them was a healing well, where the blood of St Katherine of Alexandria was meant to flow from the ground in an actual discharge of bitumen and black oil, said 'to kure and to remeid divours dolouris of the skin'. Queen Margaret was held to have started the natural flow by bringing a phial of the Saint's blood from her tomb on Mount Sinai. Certainly, the Queen ordered a chapel to be built over the balm well, while William de St Clair was knighted and given for life the lands of Roslin. Again he had become the guardian of holy things. The fact that his very name derived from a Gillermus Saint Clair with a healing well near the Epte could only have increased the identification of Sir William de St Clair or Gillermus de Sancto Claro with a bloodline that defended the Holy Light.

On the death of King Malcolm in 1093, his wife Margaret also succumbed, and the throne was seized by Malcolm's brother Donald Bane, who was brought up under Norse influence and characterised as 'an incorrigible old Celt'. He despised the Norman influence at court and resisted the counter-attack from England by Duncan, King Malcolm's son by his first wife, with a Norman army. Duncan was killed, but Edgar, the son of Queen Margaret, now defeated Donald Bane with the help of another Norman army. His uncle, Edgar the Atheling, was commanding a contingent of Scottish knights on the First Crusade. There is a record of a St Clair on that Crusade among the companions of Godfrey de Bouillon, but he may well have been one of the family still living in Normandy. Certainly, the St Clairs at Roslin remained the defenders of the Scottish Crown, and Sir William de St Clair was killed during an English raid. In the words of the later family historian Father Hay, Sir William 'rushed forward, with a design to put the enimie out of ordre, but being enclosed by the contrary party, he was slain by the multitude of his enimies, whereof he made fall many in heaps flat down before his feet.'

Sir William was showing that berserker streak in battle that was to kill so many of his heirs in reckless charges at the foe. But before his death, he had married Dorothy Dunbar, the daughter of the First Earl of March, who had given him a son Henry. A remarkable legacy of the Lords of Roslin was that the title would descend in an unbroken male inheritance for seven centuries, unique among the Scottish nobility. It added credence to their function and their name – guardians of the Holy Blood and the Holy Light. Moreover, Sir William had married his sister Agnes to Philip de Bruce, the heir of Annandale, and also from Normandy and originally from Orkney, another link between two families important in future history.

Sir Henry de St Clair was granted Roslin 'in free heritage' with the barony of Pentland, adjacent to his property. 'He was of a free nature, and candid in his thoughts and words, very wise and more given to study warre than peace, for which rare qualities, he was entrusted with the militarie commands.' He took over the duties of the defence of the southern marches, and there is evidence of a grant of land in the Lammermuir hills to the St Clair family at this time. He married Rosabelle, the daughter of the Earl of Stratherne, who bore him an heir, also called Henry. The legend of her sad drowning was to give Sir Walter Scott the inspiration for one of his poems in *The Lay of the Last Minstrel* about Roslin Chapel:

> . . . And each St Clair was buried there
> With candle, with book and knell;
> But the sea-caves rung, and the wild winds sung,
> The dirge of lovely Rosabelle.

The Third Lord of Roslin was a Privy Councillor and one of the chief commanders of King David I, who continued the tradition of the St Clairs as guardians of the holy relics of Scotland. In the Stella Templum Scotia Archive at Edinburgh, there remains a bronze reliquary with an engrailed border containing a miniature sculpture of the vision of the Holy Rood, which King David saw, as had the knightly St Hubert, after being injured in the forest of Drumsheuch during a hunt. He held that its intervention saved him from death on the horns of a wounded stag. He began the building of Holyrood Abbey and Holyrood House to safeguard the precious relic brought from Hungary. And the St Clair family of the Holy Light became its protectors and later the great benefactors of the Augustinian royal abbey.

Under King David, the Augustinian and the Cistercian Orders founded monasteries and abbeys across Scotland. Roslin itself became the home of the black monks in the Church of St Matthew, while younger members of the St Clair family were to serve as canons at the neighbouring abbeys of the white monks at New-battle and Melrose, also in religious posts at Selkirk and Kelso, Dunkeld and St Andrews, Dornoch and Dunfermline. Faith and war went hand in hand in the twelfth century, the age of the Crusades. And the St Clairs were always conscious of their duty to the Crown as the defenders of spiritual as well as secular power. King David also encouraged the Templars and gave them some of the first of more than 600 properties that they came to acquire in Scotland. They were the armour of the Cistercians and had the same sponsor, St Bernard of Clairvaux. Like the St Clairs, they served the sword as well as the soul.

The Third Lord of Roslin was sent as an ambassador to King Henry II of England to demand the restoration of Northumber-land. Although his mission failed, he remained in royal favour and married the daughter of the Earl of Mar. His son and heir was again called William, and was succeeded by a Henry, who gave way to another William, the Sixth Lord of Roslin. He was made the Sheriff of Haddington, then one of the larger towns of Scotland, and Warden of the Marches. His appointments con-firmed the long trust that had developed between the Crown and the St Clair family, which had built a castle at Roslin, named after two Celtic words, *Ros*, meaning 'a promontory', and *lin*, meaning 'a waterfall', although later members of the family saw *Ros* as meaning 'red' or 'rose' and Roslin as signifying the Blood of Christ.

'Roslin was att that time,' Father Hay observed, 'a great Forrest, as also Pentland Hills, and a great part of the country about, so that there did abound in those parts great number of harts, hynds, deer, and roe, with other wild beasts.' Hunting was the sport of kings and nobles, and the Sixth Lord of Roslin was also given the post of the keeper of the royal forests, or Grand Master Hunter of Scotland. He was esteemed by King Alexander II for his 'excellent beauty and delicat proportion of body' and was sent as an ambassador to France. His son William was also a favourite of King Alexander III, who made him the guardian of the Crown Prince and the Blood Royal, a position that was to become almost hereditary in the St Clair family. He was further made Sheriff of the whole of Lothian, and later of Linlithgow and Edinburgh and Dumfries. He was used in embassies to France and England, particularly in the wedding negotiations for his royal masters, one of whom married a de Coucy, a family related to the St Clairs of Normandy. He fought against King Haakon of Norway in the Battle of Largs, command-ing a wing of the Scottish army in the victory.

On the death of King Alexander III, Sir William de St Clair became embroiled in the struggle for the succession between John Baliol and Robert the Bruce, who chose his Norman kinsman as one of his noble supporters. The intervention of King Edward I, the Hammer of the Scots, gave the Crown of Scotland to Baliol as an English vassal. And King Edward removed the holy relics of Scotland, the Holy Rood and what he thought was the Stone of Destiny, the symbols of the divine right of the kings of the country, while the Great Seal of Scotland was broken into pieces. He demanded oaths of allegiance to himself and to Baliol, and as he held the sacred relics, Sir William de St Clair swore fealty, but then took up arms again. He and his son and heir Henry were captured at the fall of the castle of Dunbar and were imprisoned in the Tower of London, but they were released in time to help win a major battle for Scottish independence at Roslin Moor.

King Edward had sent an army of 30,000 men to subdue Scotland. The army was split into three divisions of 10,000 men. One Scottish division of 8,000 men opposed them, led by sup-porters of the fighter and martyr for independence, Sir William Wallace, if not always friends of Robert the Bruce. Sir John Comyn came from the Baliol family, but he combined with Sir Simon Fraser and Sir William de St Clair and his son to resist the English forces. The first enemy division was hardly defeated when another division appeared. After prolonged fighting, it was also destroyed. Then, as Father Hay described the great struggle:

> This victory scarce was obtained, when, behold, a new company of ten thousand men is readie to joyne in battle with them, which the Scots beholding became all dismayed; yet, through the persuasive exhortations of their captains, their courage became fresh; and anone the three captains went through all the companys where the wounded and slain were, and slew all the English that were alive, and to every Scot liveing they gave a weapon, to the end they might kill the English that came upon them, and after that, they went to prayer, desiring God to remove their offences, and to consider how just their cause was. The English thinking because they were with heads uncovered, and knees bended, that they craved mercie of them; and so, without thought of any resistance to be made, they came over Draidon Burn, where, contraire to their expectations of friends, they found foes; of men overcome, men redie to be victors. Yea, within short time, put them to flight, although the battle continued for a space with uncertain victory.

The killing at the battle was so terrible that bones are still being ploughed up there and the local names for the site are Shinbones Field, the Hewings, Stinking Rig, and Killburn. Sir William de St Clair was presented with the battleground to defend in future and also English prisoners of quality for ransom. One of them advised him to relocate his castle on the actual promontory above the North Esk, invulnerable on two sides and protected towards the north-west by marshlands called the Stanks. He began the building of the Wall Tower of the castle, which was to be completed by his heirs. He was also 'rewarded by King Robert with a sword, whereof the hand was set with stones, and the scarbard, velvet covered with plate of gold, bearing on the one side this inscription, "Le roy me donne," and on the other the following words, "St. Cler me porte".'

On the death of his father and the barbaric hanging and drawing and quartering of Sir William Wallace by the English, Sir Henry de St Clair committed himself to the cause of Robert the Bruce against the rival claims of the Comyns, who had now sworn allegiance to the English Crown. Robert the Bruce personally stabbed John Comyn in front of the high altar of the church of the Grey Friars in Dumfries. Leaving the church, he met his brother-in-law Christopher Seton, who cut down Comyn's uncle, and asked if Bruce's victim was dead. In a notorious phrase, a companion of Bruce said he would '*mak siccar*' and returned to make sure that the murder of the bleeding Comyn was completed.

One of the first long Scottish poems, *The Bruce* by John Barbour, told of the slaying of Comyn because he had given an indenture to the king of England to be his ally. That was the reason he was killed at Dumfries by Robert the Bruce:

> *Thiddir he raid but langir let*
> *And with schyr Jhone the Cumyn met*
> *In the freris at the hye awter*
> *And schawyt him with lauchand cher*
> *The endentur; syne with a knyf*
> *Rycht in that sted hym reft the lyf.*

> And there he rode at speed and set
> And so with Sir John Comyn met
> At the friary's altar high,
> And showed him with a mocking eye
> The indenture; and with a knife
> Right in that place took off his life.

If Bruce had not committed a ritual murder, he had killed in a holy place. He was excommunicated by the Pope, an act that allowed any nation to mount a crusade against him. That same year, King Edward I crushed the Scottish forces at Methven and had Christopher Seton and his brother executed along with one of Bruce's brothers and Sir Simon Fraser. Bruce was forced to flee, his supporters to lie low. There seemed to be no hope of resisting the English, particularly the dominance of their heavy cavalry. It was the age of the armoured knight, and foot-soldiers could not resist their massed charge. Without fresh resources and armaments, the cause of Scottish independence was condemned.

5

The Fall of the Templars

THE DESTRUCTION of the Templars by Philip le Bel, King of France, in 1307, with the connivance of the Papacy, was due to wealth, greed, arrogance and secrecy. By the thirteenth century, the Templars rivalled the Genoese and the Lombards and the Jews as the leading bankers of the time. They owned some 9,000 manors across Europe, all of which were free of taxes, and they provided security for the storage and transport of bullion. The treasury of the King of France was normally kept in the vaults of the Temple in Paris; the King himself took refuge there when threatened by mobs. The only cash drafts that were readily redeemable were issued by the Templars. They became the bankers of the Levant, and later of most of the courts of Europe. When King Louis VII accepted a large loan from the Order, he noted that the money must be repaid quickly, 'lest their House be defamed and destroyed'. Even the Muslims banked with the Templars, in case the fortunes of war should force them to ally themselves with the Christians. Though usury was forbidden to Christians in the Middle Ages, the Templars added to the money they banked or transported by paying back an agreed sum less than the original amount, while a debtor returned more than his debt. The Paris Temple became the centre of the world's money-market.

That an original group of nine knights in Jerusalem, instituted as an Order to protect some pilgrims on their journeys to the Holy

Places, should have acquired such power and wealth, testified to their integrity and discretion, as well as to the original support of St Bernard of Clairvaux, and the later backing of Pope Innocent III, who saw them as his private army of militant Christians. They were the shock troops of Rome, answerable to no local rulers, only to their elected masters and the Pope. Donations poured into their coffers from those feudal lords who were guilty of not taking the Cross themselves and so paid for the huge military machine which the Templars maintained in the Holy Land. Yet it was their ceasing to function as protectors of pilgrims in Palestine that led to their speedy destruction.

The European Kings, who founded their nation-states, were always short of money. They regularly turned on their bankers, Italians and Jews; they defaulted on their loans and expelled their creditors. The Templars were particularly vulnerable to such treatment. They had lost the Holy Land, their arrogance was almost royal, while their secrecy provoked slander. Something of their notorious pride can be seen in an exchange between King Henry III of England and the Master of the Temple in London. When the King threatened to confiscate some of the Order's lands for his treasury, because the knights were raving with pride and haughtiness, the Master replied, 'What sayest thou, O King? Far be it that thy mouth should utter so disagreeable and silly a word. So long as thou does exercise justice, thou wilt reign, but if thou infringe it, thou wilt cease to be King.' The implication was that he might be deposed by the Templars.

Pride or *superbia* was considered the worst of the sins in the Middle Ages. To this, the Templars added secret rituals and diplomacy, which added to the envy and hatred of them by the princes and the people. They were seen both as the poor knights of Christendom and as rich conspirators against the state and public welfare. When King Philip of France imprisoned more than 600 of the 3,000 Templars in the country in 1307, according to Inquisition records, their interrogation and torture produced confessions that corroborated medieval superstitions, but were the result of applying force and pain. They were not the evidence of truth.

Although the initiation rights of the Templars were secret, there was a Rule of the Temple. Their hidden regulations were to provide the key to their destruction, although they could hardly have existed as a proud and efficient military caste without special ceremonies to distinguish them from other Orders, such as the Hospitallers and the Teutonic Knights. The investitures were secret, being held under cover of darkness in the guarded chapter house. The Rule was clandestine in so far as it was known in its entirety to only the highest officers of the Temple. We know it only in copies, which simply describe the constitution of the Order, and the duties and ceremonies of each rank. But because of this element of secrecy, and because the original manuscript of the Rule has not survived, opponents of the Templars have always postulated the existence of a separate, secret Rule that would endorse blasphemy and sexual licence. The final prosecutors of the Templars were to accuse them of forcing their initiates to spit on the Cross and to become homosexuals; in fact, the Templars were more likely to make a novice tremble in front of the Cross and the Knights of the Order than to make him despise both. An early copy of the Rule tells of one case of sodomy among the Templars in a castle in the Holy Land. The whole group was dispersed and the guilty persons were executed.

An unbiased account of their initiation ritual gives the following details. The Master of the Temple asked the assembled knights three times if there was any objection to a particular novice being admitted to the Order; the novice himself was shown 'the great hardships of the House, and the commandments of charity that existed'. He was also asked if he had a wife or betrothed, debts or hidden disease, other vows or another master. If the novice answered these questions satisfactorily, he knelt in front of the Master and asked to become 'the serf and slave of the House'. The Master replied that many things were required of him and that the

Templars' beautiful horses and costume were no more than the 'outer shell' of their life.

> You do not know the hard commandments that are within; because it is a hard thing for you, who are master of yourself, to make yourself the serf of another. For you will scarcely ever do what you want; if you wish to be on this side of the sea, you will be sent to the other side; or if you wish to be in Acre, you will be sent to the land of Tripoli or Antioch or Armenia, or you will be sent to Apulia or Sicily or Lombardy or France or Burgundy or England or to many other lands where we have Houses and possessions. And if you wish to sleep, you will be made to stay awake; and if you sometimes wish to stay awake, you will be ordered to go and rest in your bed.

Then the novice was warned that he must not enter the Order for his own advantage, but to forsake the sins of the world, to serve Our Lord, to be poor, to do penitence and to save his soul. He took an oath to obey the Master of the Temple in everything, live all his life without private possessions, follow the customs of the House, help in the conquest of the Holy Land, stay for the rest of his life in the Order 'both in strength and in weakness, for better or worse', and never allow a Christian to be robbed of his goods. Once the novice had sworn by God and the Virgin Mary to observe all these rules, the Master accepted him into the Order, putting the mantle on him and promising him 'bread and water and the dress of the poor and much suffering and hardship'. The chaplain then recited the psalm *Ecce quam bonum*, and the knights repeated the Lord's Prayer. The novice would have no illusion, after a ceremony of this sort, that he was not engaged in an Order that demanded total obedience to the end of his days.

Guiot de Provins, the contemporary monk who belonged to many Holy Orders and condemned his own time as 'vile and filthy', testified to the Templars' integrity, praising them above all other religious orders. He found them dedicated unto death, ascetic knights whom his shrinking flesh could admire and refuse to join.

Better far be cowardly and alive,
Than dead, the most famous of them all.
The Order of the Templars, I know well,
Is beautiful and excellent and sure –
But keeping healthy keeps me from war.

Yet those brought up from birth to be knights, who had no hope of marrying or inheriting lands of their own, had often preferred to rise to the command of a Templar castle in the Levant or Spain rather than to subsist on a feudal lord's charity in Europe. Merit in battle and organization meant promotion in the Order. Rarely was feudal rank important in the election of the Grand Master of the Temple, although the increasing wealth and power of the Order tended to attract ambitious and greedy men to try and gain its leadership.

The last overt Grand Master, Jacques de Molay, was not one of these. Experienced in war, illiterate in diplomacy, he fell victim to his own limitations. Among many other French Templars, he confessed under torture to heresies and abominations. Yes, the Templars were homosexuals, forced to kiss the mouth, navel and anus of their initiator. Yes, novices were made to spit on the Cross. Yes, the Templars had worshipped the devil Baphomet, which was a jewelled skull or a wooden phallus. They also worshipped the devil in the form of a cat, in the presence of young virgins and female devils. Thirty-six of the Paris Templars died under torture within a few days of their arrest, and the remainder were only confessing to a hotchpotch of the diabolical and sexual fantasies of their age. Above all, the Templars were made the scapegoat for the loss of the Holy Land; they were accused of selling to the Muslims what they had fought to hold.

This was the only charge against the Templars that had some basis in truth. Over the years, they had become politicians of the Christian faith, more ready to accommodate themselves to Muslim rulers and customs for the sake of their own interests than to attack with the sword every evidence of Islam. This policy, combined with the facts that they spoke Arabic and, unlike other Christian

Orders, wore long beards in the Muslim fashion, played into the hands of their detractors. Opponents of the Templars did not forget that their first home had been a mosque, built on the site of the Temple of Solomon in Jerusalem. A visiting Muslim envoy had been allowed to say his prayers to Allah there, facing Mecca, though the mosque had been converted into a Christian church. The Templars themselves often pointed out that the Virgin Mary, to whom they were dedicated, had her place in the Koran. They knew of the esoteric doctrines of the East; their discipline of prayer, fasting and scourging for sins was severe enough to satisfy the most rigorous Muslim; and they knew that their position in the Levant was tenable only as long as they had Arab allies and the Arab world remained divided. When the Templars were accused of worshipping the phallic idol called Baphomet, they were really being accused of dealing with the worshippers of Muhammad.

Obscene and ridiculous as most of the charges against the Templars were, the Order was open to attack by the secular state for its pride, its independence and its secrecy. Homosexuality, and the coarse gesture of spitting on the Cross, may possibly have existed in some Temples. Yet, on the whole, the Templars suffered because the Kings of Europe wanted to centralize their states. The Kingdom of Jerusalem and the Templars were the victims of the revolutionary Kings who turned their attention to their own countries rather than to uniting Christendom. The Templars had estates all over Europe, while their income in many fiefs was greater than that of the feudal lord. When, in November 1307, the Pope ordered the Kings of Europe to arrest every Templar in their territories, only Denys of Portugal and the excommunicated Robert the Bruce of Scotland did not take the opportunity of plundering such wealth. Though the goods of the Templars were finally made over to the Hospitallers, precious little slipped out of the hands of the Kings; and the Hospitallers were careful to refuse such possessions as might lead them into conflict with the secular power.

Jacques de Molay, who had ruined his sect by ordering it to surrender and confess, ended by retracting his confessions and denying all the evil he had spoken of his Order. In 1314, when he was brought out onto a scaffold in front of Notre Dame to receive his sentence, he declared: 'I confess that I am indeed guilty of the greatest infamy, But the infamy is that I have lied. I have lied in admitting the disgusting charges laid against my Order. I declare, and I must declare, that the Order is innocent. Its purity and saintliness have never been defiled. In truth, I had testified otherwise, but I did so from fear of horrible tortures.' He was burned alive the following day.

So ended the Templars as a known power, the victims of the greed of Kings and of their own pride and wealth. As a contemporary poet asked:

> The brethren, the Masters of the Temple,
> Who were well-stocked and ample
> With gold and silver and riches,
> Where are they? How have they done?
> They had such power once that none
> Dared take from them, none was so bold;
> Forever they bought and never sold . . .

Until they were sold to satisfy the greed of Kings, in whom the state was sovereign and indivisible.

The Flight of the Templars

Although King Philip's seizure and destruction of Jacques de Molay and the French Templars was as efficient an operation as Hitler's coup against Roehm and his Brownshirts, there is no record of his finding the Templar treasure in Paris or the secret archives of the Order or its fleet, based mainly at La Rochelle in Brittany. Much evidence and some tradition point to the removal of the treasure and most of the archives on ships, with refugee Templars taking these to Portugal and to the west and east coasts of Scotland, where they were welcomed. Acting on warnings, de Molay had already had many records recalled and burned. One of the confessions, written down in Latin by the Inquisition and extorted from the French Templar Knights was the testimony of John de Châlons of Poitiers. He stated that Gerard de Villiers, the Preceptor of the Order under the Treasurer, Hugh de Peraud, knew in advance of the mass arrests and fled the Temple in Paris with fifty knights, whom he commanded to put to sea on eighteen Templar galleys. He added that another knight, Hugh de Châlons, had fled with all the Treasurer's hoard – *cum toto thesauro fratris Hugonis de Peraudo*. No Templar who knew of it had dared to confess before he had. Certainly, Gerard de Villiers and Hugh de Châlons escaped the first arrests and were captured only several days later. Whatever they had taken with them was already gone.

Those knights who managed to escape by sea proceeded to Scotland and Portugal, where they landed near Nazare and proceeded to their main stronghold at Tomar. There they were particularly well received because of their experience in navigation. In the Levant, their sailing ships had led in using the compass and the lateen sail rig, which they had adopted from Arab *dhows* and steersmen. The very word they used for a boat, *barca* or bark, was a shortened version of the Arab word *baraka*. And the innovative Portolan maps of the Atlantic coast of Europe and the Mediterranean and North Africa, so different from the Ptolemaic maps previously in European use, seem to have derived from their trading experience and knowledge of Arab cartography, since these first appear soon after the suppression of the Order of the Temple with its skills that it withheld from its commercial rivals. Whatever the Templar refugees brought with them, they were incorporated into the same Order under another title, the Knights of Christ. The ships of the renamed Order sailed under the eight-pointed red cross of the Templars. The African explorer Vasco da Gama was a Knight of Christ, and Prince Henry the Navigator was to become a Grand Master.

In other European countries, the Templars merged with the Hospitallers or left the Order and went underground. In Germany, however, where the Teutonic Knights were carving out an empire to the east, the Templars joined their ranks and accepted a slightly different ritual. The Teutonic Knights, or the Order of the Hospital of the Blessed Virgin Mary of the German House of Jerusalem, had been founded as a field hospital in 1191 at the siege of Acre. They were the remnants of the German contingent to the Third Crusade, and they had hardly reached Jerusalem. Their rule derived from that of the Templars; their headquarters in the Holy Land were at the castle of Montfort-Starkenberg.

When Acre fell one hundred years after their founding, the Teutonic Knights removed their headquarters to Venice. It was a significant choice. Venice lay halfway between the Levant and the overland trading-route from Germany and Prussia, where the knights were already constructing an empire towards the east. In September 1309, Grand Master Siegfried von Feuchtwangen moved the centre of the Order to Marienburg in Prussia. The knights held no power in Venice, the chances of a new crusade were poor, their opportunity lay on the eastern marches stretching towards Russia and they did not wish to share in the fate of the Templars in France. They would be protected in Germany as military agents of the states and the bishops on a crusade to dominate and convert the pagan Lithuanians. With its twelve bailiwicks in the Holy Roman Empire stretching from Alsace to Austria and Saxony, and its Baltic conquests as far as Livonia, the Order was a temporal force.

The Teutonic Knights were also a sea-power. Their support was necessary for the merchants of the Hanseatic League with its two trading-posts on Orkney and the Shetland Isles. Goods that were not shipped down the great rivers such as the Vistula to the Near East, or overland on the trade routes over the Alps to Venice, went on small merchant vessels to the North Sea and down to Scotland and Flanders, England and France. There was also the profit from the trade in furs and salt fish from the Norse colonies in Iceland and Greenland. The St Clair family had maintained connections with the Teutonic Knights and the Templars from the time of the

Crusades. They also had trading connections with the Baltic. It is hardly surprising that the father of Prince Henry St Clair, who was to become the first Scottish Earl of Orkney and the Shetlands, was to die in the service of the Teutonic Knights on their eastern crusade of mastery. Nor is it surprising that his son was to repeat their example in trying to found a military and religious empire in the West.

The Cistercians as well as the Templars had much influence on the development of the Teutonic Knights. Missionaries from that Order had been active in pagan Livonia from the middle of the twelfth century. A crusade was called against the heathen Slavs by Pope Alexander III, but it was unsuccessful. It was followed by the founding of a Military Order, the Brethren of the Sword, which began to defend German colonies towards the East. This Order soon merged into the Teutonic Knights, whose rules and building techniques were also influenced by Cistercian practice through the Templars. Although the charge into Russia was stopped by Alexander Nevsky's victory on the ice at Peipussee, the Teutonic Knights concentrated on taking Prussia and the east Baltic.

With the fall of the Templars and the removal of their headquarters from Venice to Marienburg, the Teutonic Knights consolidated their empire. In Prussia and Lithuania, the inhabitants were converted to Christianity by sword and the efficient administration of the knights from their fortresses. As the English philosopher and cleric Roger Bacon observed, the brothers of the Teutonic Order who laboured for the conversion of the heathens wanted to reduce them to serfdom. Resistance to the Christian knights was against 'oppression, not the arguments of a superior religion'.

Particularly significant in the German Military Order was its cult of the Virgin Mary. Her office was said daily, while a 20-foot-tall mosaic in gold of Her was inlaid in the church of the great castle of the Order at Marienburg. This was a development in northern Europe from the more oriental beliefs of the Templars, although their Rule also declared Our Lady to be the beginning and the end of their religion. The rose within the Rosy Cross within the chalice on the Templar tomb of Sir William de St Clair at Rosslyn does show, however, that the cult of Mary had also reached Scotland. For Her supreme symbol as Queen of Heaven was the foliate rose, the Rose of the centre of the World. She was also the living Grail, for She contained and gave birth to the Body and Blood of Her Son, in the same way as the carving of the chalice serves as the womb of the Rosy Cross. The tombstone further demonstrates how the Templars after their fall merged into the remaining Military Orders, the Hospitallers and the Teutonic Knights, with their variant symbols and the cult of the mystic Rose.

Sure of a welcome from the crusading St Clairs and other neighbouring landowners in Midlothian near their chief presbytery at Balantrodoch – now called the village of Temple – most of the seaborne French refugee Templars made their way to Scotland, probably with their treasury and the remaining archives from the Paris Temple. One French Masonic tradition declares that the records and wealth were taken on nine vessels to the Isle of May in the Firth of Forth near Rosslyn. Others believe that these vessels went to Ireland and then to the Western Isles of Scotland. When the authorities burst into the Irish Templar presbyteries, they found them stripped of ornaments, while Robert the Bruce was receiving new supplies of weapons before the Battle of Bannock-burn – to the cost and complaint of King Edward II of England. Indeed, a recent inquiry has discovered Templar graves near Loch Awe in Argyll by Kilmartin Church. One tombstone bears the steps of the Temple of Solomon leading up to a foliate cross beside a Crusader sword, as on the William de St Clair grave at Rosslyn. Also at the ruined chapel of Kilneuair to the east of Loch Awe, there are the remains of an ancient circular church and a gravestone with the Templar *cross patte*, as there is at neighbouring Kilmichael Glassary. And near Castle Sween lies the fallen chapel of Kilmory, where another Templar cross is carved by a sailing ship, far larger than a war galley, and by a masonic set-square – found only on the early graves of laymen of that Order. And yet, eight other Templar tombstones that have now been discovered at Currie near

Edinburgh and at Westkirk near Culross in Fife suggest that most of the Templars who fled to Scotland sailed to the Firth of Forth rather than to the Western Isles.

At the time, the excommunicated Robert the Bruce held part of Scotland with his army, fighting against the allies and armies of the English King Edward II, who ordered his officers to arrest all the Templars in Scotland and keep them safe in custody. Only two were arrested, and both of them came from over the Border. They were soon released after testifying that their colleagues had fled overseas. It was interesting that an English Templar at his inter-rogation declared that his brethren had fled to Scotland, where the writ of the English King was only partially enforced, and not to the Baltic to join the Teutonic Knights.

Robert the Bruce, of Norman and Scottish royal ancestry, had been excommunicated for the murder of John Comyn, who had defeated three English armies in one day near Roslin with the help of the St Clairs, but had later recognized the sovereignty of England and the Church of Rome. After his apostasy, the third Scottish patriot and guerrilla leader, William Wallace, had been captured and horribly executed by the English. Robert the Bruce had himself crowned on the Throne of Scone – the false Stone of Scone had been removed to England by King Edward I after his victory against William Wallace at the Battle of Falkirk, in which two leading Templars had assisted him, the Master of England and the Preceptor of Scotland. Before the battle, King Edward's Welsh archers had stayed at Balantrodoch, the principal Templar base, and had marched to Falkirk under Templar command. The victory had been won by a cavalry charge led by the two Templar leaders, although both had been killed. But now Bruce was making his stand against King Edward II and his army at Bannockburn, three months after Jacques de Molay was burned at the stake.

The battle took place near Stirling Castle on St John's Day in June, a significant date for the Military Orders. Bruce's army was outnumbered by at least three to one, 6,000 men against 20,000. His deficiency lay in mounted knights. There were some 3,000 in the English army, while the Scots could muster only 500 poorly armed cavalrymen. Accounts of the conflict are sparse and fragmentary. But they testify to two strange events. There was a charge by mounted soldiers against the English archers from a reserve kept back by Bruce. And when all the troops were fully engaged on both sides, a fresh force of horsemen appeared with banners flying and routed the English. While one Scottish legend claims these to have been camp-followers riding ponies and waving sheets and clubs and pitchforks, such a mob could never have put the English King and 500 of his knights to immediate flight. For the charge of this new squadron struck terror in the English, who recognized the force of their foe and probably their war banner, *Beauséant*. On the anniversary of Bannockburn on St John's Day, modern Scottish Templars still pay tribute to their predecessors, who fought in the battle and were martyred there in the struggle for the freedom of Scotland.

Three of the St Clairs fought alongside Bruce at Bannockburn. One of them was the Fighting Bishop of Dunkeld, who destroyed a sea raid by the enemy the following year in Fife. 'Many of the English,' Father Hay reported, 'not getting in time enough to their boats, were cut in pieces. Others, striving to save themselves by swimming, perished in the sea. Others, who were got there, for that they were alreadie too full, were made a prey either to the water which swallowed them up, or to the enimie, who slew them from the shore. Several of their boats sunk, as being too heavily loaded.'

Another of the St Clairs who fought at Bannockburn, the Lord of Rosslyn, was one of the signatories of the Scottish Declaration of Independence at Arbroath in 1320, with its defiant statement: 'So long as a hundred of us are left alive, we will never in any degree be subjected to the English. It is not for glory, riches or honour that we fight, but for liberty alone which no good man loses but with his life.' And the third St Clair in Bannockburn was Sir William, who died later with other Scottish knights in a charge against the Muslims in Spain, while taking the Heart of Bruce for burial in Jerusalem. His is the Grail and Templar gravestone in Rosslyn

Chapel. If refugee Templar Knights did enter the service of Bruce before Bannockburn, William de St Clair would have a strong claim to have been their leader. The evidence lies carved on his tomb, which shows the burial of a Master of that Military Order.

Whoever dispersed the English knights, the victory at Bannock-burn confirmed Scottish freedom and Robert the Bruce as King. The benefit to the St Clairs was immediate, the grant of more lands and a bishopric. For it was to the Firth of Forth that part of the Templar fleet had evidently sailed from France. The extensive Templar properties stretching between Rosslyn Castle and the Seton estate near Musselburgh were centred on Balantrodoch, now known simply as Temple. Its preceptory and church had been built in the middle of the twelfth century between two St Clair castles on lands under the jurisdiction of the St Clairs as Sheriffs of Midlothian. That ruined graveyard is still full of Templar and Masonic tombstones, bearing the symbols of both rites. Although Robert the Bruce confirmed by charter all the possessions of the Hospitallers in Scotland six months after his victory, he made no mention of the Templars at all, any more than he referred to them at the Battle of Bannockburn. Yet, curiously, two charters show a Seton as the Master of the Hospitallers, presiding over 'Temple Courts' at Balantrodoch thirty-two years after the English defeat.

Templar Courts and properties continued to exist in Scotland for some two centuries, and some still exist. Although the Hospitallers were given authority over their proscribed rivals, they never ingested them. Not until 1488 did an extant Charter of King James IV of Scotland confirm the union of the Templars and the Hospitallers and the grants of the lands given to both Orders in *Deo et Sancto Hospitali de Jerusalem et fratribus ejusdem Milititiae Templi Solomonis*. The Knights of the Temple in Scotland remained a group hidden within the mantles of the Knights of St John, and directed from the neighbouring St Clair castle, now known as Rosslyn, where extensive rebuilding and fortification took place, as if the family had received a sudden inflow of wealth and building skills.

The Scottish Knights Templars still commemorate their Oath of

Fealty, first taken three years after the Battle of Bannockburn and restated in 1991 at their festival for the martyrs of the Temple at Torphichen Preceptory, the Lothian headquarters of the rival Hospitallers, which the Templars acknowledge as causing 'the especial nature of the survival of the Order of the Temple in this our native land of Scotland in the fourteenth and fifteenth centuries'. The Oath of Fealty in its modern text, but unaltered in content, explicitly asserts the continuance of the Templars by Robert the Bruce:

> Inasmuch as the ancient realm of Scotland did succour and receive the brethren of the most ancient and noble Order of the Temple of Jerusalem, when many distraints were being perpetrated upon their properties, and many heinous evils upon their persons, the Chevaliers of the Order do here bear witness.
>
> Chevaliers of the Order do undertake to preserve and defend the rights, freedoms and privileges of the ancient sovereign realm of Scotland. Further they affirm that they will maintain, at peril of their bodies, the Royal House of the realm of Scotland, by God appointed.
>
> Chevaliers will resist with all might, attempts by any person, or bodies of persons, wherever or however authorised outwith the ancient realm of Scotland, to take unto themselves the ancient realm of Scotland, or any portion thereof.
>
> As we Chevaliers do fear the perils to our immortal souls, upon our Knightly Honours, we attest the foregoing, and before God we so swear.

Wishing to make his peace eventually with the Church so that a Crusade could not be declared against Scotland as it had been against the heretic Cathars of the Langue d'Oc in the South of France, Robert the Bruce required the Templars to become a secret organization, which was to originate the later fraternities of Masons. According to an old Masonic tradition, Bruce established the Royal Order of Scotland to reward the courage of the Templars at

Bannockburn with the St Clairs appointed as hereditary Grand Masters. The Sovereign Grand Master was the King of Scotland, and it still remains a royal appointment, for the Royal Order exists to this day in its secret power. Although it was not combined with the Templars, many prominent Templars became members of the Royal Order, including its Grand Master in Scotland. This would further explain the burial of Sir William de St Clair in 1328 in the Templar fashion.

Robert the Bruce is also held to have raised the Kilwinning Order of Heredom (or Sanctuary) to the status of the Royal Grand Lodge of Heredom, the prime Masonic Lodge of Scotland, located by the ancient abbey in Ayrshire near Kilmarnock. The original Kilwinning Lodge was reputed to have been founded by King David I, a generous benefactor of the Templars, who certainly have influenced all Masonic symbols and rites to this day. Curiously, the right of sanctuary in the six hundred and more old Templar properties in Scotland was preserved, even for debtors, until the nineteenth century. The Canongate Masonic Lodge in Edinburgh also took the name of the primary Lodge at Kilwinning, and the later St Clairs of Rosslyn presided there. But in medieval times, as the Earl of Rosslyn has stated in his recent book on the family chapel, 'The Barons of Rosslyn held their principal annual meetings at Kilwinning. The ecclesiastical fraternities – the Benedictine Order as at Dunfermline, the Cistercian Order which had a Monastery at Newhall, Carlops, and others, were large employers of labour, and they had many skilled builders, architects and craftsmen under their supervision during the thirteenth and fourteenth centuries, but they were largely superseded by the Masons who were held together by their oaths and customs, and who had a profound influence upon ecclesiastical architecture throughout Europe.'

The Masonic tradition was confirmed by the pretender Larminius, who assumed the post of Grand Master of the Temple in France, and excluded the new Scottish Order as *Templi Desertores*. An authority on the subject in 1912, a Mason herself, has written that 'the tradition connecting Kilwinning with the Templar Grades is persistent and is perpetually cropping up . . . It is plausible, as it explains the union of the trowel and the sword, that is so conspicuous in the high grades'. Less plausible are the names of the Templars whom Masonic tradition held to have escaped to Scotland. One of them was Pierre d'Aumont, said to have been the Preceptor of Auvergne, and later to have become Grand Master of the Templars in Scotland and to have given them the title of Freemasons, adopting the symbolism of architecture. This tradition is false. The Preceptor of Auvergne was Imbert Blanke, who fled to England and was arrested and later released. Moreover, the Templars had many masons among them for their castle- and church-building in the Holy Land, and they were fully aware of the symbolism of their architecture.

The tombstone of Sir William de St Clair indicates another Master of the Templars in Scotland after the Battle of Bannockburn, while the building of Rosslyn Chapel on the principles of sacred architecture by a later Earl William St Clair in the fifteenth century marks the passage of the knightly heirs of the Templars into the democratic Masons. For St Clairs of Rosslyn were the hereditary Grand Masters of the Crafts and Guilds and Orders of Scotland, and later of the Masons of Scotland, for nearly 500 years until the end of the eighteenth century. Through them the knowledge of medieval secret societies entered the Masonic movement. This transmutation was heralded by a sword and a Grail on a stone at Rosslyn.

6

The Search for the Stones

I FOUND a second Grail and Templar stone in the Commendator's House of Melrose Abbey. The dark crimson ruins of this Cistercian institution, the first of that Order in Scotland, was founded seven years after Hugh de Payens had come to the country in 1129 to initiate the Templar centre at Balantrodoch. It was built on the southernmost tip of a swathe of land stretching up to Edinburgh that included two Augustinian hospices on the hills at Soutra and on the coast at St Germains, the Templar presbytery and lands at Balantrodoch, another major Cistercian foundation near Dalkeith at Newbattle, the St Clair lands around Rosslyn and the Seton lands by the sea in East Lothian. Both Scottish families established Collegiate Churches of teaching Augustinian black canons, the St Clairs, as early as 1207, according to local records, as well as a nunnery to the Order of St Bernard, the founder of the Cistercians. Both families remained well connected with the Military and the Monastic Orders, and both were fundamental in the fight for Scottish independence and the support of Robert the Bruce.

So it was not incredible to find another Templar and Grail tombstone at Melrose. Even smaller than the St Clair stone in Rosslyn Chapel, its design was different. Inside the cup of the chalice was a small eight-pointed cross fleury within a large eight-pointed foliated cross. An elongated dirk pointed down beside the stem of the cup to the base, again depicted as the steps of Calvary and of the Temple of Solomon. The name of the dead knight was not engraved upon it. Nearby were other fragments from Templar graves, floral crosses contained within a circle or a disc-head, and a boss of the five-petalled rose and the symbol of the Virgin Mary. Another boss was carved with clam-shells, the emblem of the pilgrimage route to Santiago de Compastela in Spain. A diagram showed the octagonal roof arches of the original central vaulting of the Abbey, signifying the Trinity and its offshoots. It was reminiscent of the Templar practice of 'working the octagon' to reveal the secret of its ritual and its architecture. And a monk's lead badge from the Abbey was a rebus, a play on the word melrose. It showed a mason's mallet or *mel*, which contained a *rose*. Also there was a mason with his mallet carved on the exterior walls of the chapel.

The connection between the Templars and the Cistercians as the architects and Master Masons of their age was further emphasised in the Abbey, where the Master of the works in the middle of the fifteenth century, John Morow, had left his mark on the lintel of the doorway to the wheel-stair – a shield charged with two mason's crossed compasses and a fleur-de-lys. This device was surrounded by an inscription: SA YE CVMPAS GAYS EVYN ABOVTE S VA TROVTH AND LAVTE SALL DO BVT DIVTE BE HALDE TO YE HENDE Q IOHNE MORVO. This Masonic truth meant, *As the compass goes evenly about, so truth and loyalty shall do without doubt. Look to the end quoth John Morow.* Morow also left another inscription, declaring that he was in charge of the mason's work in six major Scottish ecclesiastical buildings, and he prayed to GOD AND MARI BATHE & SWETE SANCT: IOHNE TO KEPE THIS HALY KYRK FRA SKATHE. Mary and St John were also venerated by the Military Orders as the protectors of holy places from harm. The exuberance of some of the carvings on the ruined chapel at Melrose, poppies and roses and a Moor's head along with devils' masks and Green Men, also suggests the influence of Morow on his contemporary Earl William St Clair, who built Rosslyn Chapel with its profusion of stone ornaments. Certainly, the crusading St Clairs and the Cistercians kept in close touch.

The *Chronicle of Melrose*, the principal monastic record of medieval Scotland, runs for a hundred years between the late twelfth and
thirteenth centuries. Its most interesting entry deals with the
disinterment of its second abbot Waltheof, whose relics were
ascribed with the power of working miracles. When his lead coffin,
was opened, his body was discovered to be incorruptible, probably
because it had been embalmed. He had been the youngest son of
Queen Matilda and was descended from the St Clair family through
his father, Simon Senlis, the Earl of Huntingdon and Northampton.
Embalming techniques had been brought back by the Crusaders
from the Near East.

This was proved by the exhumation of another St Clair in 1779
in the Church of St John the Baptist at Danbury in Essex. Three
wooden effigies of crusading knights still exist in the church, two of
whom are St Cleres, so spelt in the town records. Masons' marks on
the walls and a Templar cross fleury on a floor slab identical to two
crosses on the floor of Seton Collegiate Church prove a connection
with the Military Orders. The eye-witness of the exhumation
wrote to *The Gentleman's Magazine* about the opening of the leaden
coffin, which 'enclosed the body of the Knight Templar represented by the effigy' of Robert de St Clere, who died early in the
fourteenth century – after his death, the family name disappeared
from the records of Danbury. Inside the coffin, the body of a 'hearty
youth' was found floating in liquid that tasted 'of catchup and of the
pickle of Spanish olives'. It was as well preserved as Waltheof had
been in his lead coffin.

More proofs of embalming techniques used at the same period
exist at Melrose. On a low wall by the ruins, a plaque reads: AN
EMBALMED HEART WITHIN A LEADEN CASKET, SUPPOSED BY MANY TO
BE THE HEART OF KING ROBERT BRUCE, IS INTERRED NEARBY. This
may well be the Heart of Bruce, which the William de St Clair
beneath the Grail tombstone in Rosslyn Chapel was carrying when
he died in Andalusia, charging ahead of Sir James Douglas and other
Scottish knights into the heart of the massed Moors. He was
showing that berserker streak in the Norse and Norman St Clairs

that made them rush to an almost certain death. The Templars had that fury in battle – a will to die in a holy war and give up the corrupt flesh for the life of the spirit. As Aytoun's poem 'The Heart of Bruce' asserted with such passion:

> The trumpets blew, the cross-bolts flew.
>   The arrows flashed like flame.
> As spur in side and spear in rest,
>   Against the foe we came.
>
> And many a bearded Saracen
>   Went down, both horse and man;
> For through their ranks we rode like corn,
>   So furiously we ran!
> But in behind our path they closed,
>   Though fain to let us through,
> For they were forty thousand men.
>   And we were wondrous few.
>
> We might not see a lance's length,
>   So dense was their array.
> But the long fell sweep of the Scottish blade
>   Still held them hard at bay.
>
> 'Make in! make in!' Lord Douglas cried,
>   'Make in, my brethren dear!
> Sir William of Saint Clair is down:
>   We may not leave him here!'
>
> But thicker, thicker, grew the swarm,
>   And sharper shot the rain,
> And the horses reared amid the press,
>   But they would not charge again.
>
> 'Now Jesu help thee,' said Lord James.
>   'Thou kind and true Saint Clair!
> An' if I may not bring thee off
>   I'll die beside thee there!'

> Then in his stirrups up he stood
>> So lion-like and bold.
> And held the precious heart aloft
>> All in its case of gold.
>
> He slung it from him, far ahead,
>> And never spake he more.
> But – 'Pass thee first, thou dauntless heart,
>> As thou wert wont of yore!' . . .
>
> We'll bear them back unto our ship.
>> We'll bear them o'er the sea.
> And lay them in the hallowed earth.
>> Within our own countrie.

The embalmed heart of Sir James Douglas was enclosed in a silver and lead casket and is in the Douglas Chapel, set in the floor beside the gigantic effigy of Sir James. Opposite are the stone figures of his great-grandson, the 4th Earl of Douglas, the husband of Beatrice St Clair of Rosslyn, who became the mother of four more Scottish Earls. Another broken Templar gravestone in the chapel proves the Douglas connection with that Military Order as well as with the St Clair family, both strong supporters of Robert the Bruce. Sir William de St Clair's heart was not preserved, but his bones were brought back from Spain to be buried under his Templar tombstone at Rosslyn. And at the nearby chapel and cemetery of Old Pentland, erected and endowed by Sir William de St Clair, but now desolate and vandalised, two gravestones 'lying flat upon the ground, the crusading cross and sword on each of them, with the inscription nearly obliterated' were also recorded in the last century. Surviving drawings of the tombs show foliated Templar crosses incised within circles, stems leading down to the steps of the Temple of Solomon or to an upturned chalice base, swords on both, but a measuring rod on the left of one stone. The connections between the Crusaders and the St Clairs, the Templars and the Cistercians, the Military and the Monastic

Orders, are all written in geography and stone from Melrose Abbey up to the Firth of Forth.

The reason that Sir William de St Clair acquired his lands on the Pentland Hills that stretched all the way west from Old Pentland Chapel to Currie on the Water of Leith remains as a legend and a poem, which also attest to his recklessness and to his attachment to Robert the Bruce. The Scottish King was hunting an elusive white hind on the hills, attended by Sir William with his two red hounds, Help and Hold. He wagered his head that his two hounds would kill the white deer before she swam across the burn. The King took the bet against all the royal lands of the Pentland Hills and Moor. Sir William prayed to Christ and the Virgin Mary and St Katherine for mercy for his rashness, and he set his hounds lose after their prey. The hind swam to the middle of the burn and all seemed lost, but Hold seized the deer in the water, and Help pulled the hind to the riverside where Sir William had ridden, and he slew the beast. So William de St Clair of Rosslyn acquired the Pentlands and built his chapel and the Church of St Katherine in the Hopes. And his risk was commemorated by the ballad, in which King Robert the Bruce held him to his bet, saying:

. . . 'But a man dare not take if he dare not lose.
    And the venture is yet to be said:
Should your good hounds fail, then ye shall not choose,
    My lord, but to forfeit your head.'

'A wager! a wager' cried bold St Clair:
    'See bring me both hound and horn.
Go saddle the bonny black Barbary mare,
    The fleetest that feeds on corn.

'A wager! a wager! on Help and Hold!
    Was never a lord of my line
But would wager his life against lands and gold:
    My liege, the broad Strath shall be mine!' . . .

'Light down! light down! thou St Clair bold!
  Or never go hunting more:
Now have at her, Help! Now hang to her, Hold!'
  And they turn her back to the shore . . .

The bold St Clair he sleeps in Spain,
  For with good Lord James he had part.
When they hewed a red path through a host of slain
  To follow the Bruce's heart.

But Help and Hold, as I've been told,
  May be seen in St Katherine's chapelle:
And scion and heir of the house of St Clair
  Still love a good hound well.

My investigation then took me from Melrose to Soutra, an Augustinian hospice on the Lammermuir Hills. The surviving barrel-vault church building was surrounded by snow-banks. This *domus soltre* was founded in the twelfth century by King Malcolm IV as a hospice for travellers and pilgrims, the poor people whom the Templars were bound to protect. Its infirmary and physic garden are now being analysed to discover what drugs from plants were being traded and used to cure the sick in the Middle Ages, what were the diseases of the time, and what treatments and procedures made up medical practice. So much blood was let – the whole of the English army was bled there before its defeat at Bannockburn – that the ground is still infectious. The sign DANGER BIOLOGICAL HAZARD marks samples collected by experts in surgical gloves. For the plague and anthrax can still strike from this infected ground beside the medieval highway from London to Edinburgh, which the English used for their invasions of Scotland, and which the St Clairs defended at Rosslyn.

Second only to the St Clairs were the Setons in their connections with the Monastic and Military Orders. The Collegiate Church of Seton adjoins the destroyed hospice of St Germains, but recent excavations have revealed the quarters of the teaching canons in the churchyard. The incomplete church is built in the cruciform shape of the intended church at Rosslyn; most Scots Collegiate Churches were built in the form of a cross, modelled on the Church of the Holy Sepulchre. At Seton, however, the octagon revered by the Templars has been added to the eastern end of the apse behind the altar to supplement the octagonal vaulting of the roof at the crossing of the church, which is similar to Melrose. Two foliate crosses are carved on slabs on the floor, pointing east. A boss depicts three carved Templar heads, wearing their eastern coifs. On a font, there is the Engrailed Cross of the St Clairs, for Katherine St Clair married the first Lord Seton and endowed the chapel, which was built at the same time as Rosslyn.

Recently, the Templars of Scotland held a ceremony there to commemorate the Seton family's help to the Order and to Scottish independence. They particularly remembered Christopher and Alexander and John Seton, all defenders of Robert the Bruce, all drawn and hanged and quartered by the English. Later, Bruce built the Crystal Chapel on Gallows Hill in Dumfries, where Christopher Seton had died so miserably. His son Alexander left the English forces on the eve of Bannockburn to give intelligence on their strength to Robert the Bruce and joined in the victorious charge of William de St Clair and the Templar knights. He signed the Declaration of Independence at Arbroath with the Lord of Rosslyn, and he was killed at the battle of Kinghorn two years after William de St Clair died in Spain. After the apparent disappearance of the Order of the Temple, the Setons continued to preside over the Templar Courts at Balantrodoch, although their official role was that of a Master of the Hospitallers. They were the Janus family, looking two ways at the authority, by which the Order of St John was given control over the Order of the Temple of Solomon, although it never assimilated the invisible and separate properties of the other organization.

I also discovered a Collegiate Church at Corstorphine near Edinburgh, with Templar and St Clair tombs and a hidden Grail.

Sir Adam Forrester had founded the chapel fifty years before the new chapel at Rosslyn, and his son John built it into a Collegiate Church at the same time as those at Rosslyn and Seton. He married Jean, the daughter of Prince Henry St Clair, the Earl of Orkney and a voyager to North America. He still lies beside his wife on a tomb in the chapel, she in a long dress with stone pleats, her Bible clasped in her hands. Below her is carved the St Clair coat of arms of ship and Engrailed Cross, matched by the Forrester arms of three bugles. On the opposite wall of the church is set a huge Templar stone with a cross fleury inside a circle and a stem leading down to the steps of Calvary and the Temple of Solomon; a Crusader sword is etched by its side. By the Priest's Door another memorial stone is inscribed to a chaplain named Robert Heriot, who died in 1443. Its only orna- ment is a chalice or Grail, which looks like two triangles set on end with the world as a ball dropping within. It was used as a model for the silver communion cups of later centuries. These are still in use at Corstorphine.

These three Collegiate Churches, which encircle Edinburgh to west and south and east, were run by the black canons, the Augustinians. The Augustinians were mainly a teaching fraternity, taking tithes from agricultural land, while the Cistercians were pioneer farmers and builders, creating abbeys and plantations from the wilderness. In Scotland, the black monks and friars were held to be English spies, reporting from Inchcolm to the English Court on all Scottish shipping in the Firth of Forth. The Bishop of Carlisle certainly served the English King Edward I, the Hammer of the Scots, as an intelligence system. He asked the Augustinians in Scotland to provide him with news of troop movements in the north. And when an English knight removed gold and silver from the Augustinian hospital at Soutra, he was forced by the Court at London to return it. Invading English armies would burn Cister- cian abbeys such as Melrose and Newbattle, while sparing Augus- tinian properties. It was to be a disaster for Prince Henry St Clair that the black friars would inform on his successes in Orkney and the Shetland Isles, and on his colonizing expedition to the New

World. For a rare English raiding expedition was waiting for his return from North America to kill this overmighty lord of the Far Northern seas.

The Cistercians, however, were farmers and merchants, and their close connection with the Templars taught the knights how best to exploit the resources of the lands that were donated to them. There were grain mills at Melrose on the Great Drain, while the New-battle monks mined coal at Tranent and exported it to France. And at Currie, south-west of Edinburgh on the Water of Leith on a bridle-path from Rosslyn over the Pentland Hills, the Templars built an industrial base, using water-power to grind flour and crush iron and silver ore from their Hilderston quarry near Linlithgow. And it was at Currie that I found the first Templar gravestones in Scotland that linked the Order to the Masonic crafts, similar to one recently discovered in the cemetery of Castle Pilgrim in the Holy Land, which has a hammer and a set-square carved beside a Templar cross.

Lying in fragments outside the Georgian church of Currie are broken carved stones, recently unearthed and set as a border to the path. Two of them are Grail and Templar stones, the chalice ending in the steps of the Temple of Solomon. One of them has a strange and beautiful cup, containing two circles with an opening between them, as if Christ's blood were pouring down into the hollow stem of the Grail. On one side, a dirk is incised, on the other a knight's sword with rounded pommel and square hilt. The other chalice encloses five circles within a star, the symbol of the Virgin Mary: only one sword is carved on the stone with a triangular pommel and down-curving hilt. Two other broken tombstones show the Templar octagonal cross within a disc-head, while one is incised with a mallet and a compass on either side of the stem of the Grail cup.

Within the church is another Templar knightly tomb engraved with sword and cross, but on either side of the church door, two primitive burial stones have been set, probably of lay brothers or squires attached to the order at Currie. Both show rough Templar octagonal crosses within jag-toothed circular heads, and both have hilts protruding from a stem that carries down the stone to an oblong base scratched with lines. Both have a pair of scissors or shears to the left, while one has a dirk with a double hilt to the right. The tools suggest work at woollen or building trades, although the dirk suggests a military role as well. But the stones at Currie prove the incontrovertible link between the Templars and the craft guilds in Scotland before the official disappearance of the Order, and its translation into the Masons through the Setons and particularly the St Clairs at Rosslyn.

The very charters of Newbattle Abbey, which range from the early twelfth to the sixteenth centuries, stress the close connections between the Cistercian monks and the Templars and the two Lothian families of knights. One series of charters shows the hereditary bakers of the Kings of Scotland resigning their lands at Inverleigh to the St Clairs of Rosslyn. Other charters dealing with the land rights were signed by a William and a Henry de St Clair and an Alexander and a Richard Seton. Another charter assigned to William de St Clair *tota terram meam que vocatur Tempil-land*, which demonstrated that the Rosslyn family were assigned the Templar property at Balantrodoch or Temple after the official disappearance of the Military Order. Six previous charters were concerned with dealings between the Cistercian monks at Newbattle and the Templars at their headquarters at Balantrodoch. Later charters of the Collegiate Church at Midlothian maintained that the Rosslyn Church of St Matthew had existed from the twelfth to the sixteenth century as a teaching organization of black canons, whose property lay north of the cemetery and west of the castle there.

In these charters, dog Latin turned to Lowland Scots speech, suddenly referring to *the quhilk day*. At the time, the rebuilder of Rosslyn Chapel, Earl William St Clair, was commissioning the earliest extant translations from French into the Scottish vernacular, *The Buke of Batailles*, and *The Buke of the Ordre of Knychthude* and *The Buke of the Governance of Princes*. As acknowledged by its translator,

Gilbert de Hay, once Chamberlain to the King of France, it was done at the request of 'our liege and myghty Prince and worthy Lord William, Erle of Orkney and Caithness, Lord Synclear, Chancellor of Scotland in his Castell of Roskelyn'. It stated clearly, 'God himself ordanyt Knychthude and honoured it and it honoured him and also all the people honours Knychthude.' Surviving records confirm the close links between the monks and the Christian warrior Orders and the two powerful Lothian families, so close in geography and history.

In the three centuries between the reigns of the Scottish King William the Lion and James II, the St Clairs or De Sancto Claros in Latin also signed fifteen charters and grants of land concerning Melrose Abbey. Their names were variously spelt DE S, DE SCO, DE SCO CLER, DE SCO CLARO and SANTCLER. One was Viscount of Edinburgh, one was Bishop of Glasgow, and one was a Rector, while two were Archdeacons of Melrose Abbey itself at the time of their kinsman St Waltheof in the twelfth century. The documents usually asked God to bless 'the Virgin Mary of Melrose and the monks there'. Henry, the father of the William de St Clair of the Grail tombstone, had also helped to win the Battle of Bannockburn with his brother, the fighting Bishop of Dunkeld, and he signed three charters at Melrose for King Robert the Bruce as well as the Scottish Declaration of Independence at Arbroath. The last charter signed by the family, before Melrose Abbey was finally destroyed at the Reformation, bore the name of the William St Clair, who was the builder of Rosslyn Chapel, and of William Seton, also the builder of the cruciform Collegiate Church in the place that still has his name. The *Munimenta de Melros* again are proof of the close connection between the Kings of Scotland, the St Clairs from Rosslyn and the Setons and the Cistercian monks. The Monastic Order in its white habits and the Military Order in its white cloaks and red crosses were founded in the same age and sponsored by the same Saint, Bernard of Clairvaux. In a sense, the Templars were the armed fist of the Cistercians. But both were architects and builders. From their example and ritual, the ancient crafts of Scotland took their guide.

My quest for Templar stones ended across the Firth of Forth in Fife. At Westkirk near the ruins of the Cistercian abbey of Culross, a cemetery and a roofless chapel lie among pastures and wheatfields. Masonic gravestones of the eighteenth century fill the graveyard as at Currie and Corstorphine and Temple with their symbols of the skull and crossbones and the hourglass of time as well as the tools of the trade, plumb and hammer and maul and set-square. But at Westkirk, shipwrights were buried, so that the stones show sailing vessels and carpenters' planes as well as hammers. Their ancestry is proved in a remarkable way. Three Templar tombstones have been used as lintels for the doorways of the ruined chapel. And beside the swords and the stems of flowering crosses, leading down to the steps of the Temple of Solomon, are carved a hammer-axe and a set-square above a measuring-rod. In four churchyards near the Firth of Forth, Templar tombstones, sometimes with mason's tools, are to be found near the grave slabs of the later Masons of Scotland, often with the same shapes of tools carved on the stone. The transference of the symbols of the medieval Military Order to the Crafts and Guilds and Masonic Orders is graven.

At the old Cistercian abbey of Culross nearby, the octagonal rib vaulting of the chapter house is like that of Melrose. The white monks were heavily engaged in the wool and salt trade for Baltic timber. The merchant's house of Sir George Bruce at Culross Harbour is called 'the Palace' and is fascinating because its wall shows the insignia of the Guild of Hammermen and Shipwrights, which met in a panelled room where there was a painting of the Temple and Judgement of Solomon. As at Westkirk, there is a direct link between the Military Order of the Temple of Solomon and the belief of the later Masons and Lodges of Scotland. Again in the Magdalene Chapel in the Cowgate in Edinburgh, there are stained-glass windows of the fifteenth century depicting Hammermen with their emblems and the Temple of Solomon. In paint and also in glass, the link between the Templars and the Masons is proven. And through their hereditary Grand Mastership of the Crafts and Guilds and Orders of Scotland, the St Clairs of Rosslyn were the family that translated hermetic and aristocratic knights into international and democratic Masons.

7

Finding the Grail

ROSSLYN CHAPEL is the Third Day of Creation in stone. It is a rebuilding of the Temple of Solomon and contains dozens of small Temples of Solomon carved within its luxuriant friezes of plants and leaves and flowers. It was also built as a Chapel of the Grail with the Knights of the Grail buried in its vaults. In my quest to decipher this secret, I had to search for what the Grail was meant to be before I could discover it at Rosslyn. Its myth also derives from the time of the Crusades.

Not until the end of the twelfth century did the Church allow the Elevation of the Host to the congregation. The sacred mystery was unveiled. All could see the chalice or the Grail. It was part of the spiritual awakening of Western Christendom at the time. There were discoveries or rediscoveries in science and mathematics and philosophy, the founding of convents and monasteries and Military Orders, chivalry and courtly love, the making of the Gothic cathedrals and the quest to reach Jerusalem and build a holy and heavenly city on earth. And from the quest of the Crusaders for Jerusalem flowered the quest for the Grail. It was a martial pilgrimage in search of the place of the Holy Spirit, of the grave of God, and of peace and plenty on earth before the vision of Heaven.

Only a knight without sin could reach the Grail, which ministered to the needs of its guardian knights in a castle on the Mount of Salvation. The way to the Grail was by trial and joust, by test and tribulation. The knight had to survive sitting at a Last Supper in the empty Judas seat, the Siege Perilous. If he was a sinner, he was swallowed up. If he was stainless, he might search for the Grail. His virtue proved the Gnostic belief that Judas was also a Saint, for without his betrayal of Jesus and his hanging of himself, Christ would not have been hanged from the Cross. Half monks and half warriors, the knights of the Military Orders saw themselves as the Knights of the Grail. Indeed, the Templars were identified as the keepers of the Grail in two of its romances.

The Grail itself changed its shape and substance. In the Langue d'Oc, the language of the troubadours in Provence, it was spelt *graal*. One of its first appearances was in 1204 in the Chronicle of a French monk, Helinandus. He wrote that the Grail was the bowl that the Lord had used at the Last Supper with his disciples. It had appeared in a vision to a British hermit 500 years before. The word *graal* derived from the Latin and French *gradalis* or *gradale*, a wide and hollow vessel made out of gold or silver, from which the wealthy used to eat portions of delicious foods. Spelt *greal* or *grazal* or *grial*, the word still means in the dialects of the Alps and the Pyrenees a cup or bowl of wood, earthenware or pottery. Other derivations of the word from *grais* or *grès*, meaning stoneware, or *grille*, a patter of ironwork, are unlikely. Grail does, however, sound much like Grace, and in the thirteenth-century romance, *Merlin*, this was made clear:

> *Et ces gens claiment cel vaissel,*
> *dont ils ont celle grâsce – Graal.*

> And these men call this vessel
> which gives them this grace – the Grail.

The writing of the Grail legend and the romances of King Arthur's knights was the work of a French cleric and poet, Chrétien de Troyes, born about 1135 while the Crusaders still held Jerusalem. He was patronised by the cultivated Countess Mary of Champagne, the daughter of the French King Louis VII and Eleanor of

Aquitaine, who later married the English King Henry II. Daughter and mother were said to have presided at a Court of Love, which insisted on a knightly code of chaste behaviour to women, as did King Arthur's Round Table. Countess Mary made Champagne the vineyard of the culture of courtly love and chivalry. But when her husband Count Henry went away to the Holy Land and died a week after his return to Troyes, she left public life and refused to marry the new patron of her poet Chrétien. He was the widowed Philip of Alsace, Count of Flanders, and eventually Regent of France. His first wife had been her cousin and a niece of Eleanor of Aquitaine. He also went on two expeditions to the Holy Land, the second time in 1191 on the Third Crusade. He died of the plague there without recapturing Jerusalem, now lost to the Muslim armies of Saladin.

Chrétien dedicated his last unfinished romance, *Perceval, or, The Story of the Grail*, to the crusading Count Philip of Flanders, whose father had even left a Chapel of the Holy Blood of Christ at Bruges – the sacred relic was his reward for valour shown on the Second Crusade. Chrétien's other sources came from classical myths such as the *Krator*, or cup, in which creation was mixed; from the Gospels and French heroic epics such as the *Chanson de Roland*; and from Celtic legends. Breton bards were popular at the Court of Champagne with their stories of Bran and Taliesin, of the speaking severed head and the cauldron of Annwn and the horn of plenty, of Finn and Lug and Cuchulainn, of Tristan and King Arthur and Perceval. There was also a French version in verse of Geoffrey of Monmouth's *History of the Kings of Britain* with its Arthurian tales. And Champagne was a crusading Court that received many influences from Sufi beliefs and the mysterious religions of the Near East, as well as from the Manichean and purist creeds of the Cathar movement in Provence – the eternal struggle of God against the Devil, the journey from the corrupt flesh to the real life of the spirit, the *consolamentum* or chaste kiss of reception into the company of the holy, led by the sinless *perfecti*. But Chrétien claimed that he had merely put into rhyme a lost book loaned to him by his patron Count Philip:

> He tried and tried time after time
> The best tale ever told to rhyme.
> The royal courts recount the tale:
> It is the story of the Grail.

In the poem, Perceval was a simpleton and a lout, who had to be trained into the ways of chivalry. When he first saw the Grail in the castle of the wounded Fisher King, his failure to ask the right question and to heal the King showed his lack of grace. The King had an incurable wound in the thigh or groin from a bleeding lance, like the one the blind Roman centurion Longinus put in the side of Christ, only to be given back his sight by the blood and water of the Saviour running down into his eyes. It was this Holy Lance that a cleric from Provence had discovered at the siege of Antioch and so had saved the First Crusade. Perceval's bleeding lance had made a Waste Land of the King's domains, but it could also cure the King's abscess and create an Eden from the desert.

The Grail was variously seen as a creation of jewels and pure gold, a platter long enough to hold a fish – the symbol of the Christian faith – also small and holy enough to contain a single wafer of Christ's body from the Mass, which was the sole nourishment of the wounded Fisher King. As in the miracle of the loaves and the fishes, the Grail could provide endless food and drink as well as be a fountain of youth. In later versions of the Grail story, the vessel became the chalice at the Last Supper, which Joseph of Arimathea used afterwards to collect the blood that flowed from Christ's wounds. It was Joseph who brought the Grail to Britain with the word of Christ, and he left the holy relic at Glastonbury, from where it reached King Arthur and the knights of the Round Table. Still another Welsh prose version of Perceval, named *Peredur*, actually reverted to Celtic legend and the martyrdom of St John the Baptist. The Grail was now held to be a platter in which a severed head floated in blood. So was it in the *Lancelot Grail*, where the text was revealed to the writer in marvellous terms:

> Here is the book of Thy Descent,
> Here begins the Book of the Sangreal,
> Here begin the terrors,
> Here begin the miracles.

Yet in the *Parzifal* of Wolfram von Eschenbach, the Grail and the source of its story were given their most intriguing form. Wolfram was a German troubadour knight, and he claimed that Chrétien de Troyes had wronged the tale, which actually derived from a Provençal cleric named Kyot, probably Guyot de Provins, a supporter of the Templars. But Wolfram further claimed that the true source of the Grail was Oriental. A Jewish astronomer named Flegetanis had recorded the story in a foreign language, most likely Arabic, in Toledo under the Moors. His identification of the Grail as a green stone fallen from the sky, after the battle of Lucifer with the Angels, had close affinities with the source of the sacred Islamic Black Stone at the centre of Mecca, a meteorite also believed to have fallen from Heaven and to be a means of communication with God. The Koran stated that it was given by the Angel Gabriel at the time of the building of the cubic shrine, the Ka'aba, where it is kept. Ibn Malik also told of a vision of the Prophet Muhammad, in which He ascended to the skies and saw a green goblet 'of such penetrating brightness that all the seven heavens are illuminated by it . . .' A voice declared, 'O Muhammad, the All Highest God has created this goblet for Your enlightenment.' Both divine stone and cup are important in Islamic belief.

In *Parzifal*, Wolfram von Eschenbach went as far as giving his perfect Christian knight a piebald half-brother Feirefis, born in the Levant. The subtext of the long romance is, indeed, the reconciliation and respect of Christian for Muslim, as is the change in the nature of the Grail to a stone fallen from heaven. *Parzifal* begins by defining lack of faith as dark and the Christian soul as white:

> As one sees the magpie's feathers, which are both black and
>   white,
> Yet one may win to blessing . . .

Eschenbach also stresses the hidden significance of his text: 'I tell my story like the bowstring and not like the bow. The string is here a figure of speech. Now *you* think the bow is fast, but faster is the arrow sped by the string.'

In *Parzifal*, Gamuret Angevin, a knight from the crusading French family of Fulk of Anjou, which produced the Kings of Jerusalem, takes up service with the Muslim Baruch of Baghdad. Dressed in his surcoat 'green as the emerald vase', Gamuret defends a black Muslim queen's city, defeating Scots and Norse and French Crusaders. He then marries the queen, returns to Europe and leaves her with their son Feirefis, striped like a humbug, 'dark and light, black and white . . . as a magpie the hue of his face and hair.' Feirefis grows up to become a supreme knight, whose surcoat of precious stones and asbestos shield and cloak of salamander can defeat knights of fire. Back in Europe, Gamuret marries Queen Herzeleide and then returns to fight for the Baruch at Alexandria, where he is treacherously killed because a he-goat's blood is poured onto his diamond helmet, which makes it soft as a sponge and vulnerable to a spear-thrust. Other Crusaders serving their Muslim rulers bury the Angevin knight under an emerald cross presented by the Baruch, while Parzifal is born to Gamuret's abandoned queen.

As in the romance of Chrétien de Troyes, Parzifal begins his career in chivalry as a fool, a rapist and a robber. So when the Fisher King with his incurable wound, whose 'life was but a dying', directs him to the Grail Castle, he is tongue-tied at the wonders that he sees. A squire carries the bleeding Holy Lance through the great hall in front of the assembled knights of the Holy Grail, while the Grail Queen bears the Grail stone on a cushion of green silk:

Root and blossom of Paradise garden, that thing that men call
     'The Grail',
The crown of all earthly wishes, fair fullness that never shall
     fail.

Unknown to Parzifal, the Grail Queen is his aunt. She lays the Grail on a pillar of jacinth, and its horn of plenty nourishes all the knights and maidens in the castle:

> It was the Grail that fed them, who before the Grail did stand.
> For the food and drink each was desiring, each might stretch out his hand . . .
>
> Food warm or cold, or dishes that known or unknown can be, Food wild or tame − Such riches you never on earth shall find . . .
>
> For the Grail was the crown of blessing, the bounty of the earth's delight.

Now Parzifal is given a mystic sword, its hilt carved from a ruby. But he does not question the mystery of the bleeding lance or the abundant Grail or the incurable wound of the Fisher King. Simpleton that he is, he wakes in the morning in a deserted castle and rides away to King Arthur's camp, where he is blamed by the sorceress Kondrie for not asking the Fisher King the question that will heal him. He is even told that his Muslim half-brother Feirefis will marry the Grail Queen on Monsalväsch, the Mount of Salvation. Parzifal leaves on the quest for the Grail again and kills a knight who is defending the Grail Castle. He is bitter against God, who has made a fool of him. But he meets a hermit, Trevrezent, who has a green shrine or reliquary, and who reveals to him the origin of the Grail and the nature of its defenders.

Here *Parzifal* specifically identifies the Knights of the Grail as *Templiesen*, wearing white surcoats with red crosses, as the Templar Knights did. The Templars, of course, had many contacts with their Muslim equivalents, the Sufis, and some of their secret practices derived from oriental mysticism, particularly a belief in selfless obedience and purity. The German romance preaches religious toleration between Christianity and Islam, especially when a Crusader may rule over a Muslim land or a Muslim over Christian believers. When Parzifal finally does ask the Fisher King the right question and heals him and himself becomes the Grail King, Feirefis is baptised from a ruby font filled with holy water by the Grail, and he marries the Queen of the castle, who gives birth to the Christian African emperor Prester John. At his baptism, these words appear as writing on the Grail, carved on the stone:

> The Templar whom God to a strange folk should send as head, Must ban all word or question of his country or home or race, If his subjects want their rights from him and would in his sight find grace,
>   They must not ask his origin, for he must leave them straightaway.

This concept of semi-divine rule on earth by a companionship of mysterious monastic Knights Templars confirmed the links between the concept of the Grail, the Crusades and the Military Orders, which were influenced by Islam because of a mutual respect bred by long diplomacy and frequent wars over the Holy Land and Jerusalem. The Knights of the Grail were the heirs of classical and oriental, Celtic and Christian tradition. And most significantly Wolfram von Eschenbach wrote of the Knights of the Grail:

> By a stone they live,
> And that stone is both pure and precious – Its name you have never heard?
> Men call it Lapis Exilis –
>   If you daily look at that stone
> (If a man you are, or a maiden) for a hundred years,
> If you look on its power, your hair will not grow grey, your face appears
> The same as when you first saw it, your flesh and your bone will not fail
> But young you will live for ever – And this stone all men call the Grail.

Wolfram von Eschenbach developed this description of the Grail as a stone taken down from Heaven by angels, who then returned on high because of the sins of mankind. On Good Friday, a Dove flew down with the white Host to lay on the stone – the body and blood of Christ.

> The stone from the Host receives all good that on earth may
>   be Of food or drink,
> which the earth bears as the bounty of Paradise.
> All things in wood or water and all that fly beneath the skies.

This fallen stone, which was all fruitfulness and gave eternal youth, was also called *lapis exilis* by the alchemist Arnold of Villanova. He identified it as the Philosopher's Stone, not as the Grail. It was not made from green emerald, but was unremarkable in appearance. This correspondence made commentators look for alchemy in *Parzifal* and presume that the author meant *lapis elixir*, the life-giving stone, or Philosopher's Stone. Certainly Wolfram von Eschenbach was influenced by oriental and Cathar beliefs. The Jewish philosopher Flegetanis, whom he declared to be the dis-coverer of the Grail and of the bloodline of King Solomon, was thought to be Thabit ben Qorah, who lived in Baghdad at the end of the ninth century and translated Greek texts into Arabic from the legendary emerald tablet of Hermes Trismegistus, the semi-mythi-cal founder of alchemy. Wolfram's authority, Kyot or Guyot de Provins, was said to have lived in Jerusalem and at the court of Frederick Barbarossa, as well as being an initiate of the Templar mysteries, including their association with the Gnostics and the Assassins, the Islamic sect founded by the Old Man of the Moun-tains, almost as important in eastern myth as King Solomon and his Temple. The Templars were believed to be the guardians both of the Grail and of the Temple of Solomon. It was perhaps significant that Solomon's Temple stood upon a rock, *lapis*, at the centre of the world, and this contained the Ark of the Covenant, the fount of the Christian faith. The cornerstone 'which the builders refused' in Psalms was another symbol of Christ. And it was also upon this *lapis* or rock that the Christian Church was founded.

Furthermore, there was a legendary treasure of Solomon, which was taken to Rome after the fall of Jerusalem, then seized by the

Western Goths. When Muslim armies captured Toledo, they asked after Solomon's Table, which was meant to be able to feed all who sat down to eat and to be made from a gigantic emerald, the sacred green stone of the alchemists. The Table was said to be hidden away in the mountains of Spain in a Grail Castle. Charlemagne was also said to have copied the Table of Solomon by having the universe made as three circles in jewels and precious metals, then set on legs of gold as another version of King Arthur's Round Table for himself and twelve knights. The Koran itself referred to another table brought down from Heaven by Jesus to feed Him and the Apostles, but this divine gift disappeared again because of the sins of mankind.

The Templars were also named as the keepers of the Grail in the anonymous romance *Perlesvaus*, but now they were crusaders against pagan Islam. The Grail was the chalice of Christ's blood, not a mystic stone, which might also signify *vas Hermetis* or the Philosopher's Stone of the alchemists, capable of transmuting all to spiritual harmony. There was no peace or compromise with Muslim chivalry or faith in the *Perlesvaus*. Its French author claimed that it was based on a Latin book written by a monk of Glastonbury; but its detailed accounts of weapons and armour and military strategy, as well as its praise of the Knights of the Grail protecting their sacred secret in their mantles embroidered with red crosses, suggested that the writer was a member of the Templar Order. The Grail was described as the Eucharistic chalice of the Last Supper brought over to Britain by Joseph of Arimathea; but that was its final and fifth form as seen by King Arthur after attending a sacrament given by hermits. The bleeding lance was also the lance of Longinus, which pierced Christ's side on the Cross and was rediscovered by the Crusaders at Antioch. Also visible was the bloody sword that had cut off the head of St John the Baptist, revered by the monastic knights. And the Grail Castle was put into transcendental terms. It was called Eden and the Castle of Joy and the Castle of Souls, as if it were a paradise on earth.

The enduring version of the Grail story, the *Queste del Saint Graal*, was probably written by a Cistercian monk, perhaps for King

Henry II of England, during whose reign King Arthur's grave was officially discovered at Glastonbury. This Monastic Order was always associated with the Knights Templar and the Spanish Knights of Calatrava. Galahad was preferred to Perceval as the man without sin who could find the Grail. It is interesting that he had to prove his descent from King Solomon to take up the mystic broken sword of David, which would achieve his quest – the Templars were the Knights of the Temple of Solomon. As Emma Jung wrote in *The Grail Legend*, 'In the *Queste*, many motifs, such as the legend of Solomon, which stem from Oriental fables are to be found side by side with Celtic motifs.' The Grail itself was a dish of plenty, when it came to King Arthur's Court at Whitsuntide. There the Round Table of the universe of the knights was said to be the third most important table in the world, the first being the square table of the Last Supper, the second, the square Grail table of Joseph of Arimathea. There was a clap of thunder and a brilliant ray of light. The Grail then appeared, covered with white velvet, floating free. 'The chamber was filled with a pleasant fragrance. As the Grail went round the table each person was served with the food he desired.' Later, it became the chalice or vessel of the Mass, holding the blood of the Saviour. The allegory was more Christian than Celtic.

In his Grail romance, *Le Morte d'Arthur*, Sir Thomas Malory told of Solomon's ship, his floating Temple. On the ship was a bed made from wood from a tree planted by Eve. When Solomon had slept on the bed, an angel had come to him and said that the ship was 'but faith and belief'. This allegory was another reference to those knights of the Order of Solomon, who were the only ones to have the wisdom and the faith to cross seas in search of the Grail of the divine grace. King Solomon and his vision were the carriers of the secret knowledge of the Christian faith.

Yet there was a strong Celtic influence in the legends of the Grail, particularly about an 'otherworld' to which the dying heroes went – Arthur to Avalon, Bran to the blessed isles to the west rather than to the Monsalväsch or Mount of Salvation on which the Grail Castle was built. All the marvels of that castle of the Fisher King were also to be found in the castle of the divine Lug, which held the treasures of the Celtic gods, including a bleeding lance – this was also possessed by the Welsh Grail Knight Peredur – a bottomless drinking vessel, a cauldron that could feed an army, an unconquerable sword, and a stone fallen from Heaven as in *Parzifal* – the Stone of Destiny or Scone, on which the Irish and the Scots Kings were crowned until the English took away its replica for their coronations of the Kings of Great Britain in Westminster.

This sacred stone was traditionally said to be Jacob's Pillow or the Stone of the Covenant. It proved the descent of the Kings of Scotland from the Kings of Judah and Israel and the House of David. In Bethel, Jacob was held to have set up his Pillow or Pillar and to have anointed it with oil. God then made a Covenant with him that his sons would always rule Israel as long as Israel recognized the Lord God. The stone Pillow or Pillar was the witness of this sacred bond. In legend, during the persecution of the Jews by Nebuchadnezzar, the holy prophet Ollam Fodhla or Jeremiah brought Jacob's Pillow to Tara, accompanied by Princess Tephi, the daughter of King Zedekiah of Judah. She married Eochaidh I, the Ardath or High King of Ireland. And the holy stone of Judah became the coronation stone of the Inch High Kings, until Fergus More, the first King of Argyle, brought the sacred stone to Scotland, to prove his anointed descent from the House of David by consecration and coronation. This confusion of the Stone of Scone with the stone before the Ark of the Covenant in Jerusalem was yet another proof of the need of the priest-kings and later Christian national Kings to prove their legitimacy and divine right to rule by deriving their authority from the most sacred rock of their religion, on which all faith should be founded. And in Scotland, as in *Parzifal*, the Templars were the traditional guardians of this holy stone, along with the St Clairs of Rosslyn, the keepers of sacred relics.

In the medieval romance of *Peredur*, the Grail was also identified with the Celtic cult of the head, which was thought to be the true home of the soul. In pagan myth, the head of the blessed and divine hero Bran was meant to be buried outside the walls of London to ensure green fields and crops as well as to protect harvests and humans against blight and plague. The Green Men carved in late Gothic chapels such as Rosslyn are shown as wild heads laughing from stone leaves. At their trials in France, the Knights Templar were accused of worshipping an idol of a severed head, which they thought would protect them and make them rich and the land green.

That sacred head, however, was not the head of the devil called Baphomet (the Prophet Muhammad). It was the head of Christ on the Veil of St Veronica, who gave it to Jesus to wipe His face when He was carrying the Cross, or it was His face on the folded Holy Shroud from His burial. And if the Templars were ever thought to be the guardians of a real Grail, it was the precious container of these relics. The head of Christ on the Holy Veil or Shroud was called the Mandylion. It came into Byzantine hands at the siege of Edessa in 943. By tradition, it was a towel with which Jesus had washed His face and which had cured a leper king of Edessa. It had been brought there after His Passion by one of the preaching Apostles. Although the Muslims had held Edessa for centuries, they relinquished the relics as a ransom to the Christians, who took them to Constantinople. Two sources suggest that there were two Mandylions, the first with only the Head of Christ on a linen Veil, the second the Holy Shroud itself, kept folded so that only the face was visible.

Three years before the Fourth Crusade seized Constantinople in 1204, the treasurer of the Pharos Chapel, Nicolas Mesarites, warned the enemies of the Byzantine Emperor not to attack his chapel (in Homer, Φαροζ meant 'shroud' rather than 'lighthouse'). 'In this chapel,' Mesarites wrote, 'Christ rises again, and the Shroud with the burial linens is the clear proof . . . They still smell of myrrh, and are indestructible since they once enshrouded the dead body, anointed and naked, of the Almighty after his Passion.' But a Crusader, Robert de Clari, saw the Holy Shroud or Veil in Constantinople in the Church of St Mary Blachernae. Here 'was kept the Shroud in which Our Lord has been wrapped, which stood up straight every Good Friday, so that the features of Our Lord could be plainly seen there.'

What was certainly true was that Constantinople was held by the Crusaders to possess more holy relics than the rest of the Christian world. By a long and elaborate process of international bribes, saintly King Louis IX of France arranged for the Byzantine Crown of Thorns in its sealed casket to be redeemed from Venice and to be enshrined in Paris within the miracle of the building of the Sainte Chapelle. Even when the Treasury of the basilica of San Marco was gutted by fire in 1231, the most holy of the looted relics were providentially spared by the flames – the wood of the True Cross, the flask of the Blood of Jesus Christ and the head of St John the Baptist. Fire forged faith. It did not destroy it.

When de Clari found the most precious of all the relics in Constantinople, the Holy Shroud or Veil, he added a description of a possible Grail. For the Mandylion of Constantinople was a cloth imbued with the blood and water of Christ. It was soaked with the fluids from His body. In the Church of St Mary, the cloth with the image of His features was contained in a rich vessel 'of gold hanging in the midst of the chapel by heavy silver chains'. That container of His blood and the image of His head may have signified the Grail to the Templars. For the Holy Shroud certainly came into their possession after the sack of Constantinople in the Fourth Crusade. When Grand Master Jacques de Molay was executed in 1314, he was burned alive with another Templar, Geoffrey de Charny, Preceptor of Normandy. One generation later, another Geoffrey de Charnay emerged as the possessor of the Shroud, for which he built a shrine at Liray near Troyes in Champagne. It was apt, for Chrétien de Troyes had written the first story of the Grail.

It is interesting that at Temple Combe near Shaftesbury, a Mandylion painting similar to the bearded Head of Christ on the Shroud of Turin has been recently discovered and radio-carbon dated to 1280, when the Templar preceptory in the village was flourishing. Copies of that image were evidently distributed to Temple preceptories and were said to be worshipped in a pagan cult of the head. This slur on the Templars at their trials in France derived from their veneration of the image of the features of Our Lord, broadcast among their centres of influence.

It is also interesting that the Mandylion of the Head of the bearded Christ, held by St Veronica as Christ carries His Cross during the Passion, is on a carving at Rosslyn Chapel. Beside it are Templar and Mason's marks on the bearded warrior figure of Pontius Pilate, washing his hands near his guard of armoured knights armed with battle-axes. These British ikons confirm the tradition of the Templars as the guardians of the Grail, and also the role of the St Clairs as the guardians of the holy relics of Scotland, ever since the first of the family to come there had been the cup-bearer of the Queen and keeper of the Holy Rood.

The tombstone of Sir William de St Clair recently discovered in Rosslyn Chapel carves the connection in stone. Not only are the Grail and the Rosy Cross incised on his tomb, but the base of the cup is shown as the steps of the Temple of Solomon. In the definitive late romance *Queste del Saint Graal*, the importance of the legend of Solomon with his miraculous cup was stressed in the pedigree of the perfect Grail knight, while *Parzifal* and the *Perlesvaus* stated that the keepers of the Grail were Templars. The Victorian author of *The Rosicrucians: Their Rites and Mysteries* was clear on this point. 'The chalice on the tomb-stone of a knight, or over the door of a castle, is a sign of the Knights Templars, of whom St. John the Evangelist was the Patron Saint. The 'cup' was forbidden to the laity, and was only received by the Priests in consequence of the decree of Pope Innocent the Third,' the supporter of the Templars, who allowed the chalice to be seen at the Mass, but who unleashed a crusade against fellow Christians, the Cathars, with their oriental beliefs.

In the case of the chalice on the tombstone of Sir William de St Clair at Rosslyn, the cup encloses an octagonal rosy cross with the flower signifying Christ's blood in the centre. It is one of the earliest representations of that symbol, held to be part of the gnostic revelations or secret Gospels known to the Knights of the Order of the Temple of Solomon and later to the Brotherhood of the Rosy Cross, which considered the heart of Jesus to be the temple where the life of the world dwelt as well as a rose and a cup. It also suggests a connection between the Templars and the Cathars, before their destruction in the Albigensian Crusade. The Cathars were also Gnostics, who were much influenced by the *troubadour* Courts of the Langue d'Oc, particularly by the seminal knightly romance epic, the *Roman de la Rose*, and the later Grail romances. In these, the Templars, riding with their red cross, were the keepers of the secret of the rose within the chalice.

The Grail on the St Clair tombstone also explains why the Grail is still held to be within the Apprentice Pillar in Rosslyn Chapel, a pillar built especially to enclose it. If Templar relics did reach Rosslyn, a communion cup or chalice within it might have been called the Grail, and left with the St Clairs for security. The present Knights Templars of Scotland possess a jewelled communion cup of the Middle Ages, which may descend from the Templar treasure carried to the Firth of Forth. And as the guardians of the Holy Rood, the St Clairs might well have been thought worthy to guard a Holy Grail.

There are said to be other true Grails in Britain. There are the remnants of a wooden cup, eroded by the lips of believers, at Nanteos in North Wales: Richard Wagner saw it before he wrote his Grail opera *Parsifal*, although that derived from the work of Wolfram von Eschenbach. There is the bronze Glastonbury Bowl, kept at Taunton, and another chalice, discovered at Glastonbury by revelation, and in private hands. There is the miracle-working goblet of St Elizabeth of Hungary, whose father was the patron of the writing of *Parzifal*, and whose ancestor St Margaret brought the Holy Rood to Scotland. But the most interesting actual Grail was an emerald bowl seized in 1101 by the Genoese after the siege of Caesarea. This trophy from the Holy Land was called the *Sacro Catino* and the Saint Graal; but when Napoleon took Genoa, he had the bowl examined in Paris, where it proved to be green glass. In the final analysis, and as the romances stated, the Grail is a thing of the spirit. The search for it is a crusade to discover the soul and the divine as well as peace and plenty upon earth. Yet a chapel was built as a Grail Chapel to hold the Knights of the Grail in their armour. And the knights are the St Clairs, and that chapel is Rosslyn.

The Search for the Grail

Rosslyn Chapel is not so much an enigma inside a riddle inside a mystery. It is a creation inside a temple inside a revelation. Its designer, Sir William St Clair, the Earl of Orkney, was an *illuminatus*. He studied the hermetic knowledge of the later Middle Ages. As a family biographer stated, he was 'more refined and less ignorant than the contemporary herd of nobles, who suspected his studies of subjects unearthly and unholy'. This is clear both in the elaborate design of the chapel and in the Rosslyn-Hay Manuscript, the most important work to survive from his library – the earliest extant work in Scottish prose, a translation from René d'Anjou's writings on Battles and the Order of Knighthood and the Government of Princes. At various times in his life, René held the title of Duke, not only of Anjou, but also of Calabria and Lorraine, as well as being the King of Hungary, Naples, Sicily, Aragon, Valencia and even Jerusalem. He was a conduit to Rosslyn of oriental, Gnostic and cabbalistic teachings, which were spreading from Medici Florence throughout Europe.

The leather binding of the oak board of the manuscript is signed by PATRICIUS LOWES – the Lowis father and son lived in Roslin village among the masons building the chapel, and worked as bookbinders for William St Clair. Thirty-three expensive metal stamps, possibly from Cologne, decorate the binding. Apart from the signature stamp, three other names are repeated twice – JHESUS – MARIA – JOHANNES. The addition of the name of St John to those of Jesus and Mary is unusual, but he was venerated by the Gnostics and the Templars. The same rare link is made on Master Mason John Morow's inscription at Melrose Abbey, rebuilt at the same time as Rosslyn Chapel – JHESUS – MARI – SWEET SANCT JOHN. Another remarkable feature of the binding is the use of the Agnus Dei, the Lamb of God, together with the Sacred Monogram, I.H.S. In Rosslyn Chapel, the Templar Seal of the Lamb of God is also carved. The stamps of the emblems of the Twelve Apostles are arranged in a filled set-square, with eight of the stamps repeated. St John is represented by the rare devices of the serpent of Gnostic wisdom and the chalice or Grail, while three other Apostles are depicted by masonic tools: St Simon by the saw, St James the Lesser by the fuller's club, and St Mathias by the axe. These last three Apostles were carved with their masonic tools in the south aisle of Rosslyn Chapel, along with St Jude with his carpenter's square and St Bartholomew with his flaying-knife. St John the Evangelist is also carved holding his chalice or Grail, but without the Gnostic serpents of wisdom, already incised at the base of the Apprentice Pillar.

Other mysterious symbols are stamped on the binding of the ancient manuscript as well as being repeated in Rosslyn Chapel. There is the quatrefoil of the Four Writers of the Gospels. There is the foliated staff of Moses, also a Templar emblem. There is a rose and a rosette, sacred to the Virgin Mary and venerated by the Templars. And most oddly, there is a unique stamp of a lion standing on its hind legs and fighting a dragon – reproduced exactly on the top of a pillar in the chapel. Evidently, William St Clair used his extensive library to institute the manufacture of more books at Rosslyn as well as to find designs for the carvings in his new chapel.

In addition to the Rosslyn-Hay Manuscript, the National Library of Scotland still possesses several important manuscripts and books annotated by the St Clairs. These include the early Irish *Rosslyn Missal*, which probably made its way there after Edward Bruce's unhappy invasion of Ireland in 1315. Written by an Irish monk in the twelfth century, it was actually annotated by Prince Henry St Clair, the grandfather of the rebuilder of the family chapel. One of his scribbles in Latin was 'who wrote after the writing?' He did. He also wrote about three sisters fleeing: 'Whoever loved x^m did not choose this world.' His spirit quested for heaven: 'Myself is a moving part – splendidly – largely . . . To you, lifting my spirit, my God.' These additions to the missal explain why he was a Crusader, nicknamed Henry the Holy. The suggestions that he did not choose this world and that his spirit could reach God directly without church or Trinity tell of his exposure to Templar or gnostic teachings.

Also surviving from the early St Clair library were *Wyntoun's Chronicle*, the *Lives of the Bishops of Dunkeld, The Roist of Tyme*, and the compendium, *Regiam Maiestatem*, a work of a thousand pages commissioned by William St Clair to include all varieties of laws and oaths and statutes. There are also sections on the rules and customs of shipping and the Guilds of Scotland. These would have been important for the Earl of Orkney, who needed a fleet to maintain his sea-power, and who was also the hereditary Grand Master of the Crafts and Guilds and Orders of Scotland, charged with settling their disputes at his annual court at Kilwinning.

In the Bodleian Library, there is another work of the period from Rosslyn, annotated by the St Clairs, sometimes in Gaelic. It bears their escutcheon of the Engrailed Cross as well as the ship of the Earldom of Orkney with its single mast and unfurled sail. It is *The Book of Troylus*, containing poems on the complaints of Mars and Venus and the Black Knight with *The King's Quair*. It also proves that the designer of Rosslyn Chapel knew of the Grail romances as well as the secret wisdom of the Middle Ages.

Unfortunately, most of the other volumes commissioned or owned by William St Clair were destroyed in a contemporary attack on Rosslyn Castle or in later assaults. So much evidence was burned that the Bishop of Orkney had to write a testimony to the King of Norway in 1446 'respecting the GENEOLOGY OF WILLIAM SANCT CLARE, EARL OF ORCHADIA' in support of his legitimate claim to Orkney. The treatise was 'translatit out of Latin into Scottis' by Dean Thomas Guild, a Cistercian monk from Newbattle Abbey close to Rosslyn. This record was necessary because of the sacking of the library at Rosslyn Castle. The Canons of St Columba at Inchcolm and the St Clair historian Father Hay were all to bear further witness to three spoilings of the Rosslyn book collection between the fifteenth and seventeenth centuries, one of them by the Puritan soldiers of General Monk and another by the Edinburgh mob. As the Bishop of Orkney wrote, charters, evidences, instruments, account books and other 'kindis of probationis war consumit be fyre, tint and alianat in the tyme of hostilitie, and of weris of unfreindfull innimiis.'

There are no portraits that survive of the scholarly William, Earl of Orkney. But at Corstorphine Church nearby there remains the effigy of his cousin, Sir John Forrester, who rebuilt his church at the same time that Rosslyn Chapel was reconstructed. Forrester's face is eroded by time, but his embroidered sword-belt and ornate armour testify to the late display of the Middle Ages. On the shields below his tomb are the three bugles of the Forresters – they were originally the foresters of the Kings of Scotland – also the Engrailed Cross and St Clair ship of the Earl of Orkney. He was descended from Jean St Clair, a daughter of Prince Henry, Earl of Orkney, who tried to colonize America nearly a century before Columbus: one of the proofs of this will be shown to be the unique old beacon tower at Corstorphine. Jean St Clair herself lies in the church beside the stone effigy of her husband, Sir John Forrester, in her embroidered coif and with her Bible in her hands.

Opposite her, a Templar gravestone is set in the wall and another tombstone by the Priest's Door – one of two in Scotland of priests bearing the chalice or Grail. As we have seen, it commemorated Robert Heriot, a chaplain of Gogar who died in 1443. It is interesting that the earliest Arabic *graffiti* carved in Scotland in the fifteenth century were incised opposite this Grail stone: Arabs were the leading physicians and alchemists of that age. The other tomb with a chalice, this time held in the hand of a priest, is at Saddell, an old Cistercian abbey in the Mull of Kintyre. As at Corstorphine, it reinforces the links between the cult of the Grail and the Cistercians and the Sancto Claro family of the Holy Light.

There are more overt Grails in the Rosslyn Chapel designed by William St Clair. On the boss of the second chapel from the north, facing south, is the Mother and Child. There, the Three Dead and Living Kings were carved, or the Three Magi bearing their gifts to the infant Jesus. Beside them on a draped trestle table, stand three chalices or Grails, and below them, a rose blooms in stone, the symbol of the Virgin Mary.

Such symbolism encrusts the whole chapel. Particularly frequent on the bosses are representations of small Temples of Solomon. Out of their twin pillars and towers, green plants spring and entwine. They suggest that Rosslyn Chapel as a whole is not only another Temple of Solomon, but also the Garden of the Temple – the Garden of the Bible and of Eden. In trying to fathom the remarkable mind of the scholar William St Clair and his plan for his chapel, it is noteworthy that books in the Middle Ages were called flower gardens or *rosaria*, arbours of roses. Illuminated by pictures, often of flowers, as in the *Rosslyn Missal*, they represented the search for wisdom and faith, as well as the cult of the Virgin Mary. One of the early physicians and philosophers, Arnold of Villanova, called his original encyclopedia *Rosarum Philosophorum*. In medieval thought, the Third Day of Creation of all biology and the sacred drawings of architecture were symbolic. The pattern of the green leaf and the shape of the dressed stone were both in the divine mind.

The planning of Rosslyn Chapel was a matter of fifty years until its execution. William St Clair grew old in the process. On a visit to Rosslyn recently, the Master Mason of New York Cathedral pointed out that the time-scale of construction from conception to foundation stone, let alone completion, was very considerable in a project of this size. From the ideas to the drawing boards to the architectural plans – and some of these are still scratched on the walls of the crypt of Rosslyn Chapel; from the development of the mystical theme in ikons to their exact placement on the exterior and interior of the building; from the import of the materials and the skilled masons to the dealings with the Crafts and Guilds; from mind to matter to achievement – this was the work of a long lifetime.

Rarely was the patron of a chapel so completely its planner. As Father Hay wrote of William St Clair:

> It came into his minde to build a house for God's service, of most curious worke, the which, that it might be done with greater glory and splendor, he caused artificers to be brought from other regions and forraigne kingdomes . . . And to the end the worke might be the more rare; first he caused the draughts to be drawn upon Eastland boards, and made the carpenters to carve them according to the draughts thereon, and then gave them for patterns to the masons, that they might thereby cut the like in stone.

The influence of other regions and foreign kingdoms on Rosslyn Chapel is on display in a room of fifteenth-century religious art in the new wing of the National Gallery in London. There hangs an altarpiece from the church of the Knights of St John, who had absorbed the Templars in Cologne. The picture is a gift from Queen Victoria, made at the request of her German husband, Albert the Prince Consort, then the Sovereign Master of the Masons of Britain. It was painted in 1445 by Stephen Lochnar at the time when the rebuilding of the new Collegiate Chapel of St Matthew by William St Clair was beginning. It shows St Matthew holding his Gospel with an angel at his feet, then the patron of the St Clair family, St Katherine of Alexandria. The wheel that broke her body lies broken about her, and she holds the huge crusading sword that beheaded her. The third figure on this painting is that of St John the Evangelist, beloved by the Hospitallers and the Templars. He carries a hexagonal golden chalice or Grail, from which rears the green serpent of wisdom, while his eagle waits at his feet. On the back of the picture is painted St Jerome with another Saint and Gregory the Great, also the figure of the donor wearing the octagonal Cross.

Beside this altarpiece hangs a painting of St Veronica carrying the Holy Veil with the face of Christ similar to that at Temple Combe, but also painted in Cologne in the fifteenth century. Opposite, from the Abbey of Werden near Cologne, there is another panel showing the knightly St Hubert praying before the deer with the Cross between its horns – the vision also seen by King David of Scotland. And near it, there hangs a section of an altarpiece of the three Magi or Wise Men, each presenting a golden Grail to the infant Christ as on the carving at Rosslyn.

In this one gallery from one medieval city in Germany, much of the symbolism that informed the builder of Rosslyn Chapel is reproduced, the Evangelist and St Matthew, the patron of the St Clairs with her sword of martyrdom, St John the Divine holding the Gnostic serpent of wisdom in a chalice, the knight kneeling before the wounded deer which is Christ, the Holy Veil or Mandylion with the head of Jesus, the three Wise Men of the East presenting the Child of God with golden Grails. The images show how widespread were the influences and secrets of the last of the Monastic and Military Orders of Europe before the Reformation. They certainly reached the crowning glory of late Scottish medieval art and faith, Rosslyn Chapel.

The construction of that whole work as a Temple of Solomon and a Chapel of the Holy Grail was the apotheosis of William St Clair. Although it was meant to be the eastern apse of a large cruciform Collegiate Church, it was contained and perfect in its own meaning. A cross-section of the building reveals that it was designed on the basis of the octagon and the hexagon and triangles contained within a circle – some of the fundamental patterns of sacred geometry and contemporary alchemy. A study of the shapes inherited by Giordano Bruno in his hermetic works repeats the plan of the architecture of Rosslyn, and is another indication of the influence of oriental and Gnostic writing on the creator of the chapel.

The eight serpents on the base of the Apprentice Pillar are further evidence of Gnostic teaching. As the early Christian author of *Testimony of Truth* wrote, 'For the serpent was *wiser* than any of the animals that were in Paradise . . . but the creator cursed the serpent and called him devil.' For he had given to Adam and Eve the knowledge of good and evil, as if they were divine. They had to be cast from Paradise in case they ate from the Tree of Life and lived for ever, or so the Gnostics taught. The Apprentice Pillar with its serpents and a complementary ornate pillar on the south of the lady chapel represented the two trees of the Garden of Eden, those of Life and of the Knowledge of Good and Evil. They symbolised the Hermetic knowledge, the secret understanding of the cosmos, given by the serpent to mankind.

The two pillars also represented Jachin and Boaz, the pillars of the original Temple of Solomon, revered by the Templars and the Masons. The serpents enshrined the Shamir, the worm of wisdom whose touch split and shaped stone. For Deuteronomy in the Old Testament confirmed Rabbinic and Arabic legend that King Solomon had built his Temple without the use of tools made of iron. It was this secret of the Shamir, which the martyr Hiram, the architect of the Temple, refused to surrender in Masonic tradition, and which remained one of the Grand Secrets of the Higher Degrees. An old ritual testified to 'the wonderful properties of that noble insect the SHAMIR, which cut and shaped all the sacred utensils and holy vessels in King Solomon's Temple . . . the wonderful creature that could cut stones'.

The Shamir, indeed, was depicted in the *Rosslyn Missal*, which was in the library of the three St Clair Earls of Orkney, including the creator of Rosslyn Chapel. Moreover, the crest of Prince Henry of Orkney was the dragon or serpent of wisdom. It showed the Norse Great Orm or Worm with the coronet of a Prince of Orkney round its neck above a knight's helmet and the St Clair silver shield with its black Engrailed Cross. It suggested that the family was the bearer of ancient wisdom, which was repeated in the design of the Apprentice Pillar.

The pursuit of the mysteries of creation was symbolised in the Middle Ages by the search for a new Temple and Garden of Solomon, also a Castle and Chapel of the Grail. The medieval romance of Wolfram von Eschenbach, *Parzifal*, was a further inspiration to William St Clair. He inscribed its hidden significance in stone on the chapel roof as his revelation that his chapel was also a Chapel of the Grail. The roof itself was a unique structure – the only large barrel-vaulted roof built in solid stone in Scotland. It was literally a stone fallen from Heaven – the *lapis exilis* of *Parzifal*, which was called the Grail.

Looking above me, I saw that the ceiling was divided into five sections stretching from east to west. In the first four segments, the flowers of Creation opened in all their glory, particularly the rose of the Virgin Mary. Then in the west, the stars of the sky clustered on high. To the south, I could see the sun that gives light and life, then the head of Jesus Christ, and then the Holy Dove flying down with the Host in its beak. And what had the hermit told Perceval or Parzifal on his quest for the Grail?

Its holiest power and its greatest, they shall be renewed today.
For ever upon Good Friday a messenger finds her way.
From the height of the highest heaven a Dove flies on her
                                                            wings,
And the Host, so white and holy, this to the stone she brings.
And she lays the Host upon it. And white as His body the
                                                            Dove
Fulfills her mission and flies on her path to the Heaven above.
Ever upon Good Friday, this happens as you hear from me,
And the stone from the Host receives all good that on Earth
                                                        may be,
All food and drink that springs here as abundant as Paradise,
All wild things in wood and water, all that moves below the
                                                        skies.
To the brotherhood of the Grail are they given, who serve
                                                God's favour fair.
His servants He feeds for ever, the Grail for their needs and
                                                        care.

Below the Dove with the Host was carved the symbol of the Grail. It looked like the bowl of a cup or a crescent moon, the emblem of Islam, the faith of Parzifal's half-brother Feirefis, the Muslim knight. Out of it poured God's grace and bounty, seen as waves or flow. Frozen in stone with green algae on the Heaven behind it, this Grail seemed to let fall all green things and wild things in wood and water that were carved in this Chapel of the Third Day of Creation. Solving the mystery of this holy place as I found the Grail among the stars above, I heard Marlowe's Dr Faustus plead in my ear:

> See, see how Christ's blood streams from the firmament!
> One drop would save my soul!

And, of course, I remembered the words of another poem, one of Sir Walter Scott's ballads from *The Lay of the Last Minstrel*. He had lived at Lasswade down the glen of the Esk and had researched into the past of Rosslyn. In his ballad of fair Rosabelle, who was drowned in the Firth of Forth making the stormy crossing from another St Clair castle at Ravenscraig, he stated as a matter of fact that twenty St Clair knights were buried in full armour in the vaults of Rosslyn Chapel. His claim that they and the chapel glowed at times of tragedy was probably a reference to the Norse tradition of burning their chieftains in their battle dress on their warships as well as the founder's legacy of having himself and his heirs buried as Knights of the Grail, forever alive in the quest for the grace of God. As Scott wrote:

> Seem'd all on fire that chapel proud,
>   Where Roslin's chiefs uncoffin'd lie,
> Each Baron, for a sable shroud,
>   Sheathed in his iron panoply.

> Seem'd all on fire, within, around,
>   Deep sacristy and altars pale,
> Shone every pillar foliage-bound,
>   And glimmer'd all the dead men's mail.

> Blazed battlement and pinnet high
>   Blazed every rose-carved buttress fair –
> So still they blaze, when fate is nigh
>   The lordly line of high St Clair.

There are twenty of Roslin's barons bold
Lie buried within that proud chapelle;
Each one the holy vault doth hold –
But the sea holds lovely Rosabelle!

My search for the Grail in Rosslyn Chapel involved the finding of
the buried knights as well as discounting the legend that an actual
jewelled chalice was enclosed within the Apprentice Pillar. This had
been the impression of two mystic writers, Walter Johannes Stein
and Trevor Ravenscroft, who also believed that the chapel was an
Apocalypse in stone, and that the complement of the Apprentice
Pillar was in the market square of Cintra in Portugal. Ravenscroft
tried to have the Pillar scanned by the latest radar devices used in an
American nuclear submarine. When permission was refused by the
Earl of Rosslyn, his wife chained herself to the Pillar in protest. I was
allowed, however, to bring in the latest radar technique developed
for modern archaeology, Groundscan, to survey the whole chapel.
The machine had the ability to detect shapes and metal objects
through stone and rubble. There was no evidence of a gold or silver
chalice inside the Apprentice Pillar.

The Groundscan of the vaults was another matter. Large cavities
were revealed below the chapel. The radar pulses also detected
reflectors, which indicated metal, probably the armour of the buried
knights. Particularly exciting was a large reflector under the lady
chapel, which suggested the presence of a metallic shrine there,
perhaps that of the Black Virgin, which still marks so many holy
places on the pilgrims' route to St James of Compostela, a sacred
way that has one of its endings in Rosslyn Chapel, where a carved
scallop-shell still commemorates the past.

The Groundscan further revealed that the foundations of a large
cruciform church had been laid beneath the present churchyard.
The existing chapel was only the eastern apse of a huge structure
intended to be built in the shape of a cross. Down at the castle,
hidden chambers were also located, although two circular stone
staircases which had recently been discovered now appeared to lead

to nothing very much. There were no metal reflectors indicating a possible buried Templar treasure; yet a more detailed survey remains to be done.

The problem was how to reach the vaults. The Groundscan had shown two stairways leading beneath the slabs. With harsh labour, one set of flagstones was lifted, rubble was cleared, and, indeed, three steep stone steps led to a vault below. I was the first to squirm into this secret chamber. It was small, the space between the foundations of two pillars. It was arched with stone, but access to the main vaults beyond had been sealed by a thick wall of stone masonry, perfectly shaped beneath the arch. The soggy wood from three coffins had been stacked in front of the blocking wall. Sifting through the debris below the broken coffins, I found human bones and the fragments of two skulls, two rusty Georgian coffin handles, a mason's whetstone – and a Grail. Yes, a Grail, as it should be in one of its many forms. It was a simple oak bowl, left there by a mason from his meal along with his flint for sharpening the tools of his craft. And that is what the original Grail from the Last Supper would have been – a wooden platter passed by the Jesus Christ of divine simplicity to his poor apostles. They were working in His cause, they were fishers of men, they were the first builders of the edifice of the Christian Church. Such a simple workman's bowl, perhaps as old as the late Middle Ages when this chapel was designed to be a Chapel of the Grail, this was a Grail as good as any other, the container of God's bounty on earth, all we eat to sustain the spirit.

We lifted the slabs to the second staircase, which might lead down to the shrine, only to discover many feet of earth and sand beneath. The Groundscan had not shown how deep down the vaults were nor the infill in the intervening spaces. It was a grave disappointment. We decided to call in core drillers in order to penetrate the roofs of the lower vaults. We would then lower a tube through the drill-hole and drop down an industrial endoscope. Its camera is the size of my little finger and is as flexible as the head of a striking snake, which can point at buried objects illuminated by a laser beam. It can operate to a depth of ten metres and passes light up glass fibres integral with the instrument. What the camera sees is transmitted in colour onto a monitor above ground.

As we drilled deeper and deeper in the centre of the chapel, we struck rubble for ten feet and then the roof of the lower vault. It was three feet of solid stone. Finally, the drill bit broke through into open space. And then it jammed. There was no way of drawing it back. In my mind's eye, I saw one of the St Clair knights reach out a mailed fist to hold the bit. They must resent our invasion after centuries of resting in peace. But after working night and day, we removed the drill and penetrated again into the lower vault and could introduce our pipe. Through it, the endoscope could drop into the chamber of the knights and film them in their armour.

So we believed. But the quest for the Knights of the Grail would prove almost as hard as the quest for the Grail itself. Again and again, we pushed the pipe down the drill hole. Again and again, infill poured into the crevices and blocked the pipe. Again we drilled through and brought back the bit. Again we introduced the pipe, this time with the endoscope inside the tube. As it almost reached the stone roof of the vault, we could see on the monitor, dust and detritus clogging up the end of the pipe, filling in our little piercing into the mystery that lies beneath Rosslyn.

After a week of work, we were defeated. The vaults of the Chapel of the Grail would keep their secret shrine. The St Clair knights would not be disturbed in their tombs. Perhaps that is how it should be. They had been buried beyond the reach of intruders. They would reappear only on the Day of Judgement, when the stone slabs would crack open.

Yet the chapel was a creation inside a temple inside a revelation. I had discovered the Grail carved on the tomb of a St Clair knight. And among the starry firmament of the roof, the Grail poured down God's mercy and bounty, while His green plenty sprang and burgeoned in the abundance of the stonework on the walls. For the Grail is the quest for God's grace. It cannot be reached, only sought. But I had found its symbols carved in Rosslyn and elsewhere on crusading Scottish graves of the Middle Ages. I had seen many Grails. And the chapel built by the genius of Earl William St Clair was revealed as a Chapel of the Grail, forever in honour of the search of our spirit for the divine.

8

Green Men and Medicine

> Thrice happy he who, not mistook,
> Hath read in *Nature's mystick Book*.

So ANDREW MARVELL wrote of himself in his green investigations. But he was also describing William St Clair, the Earl of Orkney, whose abundant instructions to the masons of Rosslyn Chapel turned it into the Third Day of Creation and the Garden of Eden and the Temple of Solomon as well as the physic garden of the Middle Ages. There, the god of nature and rebirth, the Green Man, still leaps out from every stone frieze of leaf and plant, wreath and flower. As he gorges on and spits out stem and tendril, he leers and shouts in silence, a mute mockery of the formal world. Andrew Marvell saw himself as the Green Man, the Master of the Woods. And a part of the illumination of William St Clair was the recognition of that pagan spirit of nature.

> The Oak-Leaves me embroyder all,
> Between them Caterpillars crawl
> And Ivy, with familiar trails,
> Me licks, and clasps, and curles, and hales.
> Under this antick Cope I move
> Like some great Prelate of the Grove.

The Master of the Works of Rosslyn Chapel had Norse and Norman as well as Scottish roots. Through his family and inheritance in Orkney and the Shetlands, he was exposed to Nordic culture, which had infiltrated the Gothic cathedrals of Europe with ancient fertility cults. The Green Man was associated with several archetypes, particularly the serpent or dragon of wisdom and rebirth; the sacred tree of life, which held up Heaven from the earth; and the cycle of life and death through the soil. The famed Apprentice Pillar in Rosslyn Chapel was a particular witness to Norse myth. Eight serpents with their tails in their mouths encircled its base, a tribute to the great snake that girdled the earth nine times to bind together the roots of Yggdrasil, the Norse ash tree that was the prop between the Underworld and the gods in the sky. Their divine leader Odin had himself sacrificed on the Tree of Life, hanging in the storm for nine days and nights, in order to learn the secrets of wisdom and creation from the severed head of another god called Mimir, kept forever murmuring and alive with herbs and spring water – the primal Green Man.

These masks of the earth force were carved only in the churches of the civilisations of the Mediterranean and of north-west Europe. In the seminal Gothic cathedral at Chartres, some remain, particularly on the portal of the south transept. There, three Green Men gobble and disgorge leaves of oak and vine and acanthus. All green and growing things had their symbolism in the Middle Ages. The oak was associated with a pagan past, the Druids and their sacred groves, the forest culture before the Roman invasions. The vine signified Bacchus and celebration rather more than the blood of Christ in the communion cup. And the acanthus was the herb of rebirth, the synthesis between the tree of the woods and the cultivated grape. Each of the plants and leaves that proliferate from the mouths of the seventy or more Green Men carved inside and outside Rosslyn Chapel has its own significance and meaning. In the discovery of these secrets lies the meaning of the Garden of Paradise and the Tree of Life in the Middle Ages. For Rosslyn Chapel is an Herbal in stone. It displays the monastic physic garden of the late

Middle Ages, which was largely forgotten with the Renaissance. It is the lost green medicine of its time.

The Garden of Paradise

Paradise only meant a walled garden. When Xenophon first put the word *paradeisos* in the mouth of Socrates, he was making the Athenian sage praise the Persian King for his love of pleasure gardens, 'filled with all the fine and good things that the earth wishes to bestow, and in these he himself spends most of his time.' The word came from the Persian *pairi* or 'around' and *daeza* or 'wall'. It was translated into Latin as *paradisus* and first appeared in Middle English in 1175 as a sentence in the Bible, 'God ha hine brohte into paradis.' By the time that Chaucer wrote the *Franklin's Tale*, the term was generally used to describe a flowering garden:

> May hadde peynted with his softe showers
> This gardyn full of leves and of flowres;
> And craft of manne's hand so curiously
> Arrayed hadde this garden trewely
> That never was ther gardyn of swich prys,
> But if it were the verray Paradys.

Outside medieval churches, Paradises were constructed – enclosed green spaces for prayer and meditation. In the Cistercian Order, each white monk was given his little Paradise or garden plot to cultivate. Of course, the Christians confused this new word 'paradise' with the Garden of Eden, just as the Muslims had confused it with the Garden of Allah, into which the Koran promised a way for all those who died fighting for the faith. 'There shall be two other gardens: of a dark green. In each of them shall be two fountains pouring forth much water. In each of them shall be fruits and palm trees and pomegranates. And there shall be agreeable and beautiful maidens.' In fact, the idea of a Garden of Paradise dated back to the first city-state in Mesopotamia, the Sumerian state of Uruk with its

Epic of Gilgamesh, who wandered in the immortal Garden of the Gods, where 'stands the Tree, / With trunk of gold, and beautiful to see.'

In their captivity in Babylon with its famous hanging gardens, the Jews also learned of the Garden or Paradise or of Eden and gave it the Hebrew name, *pordes*. Rabbinic tradition believed that the Garden was the blessed part of Sheol, where the just awaited the resurrection, while the olive branch brought by the dove to Noah on his Ark was plucked from the Garden of Eden, which had survived the Flood. The Jews also held Mount Moriah in Jerusalem as a sacred area on which the Temple of Solomon was built, just as the Babylonians held their stepped *ziggurats* to be holy and the Christians venerated 'the high places' of the Bible – the peaks of a possible hanging garden of Paradise.

Indeed, all the leading religions that derived from the Middle East believed in a divine Garden. It contained the Tree of Life and the Tree of Knowledge of Good and Evil. It also held the Mountain of Paradise and Salvation as well as the four rivers that divided the earth into quarters. St Augustine even called Christ the Tree of Life, while the other Saints were fruit trees, and the four Gospels were the four rivers of Eden.

Yet the Garden of Paradise had first been designed by Cyrus the Great at Pasargadae in Persia, and all Gardens of Paradise had followed his model. When Alexander the Great pursued the Persian King Darius, whose namesake is commemorated in Rosslyn Chapel, he visited the tomb of Cyrus in its grove and mourned his epitaph:

> O man, I am Cyrus
> Who acquired the Empire for the Persians
> And was King of Asia:
> Do not grudge me, then, my monument.

His true monument was his Garden of Paradise, and the flowers and fruits and herbs he grew there. Aristotle, the tutor of Alexander the Great, arranged for another pupil, Theophrastus, to write about the new specimens brought back from the East. Theophrastus had inherited Aristotle's herb gardens, and the two works he wrote about them were the first botanical guides, *On the Causes of Plants* and *On the History of Plants*. These books were of supreme importance to the scholars of the Middle Ages. Actually, the first Herbal had been carved in relief in the temple of Amun more than a thousand years before. This original record of a botanical garden depicted blue cornflower and red poppy and mandrake with its yellow fruits, the three most popular Egyptian plants, along with lotus and papyrus. Its trees showed date-palms and vines and figs, while the older temple garden at Deir-el-Bahari revealed three rows of seven sycamore and tamarisk trees planted in avenues.

Recent excavations of a rubbish dump at Saqqara, as that of Soutra in Scotland, have revealed a physic garden in ancient Egypt connected with the priests of the temple. Among the medicines in use were acacia, aloes, aniseed, apricots, caraway seeds, the castor-oil plant, cedar, chicory, chrysanthemum, convulvus, coriander, flax, hemp, henbane, mint, myrtle, myrrh, olive, onions, poppy, squills, wormwood and camomile oil, which was distilled to embalm the Pharaohs – its secret was passed on by the Copts to the Crusaders for the preservation of their dead.

Yet these sacred and medicinal gardens of the Pharaohs were unknown to the ancient Greeks, who divided their Gardens of Paradise into Arcadia for the living and the Elysian Fields for the dead. They chiefly valued two of the Alexandrian imports from Asia – saffron from the wild crocus and the rose. But many other imports were to follow, the spices and the herbs that were to become the drugs and medicines of the Middle Ages. In the Islamic Gardens of Paradise, the trees and fruit and flowers had a figurative meaning as well as a medieval use – the almond meant the eye, the quince and the apple were the chin, the pomegranate and the lemon were the breasts, the rose was the cheek, the plane-tree leaf was the hand, the date-palm was the figure, and the mandrake was the down on the skin.

In using his medieval Herbals to make Rosslyn Chapel into a stone Garden of Eden, William St Clair was particularly influenced by the *Lilium* of the Scottish physician Bernard of Gordon, who himself was strongly influenced by Arabic medicine. William St Clair was also creating a carved Garden of Paradise, a Persian or Islamic garden as well as a biblical garden. Rosslyn Chapel stands on a hill or Mountain of Salvation. Its two wrought pillars represent the Tree of Life and the Tree of the Knowledge of Good and Evil. Among its carvings are the story of Genesis and the drawing of Adam and Eve from Eden, as well as an angel with the fiery sword and another bearing date-palms. But nowhere in the Bible is there a description of the fruits and flowers and herbs of Eden. There is an account, however, of the gardens and orchards of King Solomon, who rejoiced in his labour of making them. The two wrought pillars behind the altar further represented Jachin and Boaz, the twin pillars of the Temple of Solomon, as well as the two trees of Eden. In the legend confirmed by Sir John Maundeville in his *Book of Travels*, the dying Adam sent his son Seth to beg from the angel with the sword of fire at the gate of Paradise a branch from the Tree of Life. This branch, planted on Adam's grave, produced the cedars cut by Hiram to build the Temple of Solomon, and later formed the wood that was used to make the Cross.

The cedar is represented in Rosslyn Chapel along with other biblical trees, mentioned in the Canticles and the Song of Solomon – the datepalm and the vine, the pomegranate and the fig, the olive and the almond, the hazel and the chestnut, the apple and the walnut. Among the friezes of the chapel, we find not only many of the herbs from a medieval physic garden, but also Eastern healing shrubs, some from Solomon's garden – 'Henna with spikenard, spikenard and saffron; calamus and cinnamon, with all trees of frankincense; myrrh and aloes, with all the chief spices.'

From the Bible, these would include anemones and aniseed, bulrushes and coriander, cumin and dill, flag and flax, mallow and mint, the Resurrection Flower and the Rose of Jericho, rue and wormwood. Among the vegetables also hallowed by Holy Writ were beans and cucumbers, garlic and gourds, leeks and lentils, mustard and onions. As for the trees that were sacred in meaning, there was the date-palm, also held to be the Tree of Life, the acacia (or Burning Bush) and the ash, the bay tree and black mulberry, the chestnut and the cypress, the elm and the fir, the myrtle and the oak, the sycamore and the willow.

More exotic were the aloe and the ebony and the juniper and the mastic and the olive and the sandalwood and the tamarisk trees from the Near East. Many of these real and symbolic plants from the Christian version of the Garden of Solomon may be found on the stone walls of Rosslyn Chapel, although the sprouting heads of Green Men often peer out from the branches of the friezes to bear witness to a more ancient tradition from the pagan north of Europe.

The walled chapel of Rosslyn was like the walled garden, 'a secret place, enclosing within it the mysteries of the Old and New Testaments'. So William St Clair believed when he asked his masons to carve the flowers and plants within it. He was not so strict as the early medieval historian Rhabanus Maurus, whose chapter on the Garden in his work on the Universe had excluded from the Monastic Paradise and the cloister any plant not mentioned in the Bible. To him, the garden had been the Church, which bore the fruits of the Holy Spirit and was nourished by the sacred founts of healing until it became a new Eden. But in Rosslyn, most of the carvings – if not all of them – illustrated some part of the Christian faith, a virtue or a divine lesson. The stone lily in the chapel represented the purity of the Virgin Mary and was often depicted in paintings of the Annunciation and the Assumption. The iris or fleur-de-lys was the symbol taken by the Kings of France and also a symbol of the St Clairs – it implied Christ's descent from the royal line of David, and perhaps that of the Capets and the family of Sancto Claro with its French blood. The trefoil plants of the strawberry and clover reminded the viewer of the Trinity. And so each carving of herb and plant had its esoteric meaning. Like a medieval physic garden or herbal, Rosslyn Chapel was a graven guide to the Bible through a walled garden in stone.

Most significant of all was the section of the roof carved entirely in roses next to the firmament on high with its symbols of a Grail

Chapel. It was another testament to the influence of Islam on Christianity through the Crusades. The rose had been the flower of love in the eastern Gardens of Paradise. Rose oil was the most prized of scents. The leading Arab physician Avicenna recommended the Syrian rose for its rose-water and use in medical compounds. The Persian poet Nizami told of a duel between two rival doctors: the one who used poison was foiled by the other taking an antidote, while he was killed by the scent of the blameless rose, so corrupt was he. The same death was ascribed to the famous Rabbi Loëw of Prague, the maker of the clay monster Golem: death came to him only in rose-petals, for it could not overcome him except by that sweet odour.

The famous Apothecary's Rose of the Middle Ages had been brought back from the Levant by Thibaut *le Chansonnier*, the King of Navarre and Count of Champagne, from the Crusade he had led in the middle of the thirteenth century. This import of *Rosa gallica officinalis* resulted in a profitable drug trade in rose-petals from Champagne for six hundred years, and it provided the royal flower for the House of Lancaster and the Kings of England. As a monk in York wrote by 1368, 'the red rose is ye badge of England and hath grown in that countrye for as long as ye mynde of man goeth.'

Queen Elizabeth I dared to make her royal symbol the *rosa sine spine*, the rose without thorns, which was the symbol of the Virgin Mary. The poet Sedulius had written in the fifth century:

> As blooms among the thorns the lovely rose,
> Herself without a thorn,
> For she is the glory of its crown.
> Mary the new Maiden,
> Springing from the root of Eve,
> Long ago atoned for the sin
> Of that first Maiden.

In the medieval mind, Christ was the pure Adam as Mary was the new Eve. They both still lived in a Paradise, which was a walled rose garden. The founder of the Cistercians and the consecrator of the

Templars, St Bernard of Clairvaux, pointed out that the five petals of the rose signified the five wounds of Christ as well as the five virtues of Mary, including her humility and her modesty. The first of the great medieval lays of the troubadours was called the *Roman de la Rose*. In it, the rose garden lay within the castle battlements, and there the knights offered roses to the ladies in courtly and chaste love. The great rose windows of Chartres and York showed the dominance of the shape in the mind of the time. So powerful was the image of the Mystic Rose by the period of the fifteenth century that it became the cult of the Virgin Mary, the mother of the Divine Child, and was translated into the rosary, the prayer beads used for devotion. At the Carmelite Convent of St Theresa at Avila in Spain, the beads of rosaries were made from kneaded rose-petals. And on the roof of Rosslyn Chapel, the roses in their stone heaven showed William St Clair's veneration of Mary, a cult also shared by his forefathers with their connections with the Templars and the Teutonic Knights.

The Healing Garden

While considering the characteristics of the five hundred plants that his teacher Aristotle had left him, Theophrastus of Eresos conceived ways of classifying greenery that remained unchanged for nearly two thousand years. Then the lens and the microscope would be able to penetrate more deeply into the structure of the plant. Theophrastus removed growing things from magic and superstition. For him, the flower was like leaves or hairs surrounding the organ that was to develop into the fruit or seed. His powers of description have endured in time. For instance, he compared the thickness of the stalk of the sacred lotus to a man's finger, its air passages to a honeycomb, the blade of its leaf to a Thessalian hat, the size of its flower to a large poppy; its colour was like that of a rose, its receptacle was like a round wasp's nest and its fruits were as beans. Such comparisons in nature were as accurate as they were lasting.

What Theophrastus was to botany, Hippocrates of Coos was to healing. Until his observations, the sick in ancient Greece were treated by priests in temples, but their recovery was left to the will of the god Aesculapius. Hippocrates separated medicine from religion, establishing scientific methods for curing diseases. He believed only in facts that derived from accurate observations and led to correct diagnoses. 'Life is short and art is long,' he wrote. 'The occasion is fleeting, experience is deceptive and judgement difficult.' Such pragmatism led Hippocrates to classify different illnesses by their symptoms and to recommend various cures for them, most of which were based on the herbal remedies of the classical age. As with Theophrastus, the descriptions of diseases by Hippocrates were not to be bettered for some two millennia. 'To know is one thing,' he pointed out. 'Merely to believe one knows is another.' The first was science, the second was ignorance. Hippocrates made extensive use of contemporary botanical studies. Of the four hundred simples he used, half are still a part of homeopathy, ranging from basil and bryony to verbena and willow.

When Rome conquered Greece, its botany and medicine emigrated to a language and a mentality that were less scrupulous and original. Pliny the Elder in his voluminous *Natural History* became the gardener's guide of the Middle Ages and was published in 200 editions within 350 years after the discovery of printing. His encyclopaedia was as good a guide to classical errors as it was to ancient science. But he did invent the syntax of botanical Latin – some 200 of his terms are still in use, roughly in the sense he meant them. The word 'botany' itself, however, came from the Greek word for 'herb' and was established by Pliny's follower, Isidorus of Seville, who wrote another major source book for the Middle Ages.

Galen, the physician to Emperor Marcus Aurelius, equally debased Hippocrates in his medical studies in Rome, but his work still became the doctor's manual in medieval times through the translations of Arab physicians. He recorded his successful treatments, but not his frequent failures. He did perform experiments, but he clouded his results with speculation. He took Hippocratic theories about the humours of the body to excess and so bedevilled later medical practice. As dissection was forbidden, his wild statements about the functioning of the anatomy were issued as informal truths. His overuse of drugs was also a flawed legacy, as was the pharmacopeia left behind by Dioscorides. Yet like Pliny in botany, Galen bequeathed a Latin language to medicine and to the medieval pharmacy, which is still in use.

When the Dark Ages descended on Europe, Greek practice fled to the Second Rome of Byzantium, and from there became the inheritance of the Islamic world. For 400 years after the eighth century, Arab thinkers enriched Greek studies of botany and medicine. In the Eastern Caliphate, Rhazes, the Zoroastrian experimenter on animals Haly Abbas and Avicenna added to learning. The Western Caliphate at Córdoba benefited from the studies of Albucasis and Algalzel and Avenzoar, a surgeon and opponent of Galen, and Moses Maimonides, the Jewish philosopher and physician. Jewish doctors who had studied Islamic medicine developed the first secular European medical school at Salerno. With the conquest of Sicily by the enlightened Normans and the translation of Greek and Arabic texts into Latin by Constantinus Africanus from the cloisters of Monte Cassino, Greek and Islamic learning lit up the darkness of early Christian Europe. Ironically, as scientific salvation came from the Near East, the Crusaders began to attack the sources of their new education. Ignorance and faith assaulted culture and another faith. But in Spain, where the Moors were established in Córdoba and Seville and Toledo, and in the Norman Kingdom of Sicily, Greek and Arabic scholars continued to bring the knowledge of the East to the morass of the West.

The School of Salerno produced the first European medical and herbal text, *Regimen Sanitatis Salernitum*, which eventually ran through 240 editions in prose and verse. One copy was made by Magnus MacCulloch for Lord Borthwick, the neighbour of Sir William St Clair at the time of the building of Rosslyn Chapel. As Sir John Harington's translation of 1608 counselled under the title of THE ENGLISHMANS DOCTOR, OR, THE SCHOOL OF SALERNE,

When mov'd you find your selfe to *Nature's Needs*,
Forbeare them not, for that much danger breeds,
Use three Physicians still; Doctor *Quiet*,
Next Doctor *Merry-man*, and Doctor *Dyet*.

There were also practical remedies against poisonous substances:

Sixe things, that here in order shall ensue,
    Against all poysons have a secret power,
Peare, Garlicke, Reddish-root, Nuts, Rape and *Rue*,
    But *Garlicke* Chief; for they that it devoure,
May drink, and care not who their drinke do brew,
    May walke in aires infected every houre.

After its sack at the end of the twelfth century, however, the School of Salerno was superseded by the new medical schools at Naples and Palermo, Bologna and Padua, and Montpellier. Through them, the medical literature of Islam began to heal the superstitions of the Latin West. Aristotle was rediscovered through his Arabic translation by Averroës, and his methods of observation and experimentation were passed on to such early scientists as Roger Bacon, who began to investigate phenomena directly and not receive truths through the wisdom of the Christian Fathers. The encyclopaedia of Albertus Magnus, with its sections on *De Animalibus* and *De Vegetabilibus et Plantis*, is based on Aristotle and on primary scrutiny. These were the leading scientific works of the thirteenth century, when the Crusaders were already being driven from the Holy Land. They returned, however, with some Islamic learning and techniques, including the process of embalming the bodies of knights or of dissecting these and boiling the parts to remove the skull and bones for burial at home. Although this practice was banned by Papal bull in 1300, it did not prevent the remains of Sir William de St Clair, after his death on a Spanish Crusade, from being returned for interment at Rosslyn with the Heart of Bruce, buried at Melrose.

The medical school at Montpellier in the south of France was particularly a centre of Arabic medicine, although its most famous scholar, the mystic Ramon Lull, was the instigator of crusades against heresy. He was the master of Arnold of Villanova, whose *Opera Omnia* became almost as influential as the compendia of Albertus Magnus. And most important for Scotland was his contemporary professor at Montpellier, Bernard de Gordon, whose Arabist textbook, *Lilium Medicinae*, containing *De Regimine Sanitatis*, was completed in the year that the Templars fell from grace. It was translated from Latin into French, into Hebrew and even into Gaelic. A manuscript of his work under the title of *The Book of Healers* remains in Edinburgh and would have been part of the information available to the Augustinian monks running their hospital at Soutra, and to the Collegiate Church at Rosslyn. It is notable that Chaucer in his poem *Doctour of Phisyk* acknowledged the influence of Bernard de Gordon as well as of many Islamic physicians, including Haly Abbas and Rhazes, Avicenna and Averroës:

> He knew the cause of everich maladye,
> Where it of hoot or cold, or moiste, or drye,
> And where engendred, and of what humour;
> He was a verrey parfit practisour.

Travelling Jewish doctors cared for the sick; otherwise, the monasteries were the infirmaries of the Middle Ages, aided by the Military Orders, especially the Knights of St John as well as the Teutonic Knights. The care of the sick had always been a duty of the Holy Orders. Before Charlemagne, there had been herb gardens attached to nunneries like the one made by St Radegonde when she fled the dissolute Merovingian Court and was praised by the poet Venantius Fortunatus for the green peace she had created. Charlemagne's *Capitulare de Villis* of 74 useful plants and 16 varieties of trees to be grown in the imperial gardens provided a new model for the monastic physic and kitchen garden and orchard. The design for the monastery of St Gall listed the cultivation of 34 herbs, including peppermint and penny royal, lovage and tansy. The *Hortulus* or 'Little Garden' of Walafridus Strabo of the same period added five simples, agrimony and betony and horehound and peach and wormwood, and three flowers, the violet and the lily and the rose he particularly loved. As he wrote of them,

> Better the sweeter are they than all the other plants and rightly called the flower of flowers. Yes, roses and lilies, the one for virginity with no sordid toil, no warmth of love, but the glow of their own sweet scent, which spreads further than the rival roses, but once bruised or crushed turns all to rankness. Therefore roses and lilies for our Church, one for the martyr's blood, the other for the symbol in his hand. Pluck them, O maiden, roses for war and lilies for peace, and think of that Flower of the Stem of Jesse, Lilies His words were, and the hallowed acts of His pleasant life, but His death redyed the roses.

By the twelfth century, the *Physica* of St Hildegard listed for the infirmary garden several hundred plants and nearly a hundred trees. And Alexander Neckham, the Abbot of Cirencester who died in 1217, was specific about monastic horticulture in his *De Naturis Rerum*:

> The garden should be adorned with roses and lilies, turnsole [heliotrope] and violets and mandrake; there you should have parsley and cost and fennel, and southernwood, and coriander, sage, savory, hyssop, mint, rue, dittany, smallage, pellitory, lettuce, garden cress, peonies. There should also be planted beds with onions, leeks, garlick, pumpkins, and shalots; the cucumber growing in its lap, the drowsy poppy, the daffodil and brankursine [acanthus] ennoble a garden. There should also be pottage herbs, such as beets, herb-mercury, orache, sorrel and mallows. Anise, mustard, white pepper and wormwood do good service to the small garden.

Also important was lettuce or sleepwort, on which Venus had laid the body of her lover, and which Hebe had eaten before becoming the cupbearer of the Gods.

The excavations of the rubbish dump of the old Augustinian hospital at Soutra on the Lammermuir Hills above Rosslyn have revealed 79 varieties of pollen or spores. Most of these were mentioned in the *Capitulare* of Charlemagne or in the work of Abbot Neckham, who is held to be a major influence on Soutra's horticulture, as is the mysterious Macer, praised by the poet John Gower for his knowledge of 'the strengthe of herbes'. The four chief crops cultivated at Soutra were opium poppies, hemp, flax and tormentil. Two of these produced powerful drugs for anaesthesia. A sponge soaked in opium or hashish was placed over a patient's nose during an operation: he was then revived by having vinegar rubbed on his teeth.

Drugs for surgery seemed to have been licensed in Genesis: 'And the Lord God caused a deep sleep to fall upon Adam, and he slept: and He took one of his ribs, and closed up the flesh instead thereof.' Christ Himself was meant to have been revived upon the Cross by being given a sponge soaked in vinegar. Two more of the main crops at Soutra, hemp again and flax, produced fibres for cloth and canvas and rope instead of sweet dreams. The Eastern spices excavated there were imported from Montpellier where Bernard de Gordon had taught – they were compounded in the medicines of the time as well as used on the food.

The Benedictines had established the prototype of the physic garden at Monte Cassino. The earliest design of one in the British Isles was drawn on the twelfth-century plan of the monastic buildings at Canterbury, where a large herbal garden was shown covering half the space between the infirmary and the dormitory. At Westminster Abbey, the present College garden was part of the old infirmary garden, while Vine Street nearby still records the site of the old vineyard. The *Hortulanus* in the monastic community supplied the larder and the pharmacy. The Abbey gardens both fed and healed. In the green spaces at Clairvaux, where St Bernard founded the Cistercian Order, a contemporary described how the song of the birds from the orchards delighted those who were recovering from illness. In the Gregorian chant the third 'O' of the seven announcing the advent of Christ was 'O Radix Jesse' and was always sung by the Keeper of the Gardens, who was thought to have in his care the Stem of Jesse, from which sprang the House of Judah. There was even an orchard and herbal garden between the rediscovered rock-hewn hermit's cell on the Esk and the bridge over the river toward the walls of Rosslyn Castle at the Linn, where the white waters dash between three great boulders.

The healing gardens of the classical and Islamic and medieval European ages were eventually graven in stone in Rosslyn Chapel. Its designer in the fifteenth century, William, the third and last St Clair Earl of Orkney, was the recorder of the divine garden before the advent of the Renaissance and the discovery of the plants of the Americas – although two of these were carved in the chapel, Indian corn and the aloe cactus, and serve as another proof that his grandfather, Prince Henry St Clair, did try to found a colony in the Eden of the New World and brought back specimens from that continent. Interpreting the chapel in general is reading the final medieval Herbal. And the woodcuts on the pages of the great *Hortus Sanitatus* printed in so many editions by Gutenberg's pupil Peter Schoeffer are contemporary with the plant carvings at Rosslyn and are startling in their correspondences. The walls of the St Clair chapel are the *Hortus Sanitatus*, the healing garden of the end of the Middle Ages. They are botany before the Tudors, remedy before the beginning of modern medicine.

With the discoveries in the New World and in science of the sixteenth century, the Botanical Garden would be established. While its design may have rested in biblical authority, its purpose was experiment and enquiry. The earliest Botanical Garden was founded in Padua in 1533, fifty years after the completion of Rosslyn Chapel. It was enriched by Egyptian plants collected by the university's Professor of Botany, Prospero Alpino. Florence and Bologna soon followed suit with their Botanical Gardens, as did Paris and Montpellier, which began to replace its medieval Arabist school of medicine with investigations into new plant structures. In the British Isles, herb gardens were set up in the seventeenth century at Oxford and at Chelsea in London and at Edinburgh in Scotland, at Jena in Germany, at Uppsala in Sweden, and at Leyden and at Amsterdam in Holland, which saw the founding of the last of the green physic centres in 1725 at Utrecht. For only two hundred years at the beginning of the modern age did the herb continue to rule medical prescriptions.

Curiously, tradition and religion ruled the shape of the new physic gardens. They still were designed as the Garden of Paradise or Eden, for they were laid out in the four quarters of the earth – also in the four continents of Europe and Asia, Africa and the new America. The gardens were encyclopaedias in living plants. The beds within their quarters were green pages. Looking at them was reading Renaissance botany, as looking at Rosslyn Chapel was reading the symbols of medieval plants. The difference was that these fresh healing gardens were governed by a severe Christianity and an intellectual rigour. Eve herself was excluded from these planned Gardens of Eden, where man was left alone. Andrew Marvell wrote of:

> That happy Garden-state
> While man there walk'd without a mate.
> Two Paradises 'twere in one,
> To live in Paradise alone.

The same exclusive thought occurred in the introductory poem to the catalogue of plants in the Oxford Botanic Gardens, a new Eden:

> Man then untouch'd with woman or her sinne,
> Naked like Truth, as Truth without disguise,
> Was Gardner made to Gods own Paradize.

Eve had been inside Eden, women were within the temple surroundings in the classical sites, maidens served in the Gardens of Allah, and as the rose and the lily, the Virgin Mary was the reigning goddess of the medieval paradises. In Rosslyn Chapel, Her statue and Her roof of roses were attended by wild Green Men

The St Clair Castle, on the L'Epte River in Normandy, begun in the tenth century. (This and all other photographs, unless otherwise specified, are from the author's collection.)

The St Clair Castle at Rosslyn, begun in the twelfth century.

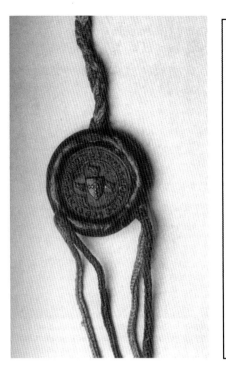

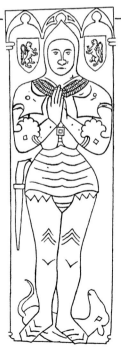

ABOVE LEFT: The seal of Sir William de St Clair (SCO CLARO) with the Engrailed Cross. (National Records, London).

ABOVE RIGHT AND BELOW: Masons' marks and knight's grave, Rosslyn Chapel.

OPPOSITE

ABOVE LEFT: The Apprentice or Prince's Pillar in Rosslyn Chapel.

ABOVE RIGHT: Melrose Abbey, begun in the twelfth century.

CENTRE RIGHT: A Templar cross made by a mason in Rosslyn Chapel.

BELOW: Rosslyn Chapel.

Supposed death mask of Robert the Bruce.

Angel bearing the Heart of Bruce.

Lucifer, falling and bound.

Templar and Masonic angel with Gospel.

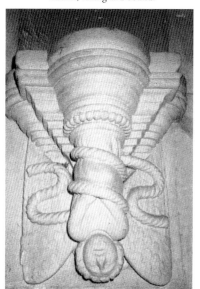

ABOVE: A reconstruction of Rosslyn Castle.

RIGHT: The earliest representation of the Knights of the Military Orders in battle against the Muslims. Godfrey de Bouillon leads the Christian knights. An engraving from a window in the Church of Saint-Denis, Paris, which was destroyed during the French Revolution.

BELOW LEFT: Muslim cavalry, from an etching by Erhard Renwick, 1486.

BELOW RIGHT: An episode from the Albigensian Crusade, depicting an attack on a Cathar castle, with naked celebrants of a heretical rite inside. A drawing from a bas-relief in the Church of Saint-Nazaire at Carcassonne.

The Dome of the Rock in Jerusalem, thought by Christian pilgrims to be the Temple of Solomon.

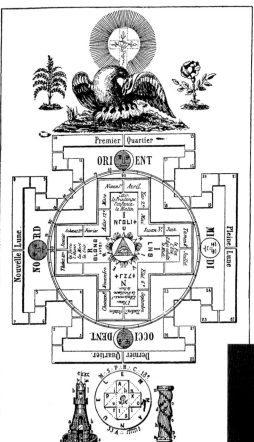

Mystical diagram of Solomon's Temple, as prophesied by Ezekiel and planned in the building scheme of the Knights Templars. The two pillars represent Jachin and Boaz from the original Temple of Solomon. The pillar on the right resembles the Prince's Pillar at Rosslyn.

BELOW: The sacred rock within the Dome of the Rock in Jerusalem.

Crusader gravestones, Saddell Abbey, Mull of Kintyre, Scotland.

Cistercian monk's gravestone with 'Grail' Chalice, Saddell Abbey.

Crusader and early Masonic gravestones, Kilmartin, near Loch Awe, Argyll. Note early compasses or shears under sword on stone on far right.

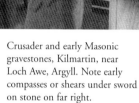

Crusader graves, Isle of Skye.

Two Templar grave slabs, Pentland, near Rosslyn, now covered.

Templar gravestones at Westkirk near Culross Abbey, Fife, with Masonic symbols.

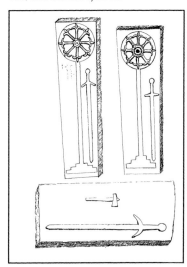

BELOW: Carvings of the Passion and the Mandylion, Rosslyn Chapel.

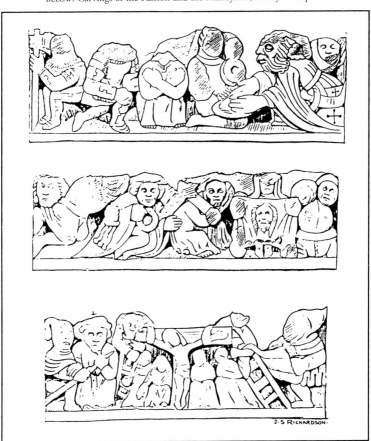

J·S·RICHARDSON·

ABOVE: A Shamir or dragon from the Rosslyn Missal.

OPPOSITE

ABOVE: The Rosslyn Missal, annotated by Earl Henry St Clair of Orkney.

BELOW: The martyred apprentice, also said to be the martyred Hiram of Tyre or St Magnus, Rosslyn Chapel.

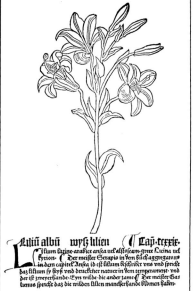

Liliū albū   wyſz lilien   ⸿ Cap̄ .ccccix.

L iliū̄ latine·arabice anſea uel aſſoſeam·grece Licina uel
lyrion·⸿ Der meiſter Serapio in dem bůch aggregatoꝛis
in dem capitel Anſea id eſt lilium beſchꝛiber vns vnd ſpꝛicht
daz lilium ſy heyß vnd druckelher natuer in dem temperament· vnd
der iſt zweyerhande·Eyn wilde·die ander zame·⸿ Der meiſter Gas
tienus ſpꝛicht daz die wilden lilien mancherhande blůmen haben·

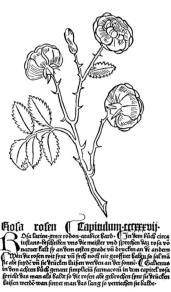

Roſa   roſen   ⸿ Capitulum·ccccxvij·

R oſa latine·grece roden·arabice bard·⸿ In dem bůch circa
inſtans·beſchꝛiben vns die meiſter vnd ſpꝛechen das roſa võ
natuer kalt ſy an dem erſten grade vñ drucken an v̄c andern
⸿ Wan die roſen roit ſynt vñ fꝛeſch noch nit geoffnet haben ſo ſal mã
ſie abe ſnyden vñ ſie drucken laiſſen werden an der ſonne·⸿ Galtenus
in dem achten bůch genant ſimpliciū farmacoꝛū in dem capitel roſa
ſpꝛicht das man als balde ſo die roſen abe gebꝛochen ſynt ſie drucken
laiſſen werde·wan ſinnet man ſie lang ſo verriechen ſie balde·

Plateariꝰ diſſer tyn̄den als groiß als dꝛy keſler gewichte geſal
ten fur die ſiben̄de der frauwen bꝛenger menſtruū vñ drytket vñ das
doꝛ tynt·   Diſz tyn̄den geſtoiſſen zů puluer vnd genutzt mit ey
nem cliſter machet flauſſen vnd rüwen fur alſk ander kunſt·

Item diſz würtzel geſotten in wyn vñ vff das gegicht gelẏgt der
glidder iſt ben werdūn ſtillen·

**Mãdragoꝛa
Capitulum**
Andrago
Die mei
ſter haben daz
ſelbe vñ die geſto
rūb beſchꝛibe ich
wan als du geſo
picſt fur diſſem·

altrun Fram
ccclviij·
ra muſter latine
ſter ſpꝛeſſen gemep̄
diſz altrun ſade die
der erſten vnd daꝛ
nit men dar von
ret hait in dem eas

ABOVE: The grave slab of Robin Hood at Kirklees,
drawn by Nathaniel Johnston, 1665.

OPPOSITE

Frontispiece and illustrations from the *Hortus Sanitatus,* a source of inspiration
for the elaborate carvings in Rosslyn Chapel.

ABOVE LEFT: Medieval doctors. ABOVE RIGHT: The Lily.
BELOW LEFT: The Rose. BELOW RIGHT: The Mandrake.

BELOW: Reconstructed Viking ship navigating from
Norway and the Shetlands to Nova Scotia.

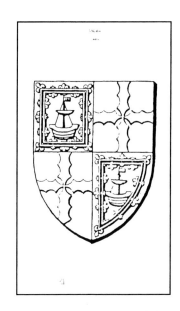

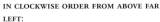

IN CLOCKWISE ORDER FROM ABOVE FAR LEFT:

Orphir Chapel, Orkney. It was built in the twelfth century on the circular model of the Church of the Holy Sepulchre in Jerusalem.

The St Clair sea fortress of Keiss, Caithness.

The shield of the St Clair Earls of Orkney.

The St Clair sea fortress of Girnigoe, Caithness.

St Magnus Church, Egilsay, the Orkneys.

OVERLEAF:
The *Zeno Map* of the North Atlantic, published in Venice in 1558.
INSET: Blow-up of the Estotiland (Nova Scotia) section of the *Zeno Map*, showing two structures.

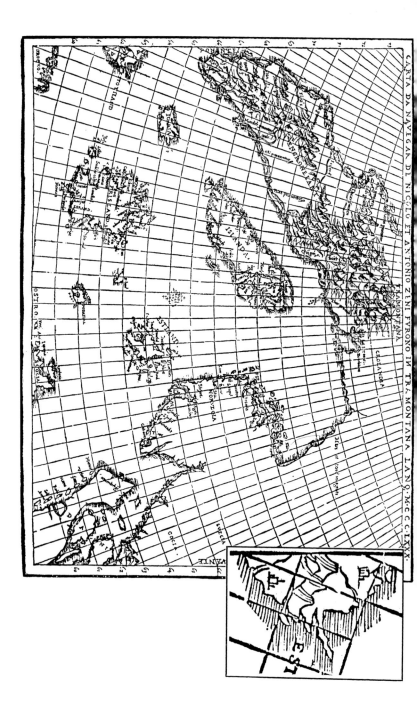

bursting from the plaits of plants and the wreaths of herbs on the walls. And yet there were no Green Women; there was hardly any recognition of the ancient cult of the Earth Goddess. One of the first in the Renaissance would be Botticelli's painting of Primavera, the flowering maiden of the spring. And yet in the end, no late Christian tradition could deny the Divine motherhood of all growing things or the beliefs about the natural world that had flourished before Christ was born.

Robin of the Woods

With the Green Man springing in the chapel, it is hardly surprising that the St Clairs of Rosslyn were also associated with Robin Hood and Midsummer Fairs. The castle itself was a haven for gypsies and strolling players. When he was Lord General of Scotland under Queen Mary, another and later Sir William St Clair not only saved gypsies 'from the gibbet in the Burrow Moore, ready to be strangled', but was their host 'in the stanks of Roslin every year, where they acted severall plays, dureing the moneth of May and June. There are two towers which were allowed them for their residence, the one called Robin Hood, the other Little John.'

Sir William had reason to be grateful to the gypsies. In 1470, two of the St Clair young women, Marion and Margaret, were decoyed from their place at Polwarth by their uncle to his castle at Herdmanston, where they were imprisoned because he coveted their estate. Marion sent a letter by Johnny Faa, a gypsy chief, to George Home, the young Baron of Wedderburn, who, with his brother Patrick and a hundred men, attacked Herdmanston. They released the sisters, who travelled home over the Lammermuir Hills to marry their Wedderburn rescuers. From this escapade came the old song 'Polwarth of the Green'. And also from it came the gratitude of the St Clairs of Rosslyn.

The gypsies who played Robin Hood at the St Clair castle were performing a subject that was widely popular in the fifteenth and sixteenth centuries. And Sir William St Clair himself annotated his copy of the *Chronicles Scotie* with some rare dating:

> 1265 rober huid ves forfaltit for fechtying againis the Kyng of Ingland at the batell of hewsham the vi zeir of Alexander iij reng
>
> Anno Domini 1287 Alexander tercius deit at Kyng-gorne the 35 or 37 zeir of his reng. In his tyme rober huid, lytill jhone, tamas Lermont or rymor and mechell schot the medycener ves al lewand.

These entries show that the legends of Robin Hood, Little John and Thomas the Rhymer were well known at Rosslyn Castle at the time when the annual May Day Festivals were still being held, before their suppression during the Reformation in Scotland. The historical dates given to Robin Hood are later than the tradition that he was alive in the time of King Richard I. The fact that Sir William St Clair was a leading judge under Queen Mary proves that he was still a Roman Catholic. Mobs from Edinburgh would soon attack Rosslyn and destroy the four altars in the Lady Chapel dedicated to the Virgin Mary and St Matthew and St Peter and St Andrew, while Reformation divines would forbid all May Day ceremonies. It was understandable. Bishop Latimer complained that nobody would hear his sermons when Robin Hood plays were being performed, while the Puritan diarist Philip Stubbes denounced Maypoles as 'stinking idols' and claimed that out of a hundred maidens who went into the woods to encounter the local Robin Hoods and Green Men on May Night, 'scarcely the third part of them returned home again undefiled'.

If Robin Hood existed in the flesh as more than a fantasy of Robin Goodfellow or Robin of the Woods or the Green Knight or the Green Man, then there is evidence of a Robert Hood of Wakefield and a Robyn Hode, porter of the chamber of King Edward II, routed by the Scots at Bannockburn. In legend, Robin Hood was meant to have been murdered by his only relation, the

treacherous Prioress of Kirklees, and until a century ago, a gravestone at Kirklees bore the name of Robert Hude, until it was
destroyed by railway navvies taking away fragments as a cure for
toothache. Fortunately, the stone slab was drawn in 1665 by the
antiquary Nathaniel Johnston. What was remarkable in the drawing
was the Templar Cross carved on Hude's grave, implying that he
was a knight of that Military Order.

In the early plays and ballads, Robin Hood does meet a poor
knight on his way to the Crusades, who rides in simple clothes
and has no money. He has had to mortgage his estate for £400 to
an abbot to pay for his mission to the Holy Land. Robin Hood
lends the knight the amount of his debt, which is repaid to the
angry abbot. Later, Robin Hood captures the cellarer of the
abbey and finds £800 in his baggage. The Virgin Mary has paid
the loan twice over. When the poor knight returns from his
Crusade, Robin Hood forgives his debt and bestows on him
another £400.

> Thus than holpe hym good Robyn,
> The knyght of all his care:
> God that syt in heuen hye,
> Grannte as well to fare!

This particular tale gave Robin Hood the reputation of robbing the
rich to give to the poor. Curiously, the Templar gravestone of
Robert Hude at Kirklees implied a recognition of that reputation.
For the Templars were dedicated to poverty, and one of their duties
was to maintain a poor man always at their cost in addition to
guarding pilgrims on their travels to the Holy Places. The Templars
also took spoils from the rich by war as well as donations. If the
Kirklees tombstone was genuine, it was Templar and contemporary
with the Templar tombstone at Rosslyn of that Sir William de St
Clair, who had helped to defeat Edward II at Bannockburn, before
dying on his Spanish crusade while trying to take the Heart of Bruce
to Jerusalem.

Fact or fantasy, Robin Hood and the Green Man were part of

the structure of belief of the St Clairs of Rosslyn. In his rhyming chronicle of Scotland, published in 1420, Andrew de Wyntoun also dated the legend to the end of the thirteenth century: 'Than litill Iohne and Robyne Hude/Waichmen were commendit gud . . .'

The St Clairs had supported William Wallace when he was a rebel and an outlaw against the English Crown, and Robin Hood's resistance to the tyranny of London made a continual appeal to a family that had helped to win the independence of Scotland. Nordic myths also contributed to the confusion between Robin Hood and the Green Man in May Day rituals at Rosslyn Castle and Harvest Festivals and masons' carvings in the chapel. Each Scottish clan was identified by a tree or plant, which may have derived from the ancient Bardic alphabet. The whin identified the St Clairs, as the bramble did the Bruces. Folk and religious beliefs twined in the Middle Ages. And the rulers of the time were not immune to that interleaving.

The green strand is evident in the legends of the Grail and is woven into the later mysteries of the Masons. The Green Knight, who cannot be killed, is a key figure in the romances of King Arthur and the Round Table. More significantly, in Wolfram von Eschenbach's medieval masterpiece, *Parzifal* – the inspiration of the design of Rosslyn Chapel – green is the colour given to the Grail itself, the stone fallen from Heaven. And green is the colour of the Grail Queen and of Parzifal's father, fighting for the Muslims in his riding habit 'green as the emerald rare'. The Grail itself is called 'the root and blossom of the Paradise Garden, the crown of all earthly wishes, the fair fullness that never shall fail'.

Rosslyn Chapel itself was built as a Paradise Garden, and its masons carved within it many of the growing plants of Creation. They were as conscious as its designer that this glen in stone represented the gifts of God to the earth. It showed the bounty of His grace, which provided their food and gave them health and cures. In its stonework, the masons also carved their ancient beliefs in the spirits of the forests, from which the northmen once had come. A thankfulness for all of Creation united Christian and pagan feelings and memories in the St Clairs of Rosslyn and in the masons, who built the chapel with its green language and medicine.

9

Sailing to the West

THERE IS LITTLE doubt that the Knights Templars wanted to create another Paradise and Temple of Solomon in a New World beyond the reach of Papal authority. Their involvement in the Albigensian Crusade against the Cathars of the Langue d'Oc was equivocal: they fought for the Crusaders, but equally many Cathar knights joined their Order. Both believed in the Holy Spirit and one God; both aspired to be *perfecti*, the sinless keepers of the Spirit of the Grail. When the Templars were also excommunicated and persecuted in France, some of them fled with part of their fleet to Portugal, where they became the Knights of Christ and pioneers in the discovery of Africa and the Far East. Vasco da Gama was a Knight of Christ and voyaged with the eight-pointed red Templar cross emblazoned on his sails, while Prince Henry the Navigator was a Grand Master of the Order.

The Templars sought to follow, however, the example of their protégés, the Teutonic Knights. While the Templars had been based in Venice throughout the thirteenth century, the Teutonic Knights set up there for only sixteen years between the fall of Acre and the excommunication of their brother Order. Fearing the same fate, they moved their headquarters to Marienburg in Prussia, and under the protection of the German Emperors and Princes, they began a crusade towards the eastern Baltic that created them an empire. The father of Prince Henry St Clair himself died fighting with a hundred men for the Teutonic Knights and their possessions.

Those Templars who escaped with their ships and resources to their properties near the St Clairs at Rosslyn; those Templars who won the battle of Bannockburn with Sir William de St Clair, who was buried as a Master of the Temple – they would have looked to the north and the west to found a new Templar empire on the model of the Teutonic empire of the east. Prince Henry St Clair with his retinue of 300 knights used Templar manpower, resources and navigational skills to conquer his birthright in Orkney and the Shetlands. But as the Fisherman's Story in the *Zeno Narrative* related, there was always the lure of the old tales of Atlantis and Arcadia and the far lands beyond the western ocean. So Prince Henry mounted an exploratory expedition under Nicolò Zen to Greenland, followed by a major colonizing expedition under Antonio Zen in the last years of the fourteenth century. He sought a new empire of the west, run by the Military and Monastic Orders. This was the logical strategy of the time. In evidence, there is the tombstone of William de St Clair in Rosslyn Chapel, the *Zeno Narrative* and its description of the voyage to the north-west, and the Vopell and Vavassatore map of the New World, with its figure of a crowned knight in Nova Scotia and its inscriptions.

In the sixteenth century, cartographers annotated their maps with drawings and a mixture of abbreviated dog Latin, Italian, Spanish, Portuguese, French, German and English. On the Vopell and Vavassatore map, which covers North and Central America and Asia, four crowned figures are drawn, all of them ruling empires or colonies of the past or the present. In Asia Orientalis, the *magus Cham Cublai* is shown on his throne: he is the Kublai Khan known to the Venetian explorer Marco Polo. Above Hispania Major, the crowned Aztec ruler *Mutzezuma* is shown, and Cortes is mentioned as his conqueror. By Florida, the Spanish King is depicted, ruling over his new colonial empire in the Caribbean. And on the Baccalearum Regio of Nova Scotia, the fourth crowned and bearded knight appears, kneeling by his shield and wearing the surcoat of the Military Orders, in testimony to some memory of a past royal or princely colony there. Above the figure is a rough square cross set on a hill. Opposite the figure, the inscription reads *Agricole proseu C. di laborador*. The words suggest *agriculture* or plantations *for* the benefit of a *labouring* rite such as a Monkish or Military Order on the cape.

It is interesting that the previous and seminal Dutch globe map called the *Gemma Frisius – Mercator* of 1537 mentions a *Promotôriû agricule seu cabo del Laborador*, or *agricultural Promontory on the cape of the Laborador*. The Portuguese word for landowner was *Lavrador* and again suggests a tradition of plantations worked in that area. This tradition was depicted on the *Frisius-Mercator* globe by three flags in the Baccalearum Regio of Nova Scotia. All of them contained a square cross surmounted by a foliate cross. They may represent the Spanish flag, for Spain was awarded the northern New World by the Pope and the remaining Military Orders were still powerful in that country. Yet the resemblance to the Templar cross on its war banner is remarkable. And as the *Frisius-Mercator* globe added the words to the area, *terra per britannos inventi* (the land was discovered by the Britons) primary evidence of a tradition of colonization by British people in Nova Scotia existed when this original globe was made.

It is also significant that St Bernard of Clairvaux had founded the Cistercian Order as well as backing the Military Order of the Temple of Solomon. One of his commands was *Laborare Est Orare* (Work is Prayer). The monks were some of the best farmers of their age, as well as some of the best builders. The Gothic cathedrals of France were constructed largely by masons called *Fratres Solomonis*, the Brothers of Solomon, directed by Cistercian and Templar master builders. Later on, these became the *Enfants de Salomon*, the French building trade guild of the Middle Ages. Anyone wishing to found a permanent colony in the New World would take with the expedition some knights and masons and farmers, preferably from the experienced Military and Monastic Orders.

In this context, it is intriguing that the *Zeno Narrative* told of the first expedition to Greenland by Nicolò Zen, who came across a trading monastery of Black Friars, since identified as St Olaf's Monastery in Gael Hamke Bay. A medieval Greenlander, Ivar Bardsen, the Steward to the Bishop of Gardar, wrote of small islands near the monastery with abundant hot water – good for bathing and the cure of many diseases. The advanced agricultural techniques of the friars included the use of a natural hot spring to irrigate a market garden that produced flowers and fruits and herbs in winter. So impressed were the Eskimos according to the *Zeno Narrative*, that when they saw these supernatural effects, they took the friars for Gods. The report of this place would have encouraged Prince Henry St Clair to include monks in his colonizing expedition, as the captions in the *Frisius-Mercator* globe and the Vopell and Vavassatore map suggested.

If Prince Henry St Clair had intended to found a colony, it would explain the inscriptions by the figure of the crowned knight set in Nova Scotia. A tradition of an early attempt to found a military and monastic Christian empire of the West in the manner of the eastern empire of the Teutonic Knights would have reached Casper Vopell in Cologne or Vavassatore in Venice, particularly through the *Zeno Narrative* and *Map*, telling of that expedition to America. There is no other explanation of the figure of the crowned knight on the map. Later, Labrador became the name of a region of Canada. It was always hard ground to farm. Recent efforts to translate the term as *La Bras d'Or* or *Labora d'or* or *gold workings*, thus connecting the term to the 'Money Pit' and old gold workings on the Oak Island off Nova Scotia, are far-fetched. It was enough for the first European settlers there to labour at planting oak trees and clearing fields and laying foundations for their buildings. There is no evidence of their working the gold-bearing Gaspereau and Gold rivers, which run across Nova Scotia between two Oak Islands.

Giovanni Andrea di Vavassatore, also known as 'Vadagnin Zuan Andre', was the leading wood-engraver and cartographer of his time in Venice. He devised his map from a woodcut of a world map in twelve sheets, produced in 1545 by Casper Vopell of Cologne, who wrongly accused him of failing to acknowledge the previous achievement. The surviving Venetian maps before the *Zeno Map* all showed Nova Scotia as part of a Bacallareum or Baccalearum or Bacalaos region, derived from the Basque word for codfish. It is still preserved in the name of Bacalieu Island off Newfoundland, then called Terra Nova. These maps shared much the same crude geography. The interest of Vopell and Vavassatore's version was that they placed their bearded and crowned knight where they did with the abbreviated commentary round it, which may explain it as the symbol of a colonizing mission. Certainly, the sophistication and accuracy of the *Zeno Map*, particularly in surveying the coasts of Greenland and in identifying Nova Scotia as Estotiland, replaced previous efforts to chart the Baccalearum region.

There is equally no question that the *Zeno Narrative* and *Map* were believed by fellow Europeans for the following 150 years. A new edition of Ptolemy's *Geography* published in Venice three years after the publication of the *Zeno Map* included its findings, as did Mercator himself in his great map of 1569. Greenland was now correctly delineated, but 'Frisland' was shown as a large island as well as the Faroes, and 'Drogeo' as another small island rather than the coastline of North America drawn on the edge of the *Zeno Map*. Estotiland, however, correctly appeared at the eastern end of Canada above Terra Corterealis, discovered by the three Corte Real brothers sailing from the Azores in the first years of the century. Below this land, Mercator placed a monastic Church building on the mouth of the St Lawrence river, apparently a reference to the city, said in the *Zeno Narrative* to have been founded by Prince Henry St Clair in the New World.

Cartographers and explorers continued to trust in the veracity of the *Zeno Map*. Ortelius used it in his *Theatrum*, published the year after Mercator's revised globe. The leading authority on exploration of the time, Giovanni Batista Ramusio, was a Venetian who knew Nicolò Zeno and published his accounts of his ancestors' polar voyages and of his great-grandfather Caterino's adventures as an ambassador in Persia; he also used the *Zeno Map* in his influential

Travels of 1574. Martin Frobisher himself trusted the same source in his accounts of his search for the North-west Passage, while Michael Lok used it in his map, published by the Elizabethan cartographer and writer Hakluyt in his *Divers Voyages*. John Davis also referred to it in his explorations, and Purchas believed the *Zeno Map* in his *Pilgrims*. It remained the standard authority as a description of the northern polar regions until the end of the seventeenth century. Many things in it must have been right, as many sailors were travelling those seas in a period when the French were settling Canada, and the fishing fleets of northern Europe were looting the rich cod banks off Newfoundland. The mathematician John Dee was so eager to see Queen Elizabeth I the mistress of a western empire that he asserted the people of Estotiland were the descendants of colonists sent out to Avalon by King Arthur – and so the subjects of the English Crown.

I myself discovered a large globe standing at the entrance of the Correr Museum in Venice. It was made in 1693 and displayed a geography of the Arctic Circle still based on the *Zeno Map*. It named the region and its discoverer: 'NUOVA FRANCIA/ESTOTILANDIA/THE NEW BRETAGNE/TIERRA DE LABRADOR DISCOVERED BY SIR ANTONIO ZEN, PATRICIAN OF *Venice in 1390 first of the other Countries of America to be made known.*'

Although the *Zeno Map* was unsigned, the engraving of it was done by a leading Venetian cartographer, probably Vavassatore or his contemporary rival Mathei Pagano, although the book was published in 1558 by Francesco Marcolini. Certainly, the world of map-making was too small for the creators of maps not to use each other's services and discoveries. The superior quality of the *Zeno Map* became the basis for polar geography after its publication. Quite simply, it was the best there was to date.

The *Zeno Narrative* confirmed how a careful survey of the coasts of Greenland was carried out after the conquest of Orkney and the Shetlands, first by Nicolò Zen after 1393 before he returned to Orkney and to death in Venice, and second by the Scottish Prince Zichmni, or St Clair, who detached support ships to complete the survey during the two years of his voyage in search of a western colony. In fact, the *Zeno Narrative* specifically credited the Prince as worthy of immortal fame for his discovery of Greenland, although it had already had Norse settlements for two centuries. The Prince should have been credited with the survey of both the eastern and the western coasts, translated to charts by Nicolò Zen's brother Antonio, and brought back by him to Venice, to be discovered more than a century later in the Zen palace in Canareggio by an ancestor also called Nicolò, who was to use them as the basis for the most accurate map of polar regions in existence.

If the charts for the *Zeno Map* did not come from the voyage of the two Zen brothers described in the *Narrative*, it is hard to know the provenance or the need to invent a false voyage of discovery to disguise the true source. The accuracy of most of the *Map* reinforces the plausibility of most of the *Narrative*. The great error in both is the description of a voyage to the fictitious island of Icaria, which has been plausibly identified as St Kilda, formerly called Hirta or Irte, or as Kerry in Ireland. The author Nicolò Zeno did state that he had destroyed as a child many of his ancestors' letters sent back from Orkney to Venice. His book was based on the surviving fragments. He seems to have confused an earlier expedition to the south-west – the inhabitants of Icaria have all the characteristics of a tribal society under an Irish High King. Unfortunately, in naming the place Icaria, Nicolò Zeno fell into the fashionable trap of giving a classical name to an unknown place that sounded much the same. Icarus certainly never fell from his flight into the sea near Icaria, nor was it settled by a King Daedalus of Scotland. No island existed where its inventor showed it to be. Other mistakes on the *Map*, particularly the large size given to Frisland (the Faroes), are explicable in terms of the *Narrative*, which sets much of its early action there. But in view of the fact that all early maps contained serious errors of geography and invented islands or misshapen continents, much of the *Zeno Map* is an advance on the cartography of the time.

The reputation of its maker must also be considered. Nicolò Zeno was a leading Venetian author as well as a public servant. He was born in 1510 in the Zen Palace at Crosichieri, went to Constantinople with his grandfather Pietro, and then returned to Venice, living to the age of fifty-five. He was acknowledged as a historian, who was devoted to the reputation of his family. He wrote an account of the wars of Venice against the Turks in four volumes. In it, he praised the role played by his grandfather Pietro in the peace negotiations. He also wrote a book on the founding of the Venetian Republic and ancient memories of the barbarians who destroyed the Roman Empire. Another treatise dealt with the origins and customs of the Arabs. As well as his *Zeno Narrative* and *Map*, he edited an account of his great-grandfather Caterino's service to Venice as an ambassador in Persia. This literary activity did not stop him from serving his country in the family tradition. He was Consul in Syria for six years, then returned to Venice to sit on the Council of Ten, holding four other posts before his retirement in 1550. His brother Ottavio was a poet and a Canon of Padua. Nicolò Zeno's distinguished family, his own writing and his public service made his word most credible in Venice. He was personally known to Giovanni Batista Ramusio, the great authority of the day on voyages and discoveries, who included the *Zeno Narrative* and *Map* in his publications. His own countrymen considered him the leading geographer of his time.

The erroneous grid that Nicolò Zeno drew on the sea charts of his ancestors to make up his map has been corrected by Miller Christy, the geologist William Herbert Hobbs, Captain Mallory and most recently Professor Charles Hapgood, who had the benefit of the Strategic Air Command survey. As sailors in the Middle Ages could use only rough latitudes, their longitudes were fantasy, compounded by the confusion of the magnetic with the true North Pole. The corrections by the four experts, however, demonstrate the surprising accuracy of the survey of the east and west coasts of Greenland by Nicolò and Antonio Zen and his Scottish Prince. In his revised edition of *Maps of the Ancient Sea Kings*, Hapgood points out that Greenland is shown rightly on the *Zeno Map* with no ice-cap and with a mountainous south and north and a flat central region. A reconstructed polar projection gives many correspondences on the ground between old Venetian and modern aerial cartography of the Arctic. Even the greater Iceland of the *Zeno Map* could well have been greater, for volanic explosions submerged whole provinces in the fourteenth century. As Hobbs declared, the Zen brothers produced a true magnetic map of Greenland and proved themselves to have been honest and reliable explorers who were far in advance of their age.

The Ships and the Instruments

The art of navigation and the construction of ships were changing in the fourteenth century. The skills of piloting the land-locked Mediterranean were being translated into the necessities of surviving a voyage on the Atlantic Ocean. By the beginning of the century, Venetian sailors had the benefit of the mariner's compass, sailing directions based on estimated distances, a nautical chart and the sand-glass and table for calculating distance at sea, the equivalent of the modern traverse table. Sailing in the Mediterranean was a system of dead reckoning based on mathematics. The absence of tides and deep basins and steep coastlines made such a method work. It was not, however, applicable to the Atlantic, where a knowledge of the tides was central, and changes of magnetic variation on the compass bearing were insignificant on long ocean voyages, particularly to the west under the North Pole.

The earliest reference to the mariner's compass dated from the twelfth century, when Alexander Neckham, an English monk and teacher at the University of Paris, described how seamen used a floating iron needle magnetized by a lodestone to determine true north, when clouds covered the sun and the stars. The divided compass card, attached to the magnetic needle and mounted on a dry pivot and enclosed in a wooden box, was developed in the Mediterranean and in China simultaneously. Its use enabled the Venetians to increase their trade voyages to the North Atlantic to two round trips every year, without the need to winter in the ports of England and Flanders.

In the same century, the development of the Portolan charts by Templar and Italian and Portuguese navigators gave the sailors for the first time a scale, based on magnetic bearings. Although applied only to the Mediterranean, this invention was a turning-point in the history of cartography. Used with the early traverse table called the *toleta de marteloio*, this dead reckoning system allowed for long ocean voyages. When taken by the Venetians to northern waters on their trading trips, these techniques supplemented the practices of North Sea sailors, who had depended on their local knowledge of tides and soundings. Norse and Scottish sailors had established their position on the continental shelf from the depth of the water and the nature of the bottom. And when they set off on long passages across the ocean to Greenland and further west, they had only the compass, the directions left by previous voyages and the interpretation of the movements of currents and birds to aid the setting of courses under cloudy and stormy skies.

New Mediterranean navigational techniques enhanced North Atlantic experience. And so did the southern practice of boat-building, particularly by the Arsenale of Venice, the major shipyard and production factory of the Middle Ages. Although Venice used mainly large rowing galleys with supplementary sails for its military operations, its merchant fleet was adopting the lateen rig with triangular sails from the Arab *dhow*. This enabled a ship to sail closer to the wind. During the fourteenth century, the square-rigged and sturdy *knorrs* of Norse trade began to add a lateen-rig on a mizzen mast to increase their potential.

There were also changes in steering and construction. Northern ships were steered by a side-rudder and clinker-built with over-lapping timbers. But the stern-post rudder was depicted on German city seals of the thirteenth century, and on the gold noble coin of 1344, struck by King Edward III of England. The bows and sterns of trading ships were also developed into small wooden towers. And the carvel or flush-built southern technique of shipbuilding, which allowed for the construction of larger vessels, also changed marine practice in the north. Rigging, too, was developed into the braces and lifts and bowlines and sheets of modern sailing. As was sung in a medieval chant from *The Stacions of Rome and the Pylgrym's Sea Voyage*:

> Hale the bowelyne! now vere the sheet!
> Cook, make redy at noon our mete;
> Our pylgryms have no lust to ete;
> I pray God give them rest!

The most significant import from the Mediterranean to northern waters was the mounted ship's cannon. Greek fire had been used in naval warfare since classical times. By the middle of the fourteenth century, the high wooden castles on poop and prow provided platforms for archers and were decisive in sea battles such as the English victory at Sluys against the French fleet. But small cannon with ringed barrels made from welded iron rods, which went under the name of *petriera* because they threw stone cannonballs, led to the Venetian defeat of the Genoese blockading armada at Chioggia and its supremacy in the Mediterranean by the end of the fourteenth century. The Venetian commander at that action was Carlo Zen, and his brothers would take Mediterranean navigational and ship-building skills along with the new guns to Orkney and the Shet-lands. And so they would provide Prince Henry St Clair with the techniques and weaponry to become a sea-power in the North Atlantic, capable of founding a colony in the unknown lands across the western ocean.

Atlantis, Arcadia and a New World

In the Middle Ages, the urge to discover a place beyond the oceans or the mountains, where there was peace and joy and heaven on earth, made the discovery of a new world a dream and a crusade. The wish to find a terrestrial Paradise was an inspiration behind the quests of explorers and the theories of philosophers and poets. To civilized communities, the hope of a golden age existing among simple people was almost as great as the fear of the onslaught of the savage and the beast against them.

The unknown could be hopeful as well as fearful. Plato deliberately created his mythical Atlantis as a mirror of the vices of Greek society. The vision of the perfect state of his *Republic* was translated in the *Timaeus* and the *Critias* to the sunken island of Atlantis, with its perfect government and convenient canals and excellent water system. Atlantis has always been more useful as a promoter of dream worlds than as a description of society. It was matched by the vision of Arcadia, the shepherd's Paradise in a place forever green and golden. And by the Elysian Fields at the world's end, 'where living is made easiest for mankind, where no snow falls, no stormy winds blow, and there is never any rain.' Lucian later added inexhaustible wine and honey and music and scent to the Elysian Fields, making them fit for hedonists rather than for heroes.

Another tradition lay behind the dream of a tangible Paradise – the traveller's tale. Where movement was dangerous and strangers rare, the fantastic had great opportunities for embroidering the facts. The Middle Ages of Europe hardly distinguished between legend and geography, between hyperbole and ethnography, between myth and fact. Thirty years after the discovery of the New World, Cortes could be instructed to look in Mexico for strange humans with flat ears or dog-like faces. Both Eden and El Dorado were considered to be discoverable in the New World, and the name of the ocean that separated it from Europe came to be called after Plato's dream of Atlantis.

In medieval times, a Paradise or Atlantis or Arcadia or Isle of the Hesperides was held to exist beyond the western ocean. It was the Avalon of the Arthurian legend: as late as the reign of Queen Elizabeth I of England, her mathematician and magician John Dee wanted her to claim the newly discovered lands of North America as the territories settled by colonists sent by King Arthur from Scotland more than a thousand years before. The Scottish and Irish legends of St Brendan and the Welsh myths of Madoc and Portuguese prehistory all described voyages to a western paradise called Brasil, while Spanish and Italian legend referred to a western island as Antilla. The very name of Orkney and the Shetlands in Latin was the Orchades or Orchadia, so similar to Arcadia.

These were the medieval stories of an unknown island or country beyond the western ocean, which were inherited by the young Henry St Clair, who was to become the Earl of Orkney and to lead an expedition to a new western world. He was the heir of classical and medieval imaginings. He spoke and read Latin, he visited the Near East, he had Templar connections along with Norse and Celtic roots. From these various influences, he would draw the power and the inspiration to endeavour to reach his Atlantis and Arcadia from the Orchadia under his control.

10

Earl and Prince of Orkney

THE BLACK DEATH spared the future Prince Henry St Clair when he was a child at Rosslyn Castle. He gave thanks to the nearby healing well of St Katherine, the patron saint of the family. The natural bitumen rising from the oil shale deposits there was meant to be a miraculous seepage from the ground. It was held to result from Saint Margaret of Scotland or her St Clair cup-bearer letting fall a drop of the precious discharge from the bones of St Katherine, taken from her tomb in Sinai. 'Als sone as Sanct Margaret saw the oulie spring ithandlie,' Bellendon wrote in his early Scottish translation from the Latin of Hector Boece, 'by divine miracle, in the said place, sche gart big ane chappell thair in the honour of Sanct Katrine. This oulie has ane singular virteu agains all manner of kankir and skawis.' So many relics of Saint Katherine were taken by Crusaders from the monastery dedicated to her that only her skull and the bones of one hand are still preserved there. It was so important a shrine that it was shown on medieval Portolan maps as the same size as Alexandria and Jerusalem itself.

If the holy oil did save the health of the heir of Rosslyn, the Black Death still killed a third of the population of Scotland, which was reduced to 200,000 souls. And when Henry St Clair was only 13 years old, his father sailed from the Firth of Forth with a new fleet and body of Scottish soldiers to fight for the Teutonic Knights on their crusade to extend their Prussian empire into pagan Lithuania.

The resources and sea-skills of the fleeing Templars were being absorbed by the St Clairs at Rosslyn, who had also profited from extensive land grants given by Robert the Bruce after the victory of Bannockburn. In Germany, the Templars had been ingested by the Teutonic Knights, while the St Clairs at Rosslyn were already involved in the Baltic timber trade in exchange for wool through the Cistercian abbeys of Melrose and Newbattle and Culross in Fife. If old alliance and commerce prompted the Scottish knights to set off on another crusade to the East, they also had to earn their share of the ransom of King David II of Scotland, then in English hands and held against an indemnity of 100,000 marks. In 1358, in a skirmish in the forests towards Russia, Henry St Clair's father was killed, and the son came into his inheritance.

He was heir to claims, chiefly to the Earldom of Orkney. His mother Isabella was the daughter of Malise II of Orkney, Caithness and Stratherne, whose previous marriage and other children had produced other pretenders to the title, chiefly the Swedish noble-man Erngisle Sunesson, and Henry St Clair's cousins Alexander de Ard and Malise Sparre. While Henry was still a boy, Sunesson had himself installed as Earl of Orkney with his title confirmed by Magnus II, King of Sweden and Regent of Norway, which had sovereignty over the Northern Isles. Sunesson was later stripped of his title after his involvement in a plot against the royal family. Alexander de Ard now intervened and took over the Earldom of Orkney, since its rightful heir, Henry St Clair, was still an adoles-cent, who would have to assert his claims at the Scandinavian royal courts as soon as he had come to manhood.

His chance came in 1363, when he had reached the age of eighteen. Haakon the VI had become King of Norway and also King of Sweden. He was to marry Princess Margaret, the daughter of King Waldemar of Denmark, in Copenhagen. Because of his Norse family connection, Henry St Clair was knighted and appointed as the Scottish ambassador to the wed-ding, and he sailed to Denmark. Most of the Scandinavian royalty and nobility would be at the ceremony. Although the bride was only ten years old, she was to become the ruler of all three kingdoms, united in her person.

At Copenhagen, Sir Henry St Clair had the lands left by Earl Malise in Orkney confirmed as his right, but he was not yet given the title of Earl by the King of Norway. He would first have to prove that he could assert royal authority in Orkney and be a faithful servant of the Norse Crown, which disliked having an over-mighty subject or a rebel on its Northern Isles. Bishop William of Orkney and the Shetlands was already appropriating royal revenues. Sir Henry St Clair's uncle Thomas was sent as Baillie to collect these monies for the King. While in Copenhagen, Sir Henry St Clair was also said to have concluded a marriage to a daughter of King Magnus, Princess Florentia: but if he did, she died young, probably before the age of puberty, and she bore no children.

On his return to Scotland, Sir Henry St Clair did marry Janet Halyburton, the daughter of the Lord of Dirleton Castle, twenty miles from Rosslyn. She was to bear him four sons and nine daughters. The parents were reputed to be the most handsome couple in the region, except perhaps for Henry's cousin Margaret Stewart, who was the ward and then the mistress of the First Earl of Douglas, who lived in his sea-fortress of Tantallon on its promontory. Along with Castle Pilgrim, it would serve as a model for Henry's own sea-fortresses on Orkney and off the Shetlands.

Douglas referred to his mistress's cousin, in a slighting way, as 'Henry the Holy'. This was because he followed the crusading example of his father and his Templar ancestors. He was recruited with other Scottish knights to join the crusade of Peter I, the Lusignan King of Cyprus. In 1365, he assembled at Venice after visiting his Norman relations on the way south through France. He may well have met Carlo Zen and his brothers during the muster of the crusading fleet or in the Near East. Certainly, the biography of Carlo Zen by his grandson, Bishop Giacomo of Padua, stated that Carlo met a Scottish prince on a pilgrimage to Jerusalem and assisted the King of Cyprus in his wars. Sir Henry St Clair would have seen the Arsenale at Venice enclosed within its fortifications, and he would have noted the lateen rigs of the merchantmen and the first mounted cannon on the war galleys, which were to take him and other Scottish knights to attack Alexandria.

When the Crusaders reached Egypt, they succeeded in occupying and sacking Alexandria. They could not hold the position and were forced to withdraw with their booty, while Sir Henry St Clair proceeded to the Holy Land, now held by Muslim forces. He went to Acre and Jerusalem under a safe-conduct for pilgrims, previously negotiated by the Holy Roman Emperor Frederick II. His pilgrimage gave him the nickname of 'Henry the Holy' on his return to Scotland.

He was powerful now at court. He was appointed to hold many state offices, including Lord Chief Justice of Scotland and Admiral of the Seas. The Scottish Queen was Euphemia Ross, his great-aunt, who had married the new king, Robert Stewart, the founder of that dynasty. This close relationship with the Scottish throne disturbed the King of Norway, who removed the St Clair Baillie and appointed the rival Sir Alexander de Ard to be the governor of Orkney and to uphold royal authority there. As with the Romans, *divide and rule* was Norse strategy. De Ard was governor for only one year, and in 1379 the Norwegian King appointed Sir Henry St Clair as the Earl of Orkney under stringent conditions. Under the Deed of Investiture, he had to agree:

To serve the King of Norway with a hundred armed men
To defend the Orkneys with all his power
To aid the King of Norway in his wars
Not to build a castle on Orkney without the consent of the
King
To uphold the rights of the islanders
Not to sell or pledge any of the islands
To welcome the King or his men on any voyage to the islands
Not to declare any war that might harm the islands
To be responsible personally for any injury to an islander
To answer the King's summons and give him counsel

Not to break the King's peace

To make no pact with the Bishop of Orkney

Not to give his son the earldom as an inheritance except if the
                                        title came from the King of Norway.

To pay 1,000 gold nobles for the title.

Other clauses confirmed that his cousins Malise Sparre and Sir Alexander de Ard would both renounce their claims to the earldom and be held as hostages in Norway. The assent of powerful Scottish nobles would be procured to confirm Henry's title as Earl of Orkney. No lands or rights of the King of Norway on Orkney would be touched. And any breach of any of the terms of the Deed would result in the loss of the earldom.

The stringent conditions of the Deed of Investiture confirmed the new Earl of Orkney as the vassal of the King of Norway. He also had to sign a bond to pay the King's Baillie in Kirkwall in Orkney two sums of 100 nobles each at Pentecost and Martinmas. This obligation compelled Sir Henry St Clair to go to Orkney in person and establish his authority there against all rivals, especially the Bishop of Orkney. He would have to build a fleet and recruit forces to control the 170 islands of Orkney and the Shetlands, where he would effectively be a Norwegian Prince.

'He was more honoured than any of his ancestors,' Father Hay wrote. 'For he had power to cause stamp coine within his dominions, to make laws, to remitt crimes; he had his sword of honour carried before him whersoever he went; he had a crowne in his armes, bore a crowne on his head when he constituted laws, and, in a word, was subject to none, save only he held his lands of the King of Danemarke, Sweden, and Noraway . . . In all those parts he was esteemed a second person next to the King.' His coat of arms was, indeed, in the shape of a sea-beast or dragon reminiscent of the prow of a Viking ship. It bore a coronet above the Engrailed Cross, the symbol of the keepers of the Holy Rood of Scotland. He was truly now a Prince.

Henry St Clair had inherited considerable resources to enforce his rights and to make himself a sea-power in the north. The Register of the Great Seal of Scotland shows Bruce and Stewart grants of land to Henry St Clair, 'our chosen defender and faithful to us', the guardian of the Crown Prince. In addition, he had absorbed many of the Templar lands and treasures from their headquarters at Balantrodoch near Rosslyn. His power and state and that of his son Henry were considerable. 'There were very few but were some way bound to him,' Father Hay wrote. 'He had continually in his house three hundred Riding Gentlemen, and his Princess, fifty-five Gentlewomen, whereof thirty-five were Ladies. He had his dainties tasted before him: he had meeting him, when he went to Orknay, three hundred men with red scarlet gownes and coats of black velvet.'

He was hardly going to a new dominion. The St Clairs were a Norse and Norman and Scottish family, which had held the name of Møre or Moray and had changed it to St Clair in the tenth century on the borders of Normandy. As the present authority on medieval Orkney has written:

> The original foundation of the Earldom of Orkney was part of the process of settlement of the Northern Isles by the Norwegian Vikings in the ninth century. Although the way in which the members of the powerful Møre family established themselves in the islands is shrouded in the mists of legendary history, there is no doubt that by the last decades of the ninth century this one family had won control of the islands and held the title of earl by virtue of their family position. Later saga material suggests that they had received their earldom and title by grant from the Norwegian kings; but the main theme running through the history of the Earldom of Orkney is one of the theoretical claims to control by the kings of Norway and the *de facto* independence which the earls seem normally to have possessed.

The Kings of Norway increasingly attempted to regard the Earls of Orkney as royal appointments, holding their title by pleasure of the crown. It was the diplomacy of Henry St Clair, which persuaded King Haakon VI to invest him as the Earl. He certainly had legitimacy, not only through his mother, but through his Møre ancestors. Many of his relations were already important at Orkney. What he had to concede was what his cousin, Sir Alexander de Ard, had already conceded four years previously to the Scottish Crown – the Earldom of Caithness, until that time linked to the Earldom of Orkney. This concession allowed the King of Scotland to accept the St Clair accession to Orkney as a vassal of the King of Norway. But the new Stewart Kings were never easy about one of their subjects also being a subject of another sovereign power. The Northern Isles should be Scottish. It was a factor in foreign policy long before it was achieved.

Without asserting his own authority in Orkney and the Shetlands, Prince Henry St Clair had to protect his own Scottish possessions, which now extended from Rosslyn to Dysart in Fife and Newburgh in Aberdeenshire. He knew that the Stewart Kings considered that he was split between two loyalties, to his home country and to the Kingdom of Norway. He induced his children to make three royal marriages: his eldest son and heir Henry to Egidia Douglas, the granddaughter of King Robert II of Scotland; his daughter Elizabeth to Sir John Drummond, the brother of the wife of the Crown Prince of Scotland; and his second son John to Princess Ingeborg, the last daughter of King Waldemar of Denmark, whose elder daughter's marriage to King Haakon VI had been attended by Prince Henry as a young man. He also secured from King Robert of Scotland the formal cession of any right to Orkney and the recognition of King Haakon's grant of the earldom to 'our beloved relative Henry of *Orcadie*'.

The first requisite for the new Earl of Orkney was a secure base for his knights and his fleet. He had seen the Arsenale in Venice and the Templar sea-fortress at Acre and Castle Pilgrim, and he knew of the Douglas castle at Tantallon, where a huge wall guarded a rocky promontory, enabling ships to sail into a defended harbour beneath the cliffs. Although his Deed of Investiture precluded him from building a castle, he did so with the help of masons imported from Lothian, who had already set up the massive red walls of Rosslyn Castle. He was under threat from the Bishop of Orkney in his fortified palace, and he could not assert the authority of the King of Norway without a stronghold. In point of fact, King Haakon died in 1380 and was succeeded by King Olaf, while Prince Henry was constructing his monumental fortress on the site of an old Norse emplacement in Kirkwall, which afforded sanctuary for ships dragged ashore. So thick were its ashlar blocks that two centuries later, one of its besiegers with cannon protested 'to God the house has never been biggit without the consent of the Devil, for it is one of the strongest holds in Britain – without fellow'.

Once his fortress was built, Prince Henry would deal with the contentious prelate, Bishop William of Orkney, whose palace was on the hill above St Magnus Cathedral a quarter of a mile away. But the problem was removed by the people of Kirkwall, who killed or burned the Bishop for his oppression of them. Equally, the released pretender Malise Sparre forfeited his claims to the Earldom of Orkney in 1387, promising 'to restore, pay and satisfy' all injuries and offences and possessions taken from Prince Henry, who would still have to kill him four years later for yet another assault on Orkney.

The death of King Olaf after a short reign confirmed Prince Henry's estimation as 'a second person next to the King'. As Earl of Orkney, he was an elector to the three kingdoms of Norway, Sweden and Denmark. So he sailed across the North Sea to confirm King Olaf's mother, the Princess Margaret whose wedding he had attended in Copenhagen, as Queen of Norway and Sweden and as Regent of Denmark. She adopted as her heir a five-year-old boy, her grandnephew Eric of Pomerania, and so sustained her power during his minority. Prince Henry's presence in Scandinavia caused him to miss the Battle of Otterburn against the English, but the peace of 1389 between England and the old allies, Scotland and France, allowed him to consider extending his power to the Faroes and the Shetlands, where he now contracted to pay rent to the

Baillie of the King of Norway at the Church of St Magnus in Tingwall, under penalty of losing his rents on two of the islands near Kirkwall. Evidently, his assertion of royal authority on the Orkneys had been so effective that he was now asked to do the same on the neighbouring chains of the Northern Isles.

Before he could begin the reduction of these far islanders, who resented paying church tithes almost as much as royal taxes, Prince Henry had to pay homage at Scone to the new King of Scotland, Robert III. He was truly a catalyst between all the nations of the north, allied by blood and trust to the ruling families of four kingdoms. His duty done, he collected a fleet of 13 ships and set sail for his campaigns to the north of Orkney. And on his voyage, design or chance would make him renew his connections with the seamen he most admired – the mariners of Venice.

11

The Zen Voyage

As a child, Nicolò Zeno played in his grandfather's palace in Canareggio and tore up most of a book written in the Shetlands and letters sent back to Venice and sea charts, the remnants of which he was later to publish as the *Zeno Narrative* and *Map*. His confession about his childish act of destruction was disarming. He regretted his mutilation of the records of his predecessor, the explorer Antonio Zen:

> All these letters were written by Sir Antonio to Sir Carlo his brother. I am sorry that the book and much else on these subjects have, I don't know how, been destroyed. For I was only a child when they fell into my hands, and as I did not know what they were, I tore them in pieces, as children will do, and ruined them. It is something which I cannot now recall without the greatest sorrow. Nevertheless, in order that such an important memoir should not be lost, I have put it all in order as well as I could in this Narrative. More than its predecessors, the present age may derive pleasure from the great discoveries made in those parts where they were least expected. For our age takes a great interest in new narratives and in the discoveries, made in countries unknown before, by the high courage and great energy of our ancestors.

The *Narrative*, indeed, began with a genealogy and a description of the high courage and great energy of the Zen line. It led into praise of Carlo Zen, who had saved Venice at the battle of Chioggia. His brother Nicolò, a wealthy man, was said to have wanted to see the world in order to serve his country better and gain reputation and honour. Equipping his own vessel in 1390, he sailed through the Straits of Gibraltar and set course for England, where Carlo was to be sent as an ambassador six years later. Caught in a terrible storm, he was shipwrecked on Frislanda, which has been identified as Fair Isle between Orkney and the Shetlands or as one of the Faroe Islands. The local people were about to kill him and the crew, who had saved the goods from the ship, when a local prince appeared with his men:

> He drove away the natives, addressed our people in Latin and asked them who they were and where they came from. And when he learned that they came from Italy and that they were men of that country, he was exceedingly pleased. Promising them all that they would not be made captive, and assuring them that they had come into a place where they would be well treated and very welcome, he took them under his protection and gave his word of honour that they were safe.

Prince Henry St Clair had a fleet of thirteen vessels – 'two only were rowed with oars, the rest were small barks and one was a ship.' He had established his authority on Orkney and was attempting to extend it to the Shetlands and the Faroes, where he took his impressed Venetians. Although the *Zeno Narrative* referred to him as Zichmni and misspelt most place names, Prince Henry was the only prince in that area at that time with a war fleet. The subsequent account of obscure fighting in the Faroes and the Shetlands would not have been known in Venice without Nicolò Zen's writing back home about the struggles and the opportunities for trade, while asking his brother Antonio to buy another ship and sail it out to the northern seas to join him. 'Since Antonio had as great a desire as his brother to see the world and its various nations, and to make himself a great name, he bought a ship and directed his course that way. After a long voyage full of many dangers, he joined Sir Nicolò at last in safety and was received by him with great gladness, as his brother not only by blood, but also in courage.'

This plausible narrative begged one question – the motives for the voyages of the Zen brothers to the north. Their descendant, Nicolò Zeno, who published the work on them, may have been ignorant or may have destroyed the evidence or may have wished to disguise Venetian state policy. Evidently, the Zen brothers sailed out not for adventure or for honour but to serve the state better. They were trying to open up direct access to the important trade in fish and furs, pitch and timber of the Far North, bypassing the stranglehold of the Hanseatic League, which even had two trading posts on the entrepôt islands of Orkney and the Shetlands. They had probably heard of the new lord of the northern seas, Prince Henry St Clair, with his Templar resources and marine skills, for the Zen family had their own connections with the Christian Military Orders in their search for power and empire in the Mediterranean and in Prussia. Now they would navigate Prince Henry's fleet on reconnaissance and colonial expeditions across the western ocean.

Voyages to the West

When Nicolò Zen sent for his brother Antonio to come and join him in Orkney with a Venetian ship, Antonio had to buy and equip it himself. There were only two trading voyages a year from Venice to the North Atlantic. So Antonio would not have received a letter from his brother until the year after the first encounter with Prince Henry St Clair. It would have taken him another year to purchase and fit and crew his vessel. He could not have sailed to Shetland before the spring of 1392. When he had joined his brother, he helped Nicolò to attack the Shetlands, where a gale scattered their ships and forced them to shelter on Grislanda or Grossey in the Orkneys, before they could resume the assault. Seven small islands were captured, and a fort was begun to be constructed on Bressay. Prince Henry himself went on a mission to the London docks under a safe conduct issued by King Richard II of England that year. Taking with him a crew of twenty-four persons, he commissioned three ships and sailed them back north. Nicolò Zen had been left on Bressay to hold the Shetlands for his Scottish Prince, while Antonio withdrew with the rest of the fleet to the other St Clair sea-fortress at Kirkwall in Orkney, where they remained for two years.

Although the *Zeno Narrative* stated that Nicolò Zen sailed to Greenland 'the next season' in 1393 'with the view of discovering land', there was a political reason for the voyage, which also became a coastal survey as well as a reconnaissance for a later colonizing expedition to the west. With two Popes in office at the time, one in Avignon and another in Rome, Prince Henry St Clair had supported the Pope in Rome, probably because the King of Norway also did. In 1392, Bishop Henry of Orkney had submitted to the Archbishop of Trondheim under pressure from Prince Henry, who wanted to be rid of this ecclesiastical rival and induced the Pope in Rome to authorize the exchange of the Bishops of Orkney and Greenland. The next year, Bishop Henry left Orkney for Greenland, most probably on the 'three small barks' equipped by Nicolò Zen for his voyage of discovery there.

Certainly, Nicolò's first port of call in Greenland was a remarkable monastery of the Preaching Friars, which used hot springs to heat the building and cook food and even grow vegetables in winter in an early greenhouse. These reports seemed fantasies to later denigrators of the truth of the *Zeno Narrative*, until a succession of modern archaeologists discovered active volcanoes and hot springs in Gael Hamke Bay on the east coast of Greenland near the ruins of the monastery of Sanctus Olaus or St Olaf, miscalled San Tomaso in the *Narrative*. It was normally the first landing place for trading ships from Trondheim, which took back fish and furs from there to Norway. The existence of the Augustinian monastery with its early central heating had been affirmed in 1349 by a Greenlander, Ivar Bardsen, who was the steward of the Bishop of Greenland at Gardar on the west coast. He also wrote of the hot springs on an island nearby in Unartoq Fjord being used for washing and for healing the sick, as well as of a Benedictine nunnery on an adjacent fjord. The surviving ruins of the medieval church at Kakortok also support the *Zeno Narrative*, as does its stone architecture with an occasional arched window of splayed stones so similar to Orkney building and to the mysterious Newport Tower in Rhode Island.

The ongoing voyage with the Bishop of Orkney to his new see would have enabled Nicolò Zen to survey the east coast of Greenland round its southern cape to the west coast at Gardar. He may also have acquired charts and a fisherman's directions from Norse sailors and the Augustinian monks to assist his passage. Certainly, he returned from Gardar the following year with an admirable survey of the east coast and some of the west. He also brought back Bishop John of Greenland to Orkney. We know of the exchange of the two bishops from the Greenland Records, which are still preserved in the Vatican Library, while we know of Nicolò Zen's survey from both the *Zeno Narrative* and the earlier *Discendenze Patrizie* of Marco Barbaro. Twenty-two years before the publication of the *Narrative*, Barbaro told of the Zen voyages to the islands under the Arctic Pole and of the going of Nicolò Zen soon after his return to Orkney.

The cold and the hardships of the Greenland expedition had proved too much for the elder Zen captain. He and his younger brother had spent only four years together in Orkney and the Shetlands, and now Antonio would spend another ten years alone there when he was not making his own voyages of discovery. For Prince Henry St Clair refused Antonio's pleas to go home. He had to take over his brother's assets and position as the captain of the St Clair fleet. 'Although he tried hard in various ways and begged and prayed most earnestly, he could never obtain permission to return to his own country.' As Prince Henry was 'a man of great enterprise and daring,' he now wanted to become 'master of the sea'.

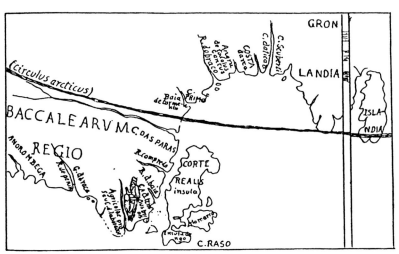

Tracing from the Bjornbo photocopy of the 1570 engraved copy of the
Vopell Map of 1545. (Courtesy of Ganong, *Crucial Maps*).
Note the King with Templar Shield.

A Venetian galley of the fourteenth century.

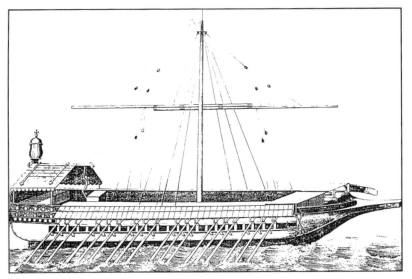

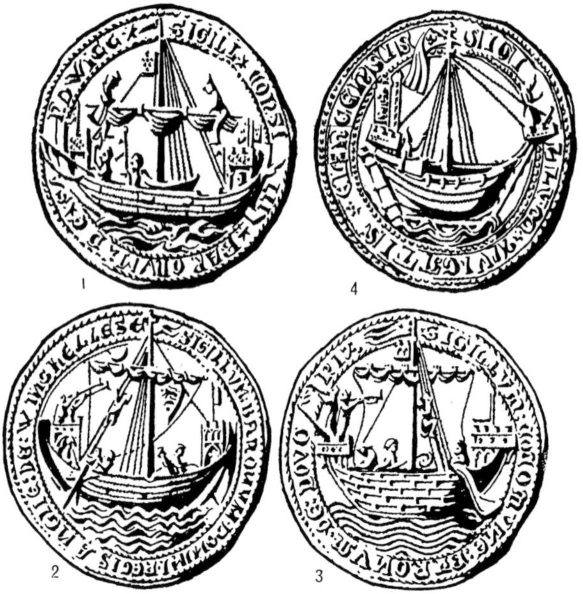

ABOVE: City seals showing ships: (1) Sandwich; (2) Winchelsea; (3) Dover; (4) Elbing. All picture North European vessels of the fourteenth century.

BELOW: Navigational techniques from an early Portuguese sailing manual.

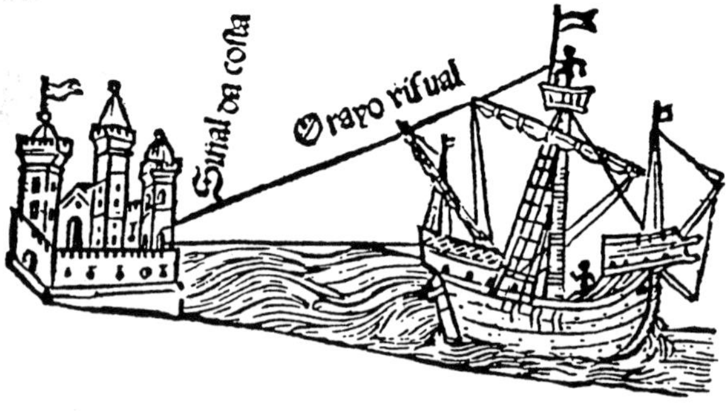

Que ha aguoa seia tambem redonda prouase em duas ma-
neyras. Ha primeyra he ponha se huũ sinall na ribey-
ra do mar: ꝛ saya dally huũa nāao podera achegar a termo em
que estando a nāo queda huũ homē posto ao pee do masto nam
veja ho dito sinal. ꝛ se sobir em a gauia vera ho sinall: ainda que

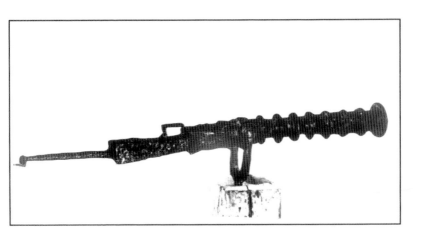

ABOVE:
Ancient cannon on display in Louisburg Museum, Nova Scotia.

CENTRE AND BELOW RIGHT:
Petriera cannon, the Naval Museum, the Arsenale, Venice. Note resemblance to cannon found in Louisburg.

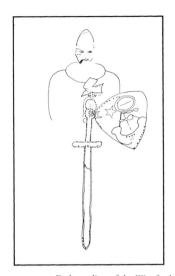

ABOVE LEFT: Early outline of the Westford Knight, made by connecting the punch marks in the rock with white chalk.

ABOVE RIGHT: Westford Knight, in situ, Westford, Massachusetts.

BELOW: Newport Tower, Newport, Rhode Island. (Photographs on this page, courtesy of Malcolm Pearson, 1946).

A petroglyph of a European ship on the coast of Maine, of a type common circa 1350–1450.

The mallet, compasses and pick, and the Grail and the Cross, from Templar graves, in Currie, near Edinburgh in Scotland.

ABOVE LEFT:
Masonic grave, Currie.
ABOVE RIGHT:
The Grail and two
swords, Templar
grave, Currie.

LEFT: Masonic grave.

BELOW LEFT:
Measuring the Scottish
Ell at Dunkeld.
BELOW RIGHT: Masonic
grave, Corstorphine.

Tomb of Sir Adam
Forrester, Corstorphine.

The aloe cactus, carved
in Rosslyn Chapel before
Christopher Columbus
reached America.

BELOW: Indian (American)
corn, carved in Rosslyn Chapel.

BELOW: The starry firmament
on the roof of Rosslyn Chapel.

ABOVE LEFT: Jesus Christ blesses the Grail, carved on the roof of Rosslyn Chapel.

CENTRE LEFT: Rosslyn communion cup, or 'Grail.'

BELOW: Knights Templars Crosses and Cypher alphabets.

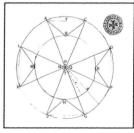

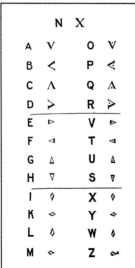

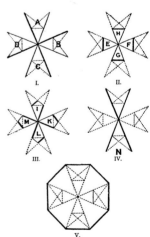

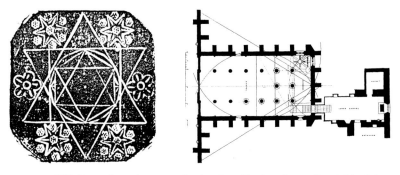

ABOVE LEFT: This figure of sacred geometry is taken from Giordano Bruno, *De triplici minimo et mensura* (Frankfurt, 1591). ABOVE RIGHT: Geometry of ground plan of Rosslyn Chapel.

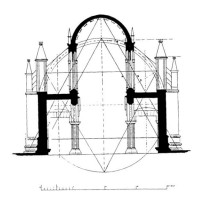

Cross-section of Rosslyn Chapel.

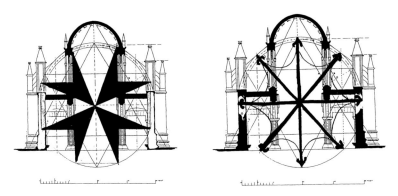

Templar geometry of Rosslyn Chapel.

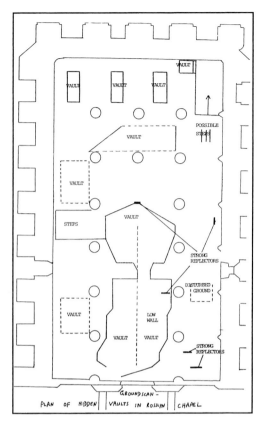

The plan of the hidden vaults in Rosslyn Chapel, from an ultrasound groundscan.

Within the plan image:
VAULT
VAULT VAULT VAULT
POSSIBLE STEPS
VAULT
VAULT
STEPS VAULT
STRONG REFLECTORS
DISTURBED GROUND
VAULT LOW WALL
VAULT VAULT
STRONG REFLECTORS
GROUNDSCAN -
PLAN OF HIDDEN VAULTS IN ROSSLYN CHAPEL

BELOW LEFT: Replica of the lost Holy Rood of Scotland in Rosslyn Chapel.

BELOW: The signal boss with Engrailed Cross pointing from the roof of Rosslyn Chapel to where the shrine, the sacred treasure, and the St Clair knights are buried in the vaults.

Gilded ceremonial armour like that in which the
St Clair Knights were buried in Rosslyn Chapel.

Scottish Knights Templar skull and
sword from their archive in Edinburgh.

Groundscan work,
Rosslyn Chapel.

Digging for the buried knights and Templar treasure.

Serpents at the base of the Apprentice pillar.

Schaw petition of 1600 of Scottish
Masons to Sir William St Clair of Rosslyn.

ABOVE LEFT: Jesus Christ blesses the Grail, carved on the roof of Rosslyn Chapel.

CENTRE LEFT: Rosslyn communion cup, or 'Grail.'

BELOW: Knights Templars Crosses and Cypher alphabets.

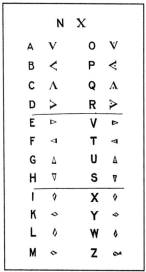

	N	X		
A	V	O	V	
B	<	P	<	
C	Λ	Q	Λ	
D	>	R	>	
E	▷	V	▷	
F	◁	T	◁	
G	△	U	△	
H	▽	S	▽	
I	◊	X	◊	
K	◇	Y	◇	
L	◊	W	◊	
M	◇	Z	◇	

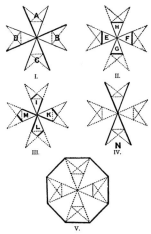

Tomb of Sir Adam
Forrester, Corstorphine.

The aloe cactus, carved
in Rosslyn Chapel before
Christopher Columbus
reached America.

BELOW: Indian (American)
corn, carved in Rosslyn Chapel.

BELOW: The starry firmament
on the roof of Rosslyn Chapel.

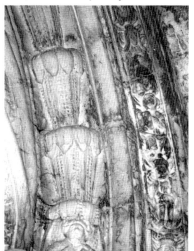

New evidence had reached Orkney of civilizations beyond the western ocean. A local fisherman had returned home with a tale that was not as tall as most fishermen's tales. Antonio Zen wrote home to his brother Carlo about it:

Twenty-six years ago four fishing boats put out to sea and encountered a heavy storm. They were driven over the sea utterly helpless for many days. When the tempest died at last, they discovered an island called Estotilanda lying to the west over one thousand miles from Frislanda. One of the boats was wrecked, and the six men in it were taken by the inhabitants and brought to a fair and populous city, where the king of the place sent for many interpreters. None could be found that understood the language of the fishermen, except one that spoke Latin, who had also been cast by chance on the same island. Speaking for the king he asked them who they were and where they came from; and when he relayed their answer, the king wanted them to remain in the country. As they could not do otherwise, they obeyed his command and stayed five years on the island and learned the language. One of them in particular visited different parts of the island and reported that it was a very rich country, abundant in all good things. It is a little smaller than Islanda, but more fertile. In the middle of it is a very high mountain, from which rise four rivers which water the whole country.

The inhabitants are very intelligent people and possess all the arts as we do. It is believed that in time past they have had dealings with our people, for he said that he saw in the king's library Latin books, which they do not now understand. They have their own language and letters. They have all kinds of metals, but especially they are rich in gold. Their foreign connections are with Engroneland, to which they export furs, sulphur and pitch. He says that towards the south there is a great and populous country, very rich in gold. They sow corn and make beer, which is a kind of drink that northern people take as we do wine. They have woods of immense extent. They make their buildings with walls, and there are many towns and villages. They make small boats and sail them, but they have not the lodestone, and they do not know the north by compass bearing.

For this reason these fishermen were highly valued, and the king sent them with twelve boats to the south to a country which they call Drogio. On their voyage they met contrary winds and were in fear for their lives. Although they escaped one cruel death, they fell into another even crueller. For they were taken and most of them eaten by savages, who were cannibals and considered human flesh as very savoury meat.

Yet as our fisherman and his remaining companions could show them how to catch fish with nets, their lives were saved. Every day he would go fishing in the sea and in the fresh water and catch a great amount of fish, which he gave to the chiefs. So he grew into favour and he was very much liked and held in great consideration by everybody.

As this man's fame spread through the surrounding tribes, a neighbouring chief became very anxious to have him and see how he practised his wonderful art of catching fish. Therefore he made war on the chief who had the fisherman, and as he was more powerful and a better warrior, he overcame him in the end. So the fisherman was sent over to him with the rest of his company. During the thirteen years he lived in those parts, he says that he was sent to more than twenty-five chiefs. They were continually fighting among themselves, this chief with that and only with the purpose of having the fisherman to live with them. Forced to wander up and down the country without any fixed home, he became acquainted with almost all that land.

He says that it is a very great country and, as it were, *a new world*. The people are very simple and uncultivated, for they all go naked and suffer cruelly from the cold. They do not have the sense to clothe themselves with the skins of the animals which they take in hunting. They have no kind of metal. They live by the chase and carry lances of wood, sharpened at the point. They have bows, the strings of which are made of beasts' skins. They are very fierce and have deadly fights among themselves and eat one another's flesh. They have chieftains and certain laws, but these differ from tribe to tribe. The farther you go south-west, however, the more refinement you meet, because the climate is more temperate. There they have cities and temples dedicated to their idols, in which they sacrifice men and afterwards eat them. In those parts they have some knowledge and use of gold and silver.

After having lived so many years in these parts, this fisherman made up his mind, if possible, to return home to his own country. His companions were in despair of ever going home again, but they bade him Godspeed and stayed where they were. He said farewell and made his escape through the woods in the direction of Drogio, where he was welcome and acceptable to its chief, who knew him and was a great enemy of the neighbouring chieftain. Again passing through the hands of the same chiefs, after a long time and with much hardship, he at last reached Drogio, where he spent three years. Here by good luck he heard from the natives that some boats had arrived off the coast. Full of hope at being able to make his escape, he went down to the seaside and was delighted to find that they had come from Estotilanda. He asked them to take him with them, which they did very willingly. And as he knew the language of the country, which none of them could speak, they employed him as their interpreter.

Afterwards he traded in their company so well that he became very rich and fitted out a vessel of his own and returned to Frislanda. Then he gave an account of the rich countries he had seen to this nobleman [St Clair]. His sailors had had much experience in hearing strange tales and fully believed what they heard. This nobleman is now determined to send me out with a fleet towards those parts. There are so many that want to join in the expedition on account of the novelty and strangeness of the thing, that I think we shall be very well equipped, without any public expense at all.

This fisherman's tale was not the first report of civilizations across the western oceans. Based on the rare accounts of sailors who had been blown off-course and had managed to return to Europe, early Venetian charts marked an island across the Atlantic, which was called Antilla, while the Portuguese called it Brasil. The fishermen who had returned to Frislanda (the Faroes) reported a people in Estotilanda (Nova Scotia) capable of laying out a city, understanding Latin and carrying on a trade with Engroneland (Greenland). The only plausible explanation for this settlement would be the Norse settlement in Markland, which has been variously located in Newfoundland, Labrador and Nova Scotia. The Icelandic Annals declared that a ship arrived from Markland in 1347 with shipbuilding supplies no longer available in defor-ested Iceland (Islanda) – particularly the pitch made from burning the resin in the stumps of pine trees. The strange letters of the people of Estotilanda could well be the Ogam script or the Runic alphabet, while Nova Scotia is rich in gold-bearing rivers. The compass might well have not reached Markland by the end of the fourteenth century, while the usual isolation of the colony would explain the loss of the ability to read Latin texts in the King's library.

The description of the voyage to Drogio suggests a passage past Florida and through the Caribbean islands, where the Caribs were cannibals, and a landing on the coasts of Mexico, where the Mayans and other tribes were still resisting the expansion of the Aztec empire. Certainly, the Aztecs had cities and temples dedicated to their idols, in which they sacrificed men. They also worked in gold and silver. The return of the fisherman on Norse trading ships, which took him from the shores of Drogio, suggests more contacts between the lost colony of Markland and Florida and the Caribbean than have been recorded, and it helps to explain why a specimen of an aloe cactus was carved in Rosslyn Chapel in pre-Columbian times.

The fisherman saved his life by teaching the American Indians to net fish rather than spear them. In Nantucket, there is still an Indian legend of the arrival of ships, a battle, and four prisoners taken, one of whom taught the Indians how to fish with nets and use fishmeal as fertilizer. In the Shetlands, large nets and marine fertilizers were widely used, and vegetable fibres for making ropes were available in New England and the Caribbean. The fisherman's story corresponds with a voyage to a Norse colony in eastern Canada and down south to Mexico. Certainly, the phrase that described his discovery of 'as it were, *a new world*' was the first time that term was printed to characterize the Americas and their peoples. He brought back to Orkney and the Shetlands an account of a New World, where Prince Henry St Clair insisted he would go with his new fleet and his Venetian captain.

Three days before the departure of the expedition to Estotilanda in May 1398, the fisherman and guide died. Prince Henry St Clair refused to give up the enterprise and pressed into his service some of the sailors who had come with the fisherman. Steering to the north-west past the Shetlands, which were now subject to Prince Henry, the fleet put in at Lille Dimon in the Faroes to rest and put on board water and supplies. At this point, the *Zeno Narrative* confused this expedition with a previous reconnaissance of St Kilda and Kerry in Ireland, miscalled Icaria. This is evident because the *Narrative* told of the expedition arriving at hostile Icaria in July, while it was also to reach Estotilanda in June. In point of fact, the fleet sailed directly from the Faroes and was scattered by a storm during the first eight days of the passage. The ships regrouped and sailed on for ten days west and south-west in rough seas with a following wind. This brought them to the New World, which they were seeking. 'Some of the crew then pulled ashore and soon returned with the joyful news that they had found an excellent country and a still better harbour. So we brought our barks and our boats in to land, and we entered an excellent harbour, and we saw in the distance a great mountain that poured out smoke.'

The Estotilanda where the Scottish expedition had landed was previously identified as Nova Scotia. The *Zeno Narrative* told of certain features: the smoking mountain, which came from a great fire in the bottom of the hill; a spring that exuded a matter like pitch that ran into the sea; and many small and timid natives who lived in caves. A geologist found oil seepages at the coastal Stellarton mines in Nova Scotia at a place now called Asphalt, where the Coal Brook carried the greasy residues down to the sea at Pictou Harbour. There were regular fires in underground coal seams in the Stellarton region in the nineteenth century, which produced smoke from the bottom of the hills. The local Micmac tribes were small and not as warlike as the neighbouring Algonquins, and they had legends of the coming of a god called Glooscap in a wonderful granite canoe like a forest. Glooscap had taught them to fish with nets like the fisherman in the tale in the *Zeno Narrative*, and sinkers and floats for nets dating from about 1400 were found on the sites of Micmac coastal camps. Prince Henry's probable harbours were established at Pictou, Guysborough and Advocate harbours, the latter near Cape d'Or.

There was one problem about these theories on Prince Henry's landing places. There was no hard evidence. Later, some rubble-stone foundations at The Cross in Nova Scotia near gold-bearing rivers and on the controversial Oak Island, where pirate treasure was said to be buried in a Money Pit, prompted speculation that these were the sites of Prince Henry's colonies or fortresses in Estotilanda. But rubble cannot be dated. On Oak Island, a log wharf was discovered marked with Latin numerals, which suggested its use as a harbour by Norse or other traders from Markland. And the fact that there were mature oak groves on the island when the platforms in the Money Pit were made and when the French explorer Champlain reached Nova Scotia in the early seventeenth century led to the thought that these had been planted at least 200 years before. Acorns do not float, and

Champlain remarked that the island groves appeared to have been created for the pleasure of man.

Yet all was still presumption and speculation. Then I was shown the photograph of a 'pre-Columbian cannon', said to be in the fortress of Louisburg on Cape Breton Island. It was a primitive weapon with eight rings welded round its narrow barrel to keep it from bursting and a detachable breech with a handle for its loading with gunpowder and a spike at its base. I could hardly believe my eyes. While wandering round the Naval Historical Museum at the mouth of the Arsenale dockyard in Venice, I had noticed in glass cases the remnants of four similar cannons with seven or more barrel rings and breeches and base spikes and iron mountings onto wooden gun-cases. These had recently been dredged from the Arsenale itself. On my next visit to Venice, I spoke to the head of the Naval Museum, Admiral Gottardo, and he confirmed that these were the first type of ship's cannon, that they were certainly used by Carlo Zen at the Battle of Chioggia, and that they were obsolete by the end of the fourteenth century. By that time, cannon could be cast in one piece in bronze or iron, and rings were no longer necessary to keep the welded rods of the barrels from breaking. Admiral Gottardo also showed me pre-Columbian and Venetian Atlantic maps, which marked an island called Antilla on the site of the Americas.

I studied then a modern map of Nova Scotia prior to another visit there. I saw that Louisburg Harbour, where the cannon had been found, was on the south of Cape Breton Island. Above it, coal mines ran into the sea for thirty miles some of the way up to the mountainous north and a headland called Cape Smokey. Furthermore, four Micmac Indian reservations still existed round the central sea loch called Le Bras d'Or. It was almost too apposite. A Venetian cannon of the right period, coastal coal mines, a smoky mountain and a large Indian presence. Above all, Cape Breton was an *island*, as the *Zeno Narrative* declared it was, while Nova Scotia itself was joined to the mainland of Canada.

My quest after the truth of the landing of Prince Henry St Clair in the New World led me almost certainly to where he had stood with his Venetian captain and cannon. The identical weapon to those found at the Arsenale was in the cellars of the Louisburg fortress, relegated there because the French Canadians did not relish the idea of a predecessor. It was, indeed, a breech-loading *petriera*, which cast small stone cannon-balls through its welded and ringed barrel. I was then introduced to a local marine explorer, Alex Storm, who had himself discovered two wrecked treasure ships off Louisburg. He told me that the Louisburg *petriera* had been found as long ago as 1849, far too early for any forgery of such a weapon, or even knowledge of how to forge it. He then took me to the place where the cannon had been discovered in sand off a beach. He stood on a small grassy mound at a place where a freshwater spring forked in a little moat before running into the sea a mile inside the bay across from the fortress of Louisburg on its promontory. He said that below him was the broken base of a small round stone tower or fortification built centuries ago and never excavated. It was the size and shape of the many round forts and church towers I had seen in the Orkneys and the Shetlands.

A later dig would assert that it was a gunsite. Alex Storm showed me further evidence that another *petriera* had been discovered at the portage of nearby St Peter's, although it had unfortunately been broken up. A Victorian who saw it described it as 'an archaic cannon formed of bars of iron fastened with iron bands or hoops'. Curiously enough, the French had chosen Louisburg and St Peter's as the sites of their first two settlements, because these two harbours were the best on the south coast of Cape Breton Island. Prince Henry's logic would have led him to the same conclusion. There was also a Micmac tradition that grassy mounds at St Peter's were the remnants of the houses or sod huts of white men, who had colonized the area before the later coming of the French settlers.

According to the *Zeno Narrative*, the mountain that poured out smoke was visible from near the harbour called Trin. Cape Smokey is visible from the mountain crests that run north-west from St

Peter's to Louisburg. The area is still abundant in fish and sea-fowl and birds' eggs, which the Scottish sailors ate until they were stuffed full. And the eight days' march of the hundred soldiers and the Venetians sent by Prince Henry to explore the island would have taken them to Cape Smokey and back again. On the way myself by the coastline to the Cape, I discovered at Point Aconi what the Scottish soldiers had also discovered, 'a certain matter like pitch which ran into the sea'. Oily residues from the open coal seams in the cliffs and from the underwater workings of the Princess Mine still pollute the beaches.

They are, indeed, like the black and oily waters of St Katherine's healing well near the St Clair castle of Rosslyn. These were meant to cure all skin diseases. St Katherine herself was the patron saint of the St Clairs as well as of the Scottish Guild of Wheelwrights – she had been broken on a wheel in Alexandria, where Prince Henry had gone on his crusade. The bitumen in the black water of the healing well was meant to have saved him from the Black Death as a child, although it fouled my fingernails for days when I plunged my hand into its black grease. Yet for Prince Henry, the finding of bitumen by his soldiers was a good omen that brought something of the Old World to the New.

His troops reported that the smoke from the mountain came from a great fire at the bottom of the slope. Actually, the Cape is now called Smokey because clouds almost always wreathe its crests. But there are on Cape Breton Island and in Nova Scotia natural gas and coal seams burning underground, while the Micmac Indians used slash-and-burn techniques to clear 'meadows' to attract wild game to graze there as an easier prey for their arrows. These 'meadows' among the woods and on the shorelines were to be most attractive to future European settlers. And whether the soldiers saw an underground fire or a burning 'meadow' beneath Cape Smokey, they did meet 'great multitudes of people, half-wild and living in caves. These were very small of stature and very timid . . .' There are sacred Indian caves in the sea-cliffs on the coastal route to the north of Cape Breton Island, particularly near Bras d'Or, the modern name for the huge land-locked sea lake round which most of the Micmacs still live.

When the hundred soldiers marched back to Prince Henry at Louisburg Harbour, they discovered that he wanted to found a city in this New World. Antonio Zen wrote back to his brother, the great Admiral Carlo in Venice, about Prince Henry's decision:

> But his people had passed through a voyage so full of hardship and began to murmur, saying that they wished to return to their own homes. The winter was not far off, and if they allowed it to set in, they would not be able to get away before the following summer. He therefore kept only the row boats and those people who were willing to stay with him, and he sent all the rest away in the ships. He appointed me against my will to be their captain. I had no choice, and so I departed and sailed twenty days to the east without sighting any land. Then I turned my course towards the south-east and reached land in five days . . .

The voyage from the Faroes to Estotilanda with storms and following winds had been sailed at an average of four knots, while the return voyage against the prevailing winds averaged three knots. Antonio Zen could report that his Scottish Prince was still alive, but he did not know what Prince Henry was doing in the New World. The end of the *Zeno Narrative* included the tantalizing opening of the last recorded letter sent home by Antonio Zen:

> The things you want to know from me about the people and their habits, the animals and the countries nearby, I have written in a separate book, which, please God, I shall bring with me. In it I have described the country, the monstrous fishes, the customs and laws of Frislanda, of Islanda, of Estlanda, of the Kingdom of Norway, of Estotilanda and Drogio. Lastly I have written the life of our brother, Nicolò the Chevalier, with the discovery he made and all about

Greenland. I have also written the life and exploits of Zichmni, a prince who deserves immortal memory as much as any man that ever lived for his great bravery and remarkable goodness. In it I have described the survey of Greenland on both sides and the city that he founded.

On the *Zeno Map*, however, two cities are marked in Estotilanda. If one was founded by Prince Henry St Clair at Louisburg Harbour by the fresh-water spring, or possibly at St Peter's, the other may well have been founded in New England. For there is compelling evidence that he and his men went onward to the West.

More American Evidence

High at the top of a hill with a commanding view over Massachusetts, the Westford Knight was first recorded in a history of that small town in 1883. The Revd Edwin Hodgman wrote about a broad ledge of gneiss, which cropped out near the house of William Kittredge. On the surface of the rock were grooves made by glaciers in some distant geological age. 'Rude outlines of the human face have been traced upon it, and the figure is said to be the work of Indians.' On their way to high school, Westford boys sometimes did a war-dance on the Indian's face to show off their daring, while the girls admired their antics in a ring around the rock. At one point one of the boys, Thomas Fisher, used a cold chisel to add a pipe of peace onto the Indian head, later called a falcon crest, to make it look more authentic.

That was that, until an amateur archaeologist and a photographer became interested in the carving on the gneiss before and after the Second World War, at a time when searching for the Nordic origins of odd structures such as the Newport Tower was becoming fashionable. What they saw on the rock was a hilted sword and rather more. Michael Pearson, who had a house near Westford, photographed the shape on the gneiss, and W.B. Goodwin published two photographs and a line drawing of it in his *The Ruins of Greater Ireland in New England*. He interpreted the shape in the middle of the glacial rock as an eleventh-century Norse sword, broken as the memorial of an exceptionally brave warrior.

Goodwin's publication came to the attention of T.C. Lethbridge, the contentious archaeologist for the town Antiquarian Society in Cambridge, England. His opinions and findings were as much discounted by academic university archaeologists as were those of Goodwin and his successor Frank Glynn by the professors at Harvard University and by the Massachusetts Archaeological Society. Goodwin died, but Glynn was in correspondence with Lethbridge, who identified the sword hilt on the stone as the large, hand-and-a-half wheel-pommel sword of the thirteenth and fourteenth centuries. Unfortunately, Goodwin had not revealed where the rock carving was located, and Glynn spent years in tracking it down; when he reached it, he had to strip turf and moss from the gneiss, which was badly weathered. He discovered that the images on the stone were made through a series of punch-holes and hammer blows, which could have been struck in the rock by a medieval armourer. With excitement, Glynn discovered that the punch-holes ran nearly to the top of the rock and to the side, suggesting that the funeral effigy of a helmeted knight-of-arms had been punched into the gneiss along with the shapes of his shield and his sword to act as his memorial tomb.

The letters from Lethbridge to Glynn reveal a fascinating case of influence by correspondence. What Lethbridge suggested might be there, Glynn found was there, by linking up the punch-holes with chalk. In their letters, Lethbridge and Glynn identified themselves as early Celtic Saints and heroes, signing themselves as Brendan and Finbar. 'Isn't there some more on this stone than a sword?' Brendan asked Finbar in 1954. 'Can't it be a medieval knight holding a sword? . . . There are many effigies in this position in the Hebrides and Ireland . . . You may have got a funerary monument to one of Sinclair's men.' Lethbridge was referring to the *Zeno Narrative*. He even drew a tracing of what Glynn should find in the rock, a knight in a pointed bassinet helmet, in quilted armour with a large sword or claymore. And that is what Glynn found by his joining together of the punch-holes in the gneiss. But he required more guidance from Lethbridge, which he duly received. Lethbridge wanted him to look for a rather misshapen figure, perhaps six feet long or more, in a quilted skirt. He also suggested that there might be a relatively permanent settlement close at hand, 'a wintering party or something like that'.

By his method of joining the punch-holes with chalk lines or dusting with talcum powder, Glynn discovered on the rock an effigy remarkably similar to the sketch of what the effigy should look like in the letter sent to him by Lethbridge, who had merely described it as 'the wildest guess'. It was the first of a dozen different outlines of the possible shape of the knight, which Glynn was to conjure out of the stone in the following decade. 'Once again,' he wrote back to Lethbridge, 'that intuition of yours was hot. The whole figure is there, about six feet long. Now, I think I've found his shield . . .'

That small shield was set askew from the body of the knight and bore a coat of arms. The final shape of this also was suggested by Lethbridge, who wrote that he could not 'picture the arms in a chap's shield being arranged quite like that', and drew a general coat of arms belonging to the younger son of a Scots lord. Again, Glynn found particular armorial devices in the right quarterings of the shield, and Lethbridge had them identified by a leading Scots genealogist called the Unicorn Herald, Sir Ian Moncreiffe of that Ilk. The heraldic galley at the bottom of the tracing of the shield of the Westford Knight, the star and crescent at the top on the right, and the large and round brooch at the top on the left were identified as the arms of a Gunn Knight from Caithness, who might well have been taken on his voyage to the west by Henry St Clair. This certification was hailed by members of the clan Gunn in Massachusetts, and one of them even painted the supposed Gunn shield and coat of arms on the rock to prove the case.

By this time, Lethbridge himself was in difficulties at home.

Using a larger method of punch-holes by probing down to a chalk layer on the Gogmagog Hills of Cambridgeshire, he claimed to have exposed three figures of ancient gods like the known Giant of Cerne Abbas and the Long Man of Wilmington. He sent to Glynn the drawing of one of them, the wild and flowing shape of Epona, the Celtic goddess of horses. 'You can see nothing on the surface,' he wrote to Glynn, 'except the old artichoke sticks I have put in as markers. *When you come to plot it on paper however, it appears like magic painting.*' Indeed it did, as did the outlines of the Westford Knight. But Lethbridge knew his fate at the hands of the academics, writing, 'I shall be in trouble over this!' And he was, losing the last shreds of his archaeological reputation at the hands of the professionals. Not that he cared too much, writing to Glynn that he had been engaged in tribal war. 'So watch your pundits over there,' he advised. 'Anthropologists and archaeologists are doubtful characters.'

Now Glynn came up with the discovery of the wintering place of the St Clair expedition that Lethbridge had suggested should be found. The later chronicler of the St Clair expedition to the New World, Frederick J. Pohl, who was trying to find the sites of the landing of the early Scotsmen in Nova Scotia, had joined forces with Glynn. They came across a carved stone, which a local farmer had unearthed at the fork of tracks to the sea near Westford. The stone showed the shape of a ship with twin sails on a single mast, eight portholes or rowlocks, an arrow with four feathers on each side of the shaft and the number 184. On advice from Lethbridge that the numerals signified paces, Glynn discovered within a radius of 184 paces 3 roughstone enclosures, which might have been the dry dock for small Norse ships or Lethbridge's 'snug little corner where Sinclair's bothy, hut, tent or whatever, was set up'. At a distance, Lethbridge identified the enclosures as similar to the stone buildings in Greenland called *Storhouses* and the ship on the rock as a Norse *knorr* or merchantman. He claimed that the Scots knew of Arabic numerals by the fourteenth century and would not have written distances in Latin numerals, although the Venetian account

of the St Clair expedition to the New World asserted that its leader
Henry St Clair spoke in Latin and the map was dated in Latin
numerals.

The town of Westford itself split over the authenticity of the
Westford Knight and the carved ship stone, which was transferred
to the small library there. Two camps appeared, one stating that
four Fisher boys had chiselled the carving of an Indian tomahawk
and peace-pipe in the late nineteenth century, and all the other
marks were the result of natural weathering. As for the ship stone
with the arrow and the number 184, it was carved early in the
nineteenth century to inform Indians that a fur-trading ship had
arrived in Boston Harbour. But the other camp insisted on the
truth of both carvings as proof that the St Clair expedition had
reached Westford in 1399, and had left a knight's memorial in
punch-holes there. They cited the evidence of two geologists,
Austin Hildreth and H.J. O'Mara, who compared the deteriora-
tion of the punch-marks with those of early gneiss gravestones and
concluded that the sword and profile on the rock were probably
five to eight hundred years old.

In the middle of this war of opinion, I arrived at Westford, trying
to prove the truth of the *Zeno Narrative* of the early colonizing
expedition of Henry St Clair to the New World nearly a century
before the voyage of Columbus. With me was Marianna Lines,
whose extraordinary method of rubbing stones with vegetable and
floral juices as well as beeswax has revealed wonders and details from
eroded surfaces. She had already brought out the tombstone of
William de St Clair in the chapel of Rosslyn. She had shown on it
the burial of a Grand Master of the Templars, the Holy Grail, the
Rosy Cross and a broadsword similar to that on the gneiss of the
Westford Knight. She set to work on a cold day in Massachusetts,
aided by James Whittall of the Early Sites Research Society, who
had taken over the mantle of Frank Glynn as the leading local
archaeologist.

Using beetroot and cabbage leaves as well as chrysanthemums
and hibiscus flowers, Lines brought out a credible shape for the

effigy of the knight. The shield with the Gunn arms of previous reconstructions had always looked askew and toylike, a primitive effort by an armourer, who did not know of the conventions of medieval military burial. But the cloth impression showed a large shield of arms set squarely below the left shoulder of the figure, with two quarterings at the top, and a ship at the base of the shield similar to the St Clair ship on the coat of arms of Prince Henry's daughter, Jean St Clair, whose effigy lies at Corstorphine Church near Edinburgh. This larger shield was balanced by an insignia on the right side of the figure that resembled a rose.

Although acid rain and erosion had severely damaged the markings since the earlier investigations of the Westford Knight, the rubbing showed a helmeted knight wearing the habit of the Military Orders with his shield and his sword engraved on the rock in the formal style of the late thirteenth or early fourteenth century. The outline of the sword has remained strong. It points due north and suggests a ritual burial. It is shown as broken twice below the hilt. The custom of the time was to break the sword of a knight of great courage and distinction, and to bury it with his body. The effigy of the Westford Knight is some seven feet tall and depicts a powerful man, although it is not as large as the huge effigy of Sir James Douglas, who died with the Heart of Bruce and Sir William de St Clair in Spain. The figure appears to have been laid down in his armour and habit and outlined by punch-holes on the stone. After his body was removed for burial, his broken sword and shield were also outlined, before their removal for burial with the knight. Then the final details were punched into the gneiss.

Yet the Westford Knight is evidence only of an *inland* expedition into New England by a crusading group in the late fourteenth century. The question is where they might have landed by sea. And an answer exists in the curious stone tower, which is still preserved at Newport in Rhode Island. Unless that tower of two storeys is understood as part of the second city that Prince Henry St Clair began to build in the New World, it is hard to explain. It is certainly based on the stone architecture of northern Europe in the Middle

Ages. It is constructed as the Templar round churches were on the model of the Church of the Holy Sepulchre and the Dome of the Rock in Jerusalem. When there was an eight-pointed cross built in regular pillars within the diameter of a tower, this was also a Christian model of the Temple of Solomon. It was the octagon within the circle, eight arches within a round tower. Round churches are rare. The only one in Scotland was built in the twelfth century on the model of the Church of the Holy Sepulchre and is in Orphir in Orkney, where Henry St Clair was the Earl. The arch of its one surviving window is constructed in the same fashion as those of the Newport Tower.

Moreover, the unit of measurement of the Newport Tower is not the English foot or yard, nor a Portuguese or Dutch standard. It is the Scottish ell, a cloth measure used in England until Shakespeare's time and one half of the Norse fathom and the equivalent of the Hanseatic yard – just over 37 inches. The diameter of each column in the Newport Tower is exactly 1 Scottish ell, the diameter of the circle surrounded by the columns is exactly 6 Scottish ells. I have personally measured the Newport Tower and checked the measurements with the standard of the Scottish ell kept on a gravestone at Dornoch Abbey and at Dunkeld Market near the cathedral where a St Clair was the Fighting Bishop at the time of Bannockburn, and where another St Clair presided at the time of Prince Henry's voyage to North America.

The Newport Tower resembles not only Templar architecture, but Scottish architecture of the period. One feature precludes its use as the windmill that some suppose it to be. On the first floor, a fireplace was made to a fourteenth-century design, which would burn down any flour mill. The design is reproduced in the St Clair church at Corstorphine, where Prince Henry St Clair's daughter Jean is buried in effigy. Also there is a similar beacon tower, where the firelight was reflected on the second storey to guide the way for travellers by land or sea.

For that is what the Newport Tower was. A Templar Church, a lighthouse onto Narragansett Bay and a watchtower. There is evidence to date it before the British colonization of Rhode Island. In his map of the first recorded European discovery of these coasts, Verrazano with his Italian crew marked in this area a 'Norman Villa'. A member of his expedition also noticed that the natives were unlike others in Connecticut and Massachusetts. 'This is the most beautiful people and the most civilized in customs that we have found on this navigation. They excel us in size; they are of bronze colour, some inclining more to whiteness.' These suggestions of a lost European colony, which had intermarried with the local tribes, were substantiated by an old map made by William Wood after 1629, which sited New Plymouth correctly in Massachusetts, but listed an Old Plymouth in Narragansett Bay. Furthermore, a text from the Public Records Office in London mentioned an existing 'round stone towre' in 1632, seven years before Newport in Rhode Island was founded. It was one of the 'Commodities' that should attract settlers to Sir Edmund Plowden's proposed colony. It would house 30 soldiers or gentlemen, who could then guard the settlers in their 'trucke and trafficke by tome with the Savages'.

The Newport Tower was later adapted as an extremely inefficient flour mill by Governor Benedict Arnold. But it had been constructed centuries before its misuse, and it had been built as a church and a beacon and a fortification. It was originally covered with plaster; the remains lie now in its foundations. Old windmills are solid in their structure in Orkney. The Newport Tower is an engineering folly as a windmill. Its purpose was sacred. It corresponds almost exactly with Templar churches in Paris and Laon, the Church of the Holy Sepulchre in Cambridge in England and at Neuvy in France, and the round church of the twelfth century at Orphir in Orkney, from where Prince Henry St Clair sailed to found his lost colony in the New World. In 1950, the director of the National Museum in Denmark remarked on the Newport Tower, 'There remain as typically Romanesque architectural details the pillars, the arches and the double splay. These medievalisms are so conspicuous that, if the tower were in Europe, dating it to the Middle Ages would probably meet with no protest.'

St Magnus Church on Egilsay near Orkney was built in the twelfth century to commemorate the murder there of the Saint, then Earl of Orkney, by his rival Earl Haakon. It has a round tower and arches and splays similar to the Newport Tower. A recent paper on it concludes that its design belongs to a family of buildings originating in North Germany and linked by the North Sea. The martyrdom of St Magnus has curious affinities to that of the Masonic martyr Hiram in the Temple of Solomon. He is lured onto the island of Egilsay, where he finds that Earl Haakon has eight ships and many armed men. To save his life, Magnus is offered three choices – to go on a pilgrimage to the Holy Land, to go into exile in Scotland or to let himself be mutilated and blinded. He finally insists on his death, but only the cook of Earl Haakon will strike the fatal blow with an axe to the head.

The relics of St Magnus lay in three places: at Egilsay; at the monastery of Eynhallow or Holy Isle, which still has arches of thin packed stones identical to those at Newport; and at St Magnus Cathedral at Kirkwall, hard by the Bishop's Palace, which also was constructed with the 'typically Romanesque architectural details' of the Newport Tower. In 1919, the finding in a pillar in the cathedral choir of some bones and the skull of a man killed by an axe-blow to the forehead allowed the belief that St Magnus had been discovered again. And the carving in the St Clair chapel at Rosslyn of a man with a mark on his brow – a carving ordered by Prince Henry's grandson – suggests a memorial to St Magnus as well as to the martyr Hiram and to the Apprentice said to be murdered by his master for carving the admirable pillar there.

The cloth impression of the Westford Knight is definitely that of a knight of the Military Orders wearing his long surcoat. The pommelled hilt of the broken sword has been identified by armorial experts as Scottish from the period of the late fourteenth century. It is difficult to conceive that this figure on the rock is the result of forgery in the Victorian age or a freak of the erosion, which has largely destroyed the view of the effigy to the naked eye. Equally, the Newport Tower, with its eight arches and round shape and high fireplace, was never built as a windmill, but as a beacon for ships and a fortified church. Its models across the Europe of the Templars and particularly on Orkney and Egilsay, its Romanesque details and packed stone arches all point to the architecture of the North Sea. The colonizing expedition of Prince Henry St Clair described in the *Zeno Narrative* is the best explanation for the punch-holes of the Westford Knight and the eight arches of the round Newport Tower. Further supporting evidence also comes from the recent discovery on a whaleback ledge jutting into Machias Bay at Clark's Point, Maine, of the petroglyph of a cross incised beside one of a European ship of the late fourteenth century with a single sail and stern rudder. In stone, the story of the expedition is preserved.

The Lost Colony

After Prince Henry's expedition to what would be called New England, where he may have left a second fort and colony at Newport, he returned across the Bay of Fundy to his first colony at Louisburg. He had been two years away from Orkney, and he knew his authority there would be under threat of attack. The farming monks he had left on Cape Breton Island would have already gathered their first crops, while the seamen there should have completed the survey of the west coast of Greenland, for which the *Zeno Narrative* was to praise him. He would have had to construct an ocean-going fleet from the resources of Nova Scotia; but there was timber and pine tar and fibre for ropes in abundance. And he had brought shipwrights from Fife and Orkney with him, as well as masons to construct his defences.

The abiding Micmac legend of the divine Glooscap coming over the sea and departing is similar to the Mayan myth of Quetzalcoatl, the winged white god who was identified with Cortes and assisted his conquest of the Aztec empire. But if Prince Henry's coming enhanced the Indian belief in Glooscap, it could only have been by his good behaviour. He brought no conflict, he took no slaves, he taught the arts of fishing and agriculture. The Reverend Silas Rand, who first recorded the Micmac language, also wrote down the abiding legend of Glooscap in Victorian times:

> The tradition respecting Glooscap is that he came to this country from the east – far across the great sea; that he was a divine being, though in the form of a man. He was not far from any of the Indians . . . Glooscap was the friend and teacher of the Indians. All they knew of the arts he taught them. He taught them the name of the constellations and stars; he taught them how to hunt and fish, and cure what they took; how to cultivate the ground. He was always sober, grave and good. All that the Indians knew of what was wise and good he taught them. His canoe was a granite rock.

The descriptions of Glooscap's sea transport were the most convincing evidence that Prince Henry St Clair's expedition to Cape Breton Island was remembered in Micmac legend. He was said to have crossed the ocean standing with his feet on the backs of whales – a traditional Indian term for decked ships. His vessel was variously called a stone canoe and a floating island with trees on it, very manageable and able to go like magic. This suggested a ship with two masts and cross trees, able to steer with a rudder and sail to the wind. When he did finally leave, he stated that he would not return to rule over the Indians – and Prince Henry never did. As a Micmac song, also recorded in Victorian times, chanted of the going of Glooscap:

> Some say that he sailed away
> In his marvellous stone canoe,
> Afar beyond the sea,
> To the country of the East.

> Some that he went to the West.
> And it is said in days of old
> There were men who knew where he lived,
> And they made a pilgrimage,
> And got from him what they sought . . .
>
> And they say that, even now,
> If you travel ever on,
> Travel in perfect faith,
> You'll find at last our Glooscap . . .
>
> That is the great Sagamou,
> The greatest of all lords.
> 'Is Glooscap living yet?'

Prince Henry St Clair did not live a year after his return to Orkney in 1400. In August, King Henry IV of England invaded Scotland and reached Edinburgh, for Prince Henry was not at Rosslyn to hold the southern road from London against an English incursion. Marine raiders from East Anglia beat off a counterattack and captured the Scottish commander, Sir Robert Logan. They then proceeded up to Orkney to challenge the new sea-power of the St Clairs. They pillaged several of the islands and made a surprise attack on Kirkwall. In his description of the family, Father Hay wrote of Prince Henry's death: 'Resisting them with his forces, through his too great negligence and contempt of his ound friendly forces [he was] left breathless, by blows battered so fast upon him, that no man was able to resist.' An account of 1446 stated tersely that he 'deit Eirle of Orchadie and for the defence of the countrie was sclane their crowellie be his innimiis.'

Even with the death of the surveyor of Greenland and founder of Scottish colonies in the New World, relief ships might have been sent out to the settlers, who would then have escaped the future fate of Sir Walter Raleigh's 'lost' colony at Roanoke in Virginia. But Prince Henry's son, Henry, who succeeded as Earl of Orkney, was fulfilling his hereditary duty as guardian of the Crown Prince of Scotland. When King Robert III had his eldest son murdered by a pro-English faction, he decided to send the new Crown Prince James to safety in France, accompanied by the new Earl of Orkney. He trusted them, according to Father Hay, 'to the sea's mercie; but when they had sailed a little space, Prince James not being able to abide the smell of the waters, desired to be att land, where, when they were come, (for they landed att his request upon the coast of England) upon their journey to the King, they were taken and imprisoned, till afterwards . . .' Gaoled for many years, the new Earl of Orkney could do nothing for his father's colonies in America. And so the relief of the New World was lost in a prison cell.

The capture of his new master by the English in 1406 at last allowed the escape of Antonio Zen back to Venice. He did not have to plead for his return after fourteen years in the north. He sailed home, either with the spring Venetian trade ships or aboard one of the vessels he had built for the Orkney fleet. Soon after his arrival and his report to his powerful brother Carlo, then second-in-command of the Republic, Antonio Zen died. His discoveries with his brother Nicolò 'made in countries unknown before' were commemorated 150 years later by the publication of the *Zeno Narrative* and *Map*, a tribute 'to the high courage and great energy of our ancestors'.

The finding of identical early ship's cannon at the Arsenale in Venice and at Louisburg on Cape Breton Island, the new cloth impression of the Westford Knight, and fresh correspondences in measurement and building methods between the Newport Tower and Norse-Scottish medieval constructions have established the main truth of the *Zeno Narrative*. If Prince Henry St Clair had not *discovered* America any more than Columbus had, he did try to plant colonies there 96 years before the sailor from Genoa. The Vikings had preceded his attempt by some four centuries, but Prince Henry had continued their tradition of pushing outposts of trade and settlement across the western ocean to a New World. His effort failed with his sudden death. The Innuit, indeed, attacked and wiped out the last Norse colonies in Greenland, while the one in Newfoundland died of isolation. For most of the fifteenth century, the Americans were free of the influence of Europe. And Prince Henry's grandson, the third and last St Clair to be Earl of Orkney, built in stone his Arcadia and Garden of Paradise, not in a New World, but back in Rosslyn above the green glen.

12

The Templars and the Masons

As JERUSALEM is crowned by the Dome of the Rock, London is crowned by the dome of St Paul's. The son of its supreme architect, Sir Christopher Wren, had no doubt where his father had found his inspiration. He was told of the origins of the Masons and of sacred architecture:

> What we now vulgarly call *Gothick* ought properly and truly to be named the *Saracenick Architecture refined by the Christians*, which first of all began in the East, after the Fall of the *Greek* Empire, by the prodigious Success of those People that adhered to Mahomet's Doctrine, who, out of Zeal to their Religion, built Mosques, Caravanserais, and Sepulchres wherever they came.
>
> These they contrived of a round Form, because they would not imitate the Christian Figure of a Cross, nor the old *Greek* Manner, which they thought to be idolatrous, and for that Reason all Sculpture became offensive to them.
>
> Then they fell into a new Mode of their own Invention, tho' it might have been expected with better Sense, considering the *Arabians* wanted not Geometricians in that Age, nor the *Moors*, who translated many of the most useful old *Greek* Books. As they propagated their Religion with great Diligence, so they built Mosques in all their conquered

Cities in Haste . . . They thought Columns and heavy Cornices impertinent and might be omitted; and affecting the round Form for Mosques, they elevated Cupolas, in some Instances with Grace enough. The Holy War gave the Christians, who had been there, an Idea of the Saracen Works, which were afterwards by them imitated in the West; and they refined upon it every Day as they proceeded in building Churches. The *Italians* (among which were yet some *Greek* Refugees), and with them *French, German* and *Flemings*, joined into a Fraternity of Architects, procuring Papal Bulls for their Encouragement and particular Privileges; they stiled themselves Freemasons, and ranged from one Nation to another as they found Churches to be built (for very many in those Ages were everywhere in Building, through Piety or Emulation). Their Government was regular, and where they fixed near the Building in Hand, they made a Camp of Huts . . .

Sir Christopher Wren was himself a Grand Master Mason and had access to early documents of the craft. He had no doubt of the importance of the Knights of the Order of the Temple of Solomon and other Crusaders in bringing back Muslim ideas on architecture from the Near East, which then became widespread throughout Europe. The *Old Charges* of the Masonic movement, which date back to the early fifteenth century, also stressed the influence of the Levant, particularly the medieval tradition of the building of the Temple of Solomon – so often confused by pilgrims with the Muslim shrine of the Dome of the Rock. The tradition was that King David had begun the building of a Temple of the Lord God in Jerusalem. He had made himself a patron of the Masons and had showed how highly he valued their craft. He had even given them a charge and control over their rules, and he had increased their wages.

When Solomon reached the throne of Israel, he pushed forward the completion of the Temple. He invited skilled workmen to

Jerusalem from all the countries of the Near East. Among them were 80,000 stone masons. King Solomon selected 3,600 of these to be Master Masons and direct the holy work. Hiram, King of Tyre, showed his friendship by providing the imperishable cedarwood for the Temple as well as his most skilled architect, also called Hiram. An expert in the sacred geometry of Euclid, the artificer Hiram was also a master of carving and engraving copper and brass. As the Book of Chronicles stated, he was:

> The son of a woman of the daughters of Dan, and his father was a man of Tyre, skilful to work in gold, and in silver, in brass, in iron, in stone, and in timber, in purple, in blue, and in fine linen, and in crimson; also to grave any manner of graving, and to find out every device which shall be put to him . . .

Both the Books of Chronicles and Kings took whole chapters of the Bible to detail the wealth and beauty of the Temple of Solomon with its golden palm trees and brass oxen and lions and cherubim and flowers and wheels and axletrees. But Hiram's special work included the casting of a molten sea, four hundred pomegranates in two checker networks, pots and shovels and bowls and candlesticks and snuffers, and his particular legacy to the Masonic movement, the two great pillars of the Temple.

> And he set up the pillars in the porch of the temple: and he set up the right pillar, and called the name thereof Jachin: and he set up the left pillar, and called the name thereof Boaz.
>
> And upon the top of the pillars was lily work: so was the work of the pillars finished.

King Solomon himself declared that the Temple was the house of God, and that He would look on it with favour and give it His holy name:

> Then spake Solomon. The Lord said that he would dwell in the thick darkness.

I have surely built thee an house to dwell in, a settled place
for thee to abide in for ever . . .

That thine eyes may be opened towards this house night
and day, even toward the place of which thou has said, My
name shall be there . . .

King Solomon was also held to have instituted the customs and
practices of the medieval masons and other craft guilds, who had
built his Temple. 'Solomon confirmed the Charges that David his
father had given to Masons,' the early Masonic document, the
Cooke Manuscript of 1410, declared. 'And Solomon himself taught
them their manners, but little differing from the manners now
used.' He was the Grand Master of the primal Lodge at Jerusalem,
while Hiram was the Deputy Grand Master, the most accomplished
Designer and Operator on Earth.

In nearly all of the earlier Masonic catechisms, the Question and
the Answer confirmed the tradition of the founding of the first
Masonic Lodge at the west end of the Temple of Solomon, where
two pillars of brass had been erected by Hiram. He was now given
the further name of Abiff, which derived from the Hebrew word
for Father, as if Hiram were the father of all masons. He was said to
have been martyred by three jealous fellow masons, because he
would not tell them the secrets of the craft. In a catechism called
after the two pillars of the Temple of Solomon, *Jachin and Boaz*, the
examination ran:

Question: *What support our lodge?*
Answer: Three pillars.
Question: *Pray what are their names, brother?*
Answer: Wisdom, strength and beauty.
Question: *What do they represent?*
Answer: Three grand masters; *Solomon*, King of Israel; *Hiram*,
King of Tyre, and *Hiram Abiff*, who was killed by
the three fellow-crafts.
Question: *Were these grand masters concerned in the building of*
Solomon's Temple?

Answer: They were.

Question: *What was their business?*

Answer: *Solomon* found provisions and money to pay the workmen; *Hiram*, King of Tyre, provided materials for the building, and *Hiram Abiff* performed or superintended the work.

Masonic historians chose several routes for the direct transmission of rites and practices from King Solomon's Lodge at Jerusalem to the present day. The Cooke Manuscript stated that the foundation of masonry was geometry, the first of the Seven Liberal Arts. Abraham taught Euclid geometry, and he taught the Israelites practical masonry in Egypt. These skills built the Temple of Solomon. The earliest four masons, the *Quatuor Coronati*, were killed by the Emperor Diocletian. Charles Martel or Charles 'the Hammer of France' organized masonry there, while St Alban and King Athelstan founded the craft in England.

Later historians looked to Byzantine corporations as absorbing the teaching of the Jewish fraternities of masons. The Emperor Justinian himself was said to have exclaimed after the building of Sancta Sophia: 'I have surpassed thee, O Solomon!' This influence was then passed on to the Teutonic guilds of *Steinmetzen*, which were certainly formed by the middle of the thirteenth century. The connection was demonstrated by the known use of spiral columns in the architecture of the Byzantines and the Hebrews as well as in later Masonic lodges – and at Rosslyn, where the legend of the famed Apprentice Pillar referred to the Hiramic tradition in masonry.

Another provenance was through Roman building guilds learning from Jewish practices after the fall of Jerusalem and the final destruction of the third Temple there. Diocletian may have tried to destroy Christianity, whose founder was a carpenter, but he was lenient to the Collegia or guilds of Rome, many of whose members were already Christians. He did martyr four aristocratic patrons of building and also four masons with one apprentice, Claudius and

Nicostratus and Simphorianus and Castorius and Simplicius. They were to become the patron saints of Lombard and Tuscan builders and later of the medieval masons of France and Germany and England. Their emblems are found at Rome and Florence, Nuremberg and Antwerp and Toulouse – the saw, hammer, mallet, compasses and square. Their confrontation with Diocletian was commemorated in an early poem:

> . . . These holy martyres fowre,
> That yn thys craft were of gret honoure;
> They were as gode masonus as on erthe shul go,
> Gravers and ymage-makers they were also.
> For they were werkemen of the beste,
> The emperour hade to hem gret luste;
> He wylled of them a ymage to make,
> That mowt be worscheped for his sake . . .

The emblems of these Roman martyrs were also those of the Collegia and have recently been excavated in Pompeii, carved on stone. There are more of them, the cube and the plummet, the circle and the level. These symbols and the rules of the craft were bequeathed to the mysterious *Magistri Comacini*, a guild of architects who lived on a fortified island on Lake Como at the break-up of the Roman Empire. These were held to have taught the secrets of sacred geometry and construction methods to the Italian builders of Ravenna and Venice, and through them, to the art and trade guilds of the Middle Ages. Certainly, an Edict of a Lombard king of 643 gave privileges to the Comacini and their colleagues. Their meeting-places were called *loggia*, from which the word 'lodge' was said to come. Their symbols included King Solomon's Knot and the endless, interwoven cord of Eternity.

Their heirs in France were given a pedigree. Their generic name was the *Compagnonnage*, and part of them were called *Enfants de Salomon*, the Children of Solomon. Along with later English masons, they believed that King Solomon had given them a charge and incorporated them fraternally within the precincts of his

Temple. They also believed in the death of the martyr Hiram and the *Quatuor Coronati*. They were the craft guilds that constructed the greater Gothic cathedrals, sometimes under the guidance of Cistercian or Templar Master Masons, called the *Fratres Solomonis*. They first congregated in the twelfth century at the building of Chartres Cathedral. There, the stained-glass windows still commemorate the carpenters and the masons who built it, and the tools and emblems of their trades.

The early building of abbeys in England under St Alban and King Athelstan gave rise to a tradition of earlier masonic guilds than in France. The *Old Charges* considered that King Athelstan, the grandson of Alfred the Great, built castles and abbeys, 'for he loved Masons well'. He was meant to have called an assembly of Masons at York and to have issued them with a Charge. What was more likely was that, after the Norman Conquest, French masons and their practices were imported to assist in the building of cathedrals and abbeys, as happened at Melrose and six other abbeys and churches in Scotland, when John Morow was the Master Mason. In the five hundred years after the conquest of England, over a thousand abbeys, priories, hospitals and colleges were founded, all built by masons. By the fourteenth century, the word 'lodge' was used of the meeting-places of the craft. The *Halliwell Manuscript* advised a mason to keep secrecy:

The prevystye [privacy] of the chamber telle be no mon,
Ny yn the *logge* whatsever they done.

And the very word *Ffre Maceons* or *Fremason* appeared at the end of that century, referring to a worker in freestone, a term already used for two centuries in the trade.

Other inquiries into Masonic origins predated the knowledge of the craft into Babylonian or Egyptian or Greek times. In a reference to the Tower of Babel, one early Masonic catechism gave the answer: 'We differ from the Babylonians who did presume to Build to Heaven, but we pray the blessed Trinity to let us build True, High and Square, and they shall have the praise to whom it is due . . .' Some historians believed that the Temple of Solomon was built by masons who knew of the Dionysian and Eleusinian mysteries as well as divine geometry from the gods and the golden mean. To them, the Masonic mystery of the martyr Hiram was merely a reworking of the myth of the death of Orpheus, the great creator, in the Bacchic religion.

Still other diggers into the dust of the past looked to the Greek god Hermes, whom the Romans called Mercury, as the source of sacred geometry. The Christian Father Cyril of Alexandria had asserted the Christian Hermetic tradition: 'Have you not heard that our native Hermes of Egypt divided the world into tracts and divisions, that he measured the country with a string, made ditches and canals, made laws, named provinces, set up contracts and agreements, re-discovered the calendar of the rising of the stars, and handed down certain crops, numbers and calculations, geometry, astrology, astronomy, and music, and, finally, the whole system of grammar which he himself invented?' Hermes was the creator of the Seven Liberal Arts, of which the greatest was geometry.

At this point, the Greek god became confused with Euclid and Pythagoras in medieval Masonic thought, never very good on names or the periods of great men. Another tradition, recorded by the Jewish historian Josephus, that the arts of astronomy and music were carved on two pillars by Adam's son Seth, also became part of Masonic tradition – these pillars were to be recast by Hiram in the Temple of Solomon. Zoroaster, the ultimate Magus, was also held to have inscribed all the seven Liberal Arts on fourteen pillars, half of brass and half of baked brick. It was these pillars and those of the Greek god Hermes, on which all true knowledge was inscribed, that were held to be rediscovered by Hermes Trismegistus, the founder of alchemy and the hermetic doctrine, which was so much to influence the Knights of the Order of the Temple of Solomon and, through them, the Masons. Later, fourteen pillars were to be set up in Rosslyn Chapel, surrounding the two significant carved ones representing the pair from the Temple of Solomon.

The Templars saw themselves as the Warrior-Masons of Zer-ubbabel, who persuaded King Darius to allow the rebuilding of the Temple of Jerusalem. They inherited the belief from the Gnostics and St John that the Temple was the mystic centre of the world, and so they secretly resisted the power and authority of the Popes and Kings of Europe. The black-and-white devices of their Order, black octagonal cross against white habit, showed their Gnosticism and Manicheanism, the belief in the continuing struggle of the devil's world against God's Intelligence. They bequeathed to the Masons the black-and-white lozenges and Indented Tessels of their Lodges. And before his death, the last of the official Grand Masters, Jacques de Molay, 'organised and instituted what afterwards came to be called the Occult, Hermetic, or Scottish Masonry.'

What all these theories of conspiracy and myth mixed with history had in common was that Masonic beliefs derived from the mysticism of the near East as well as from the Old and the New Testaments of the Holy Bible. A perfect catalyst between the legendary and the practical was the building of the House of the Lord by King Solomon. Certainly, in the romances of the Middle Ages, Solomon and his Temple were second only to King Arthur and the Grail as a source of inspiration. 'And it was precisely at that time,' the leading researcher into the Temple of Solomon has written, 'that the framers of the Masonic Legend were at work in developing the various aspects of the traditional history of their Craft.'

It was also precisely at that time that the Knights of the Order of the Temple of Solomon guarded what was thought by pilgrims to be the King's Temple in Jerusalem, the octagonal shrine of the Dome of the Rock. Its builder, Caliph Umar, had cried on its completion: 'Behold a greater than Solomon is here.' The Templars passed on to the troubadours and craft guilds of Europe much of the Rabbinic and cabbalistic lore about King Solomon, which had come from ancient times. Solomon was thought to be a Magus or wise man, a magician and a worker of wonders. He was meant to have foreseen the destruction of his Temple by the Babylonians and to have constructed a secret vault within the walls for the burial and the preservation of the Ark of the Covenant – a sacred treasure that has been the object of innumerable quests ever since its disappearance.

The Christian Fathers Clement and Eusebius had written of King Solomon's power over demons, and Gregory of Tours and Bede wrote of the wonders of the Temple and its significance. 'The House of God which King Solomon built in Jerusalem represents the Holy Universal Church, which, from the First of the Elect to the last man who shall be born at the end of the world, is built daily by the grace of her peaceful King, that is, her Redeemer.' As Mount Moriah in Jerusalem was venerated as the stepping-stone of the Prophet Muhammad on his flight to Heaven and Paradise, the Temple of Solomon was also venerated by Muslims, who built the Dome of the Rock in its place. The mysticism of the Sufis and the Manicheans and the Gnostics permeated the Christian crusading guardians of Mount Moriah with its converted mosques and shrines, so that the Military Order of the Temple of Solomon believed that it was the keeper of a house of God on earth, built by the Great Architect of the world.

In another of their roles, the Templars were literally Master Masons. They directed the building of their formidable castles such as Castle Pilgrim and ordained the shape of their octagonal chapels and circular towers. There is some evidence that, as the *Fratres Solomonis*, they introduced holy geometry from the Near East into the building of the Gothic masterpieces of France such as Chartres Cathedral. But there is no question that their secret ritual involved a belief in a sacred architecture, a single Creator of the world, and the actual regulation of the teams of masons who built their thousands of preceptories and churches across Europe and the Levant.

We have already shown that some of the French Templars fled with their treasure and fleet to Scotland after their downfall and before the Battle of Bannockburn, a victory that was to cause Robert the Bruce to create two Orders in which the Templars could merge. The first was the hidden Royal Order of Scotland; its

Grand Master was the King. The second was the change of the Order of Heredom (or Sanctuary) of Kilwinning – traditionally the first Scottish Lodge of Masons who had built the abbey there under King David – to the Royal Grand Lodge of Heredom. Over its annual court, the St Clair family of Rosslyn would preside in a hereditary role as protectors of the King and the Crown Prince, and also as the powerful neighbours and friends of the Templars at their headquarters at Balantrodoch. Within these Orders would disappear the condemned Order of the Temple of Solomon. Their secret doctrines would become the practice of the later Masons.

One medieval document still at the Temple in Paris, the *Léviticon*, suggests the beliefs that the Templars brought from the Near East. Its history and their religion were interwoven. 'There is no other religion than the religion of nature, preserved in the Temples of Initiation of Egypt and of Greece.' Moses had initiated the Chiefs of Israel, the Levites, into these mysteries, and they formed the basis for the building of the Temple of Solomon, the house of God. Taught by the Essenes, Jesus pointed out how far the Levites of His time had departed from these ancient mysteries and sacrificed Himself as a divine martyr and returned to life eternal. St John the Beloved Disciple stayed in the East and kept alive the mysteries, while St Paul and the other disciples set up churches that forgot them. Certain Patriarchs and wise men and even Sufis kept alive the traditions and the rites until Hugh de Payens was initiated into them in Jerusalem and founded the Order of the Temple of Solomon. From that time, the Templars were the custodians and transmitters of this religion of nature.

There was no distinction between animal, vegetable and mineral, according to this pantheistic and mystical belief. As the *Léviticon* declared:

God is all that exists, each part of all that exists is a part of God, but is not God. Unchanging in His essence God is changing in his parts . . .

God being the Sovereign intelligence, every part that is constituted is endowed with a portion of His intelligence in proportion to its destiny – from which it follows that there is an infinite gradation of intelligences, resulting in an infinite combination, of which the reunion forms the great whole of the worlds. This is the great *all* of God, which alone has the power to form, to modify, to change, and to rule all the orders of the Intelligences according to eternal and immutable laws which are infinitely good and just.

There was also a belief in the nature of the Trinity different from that of the Catholic Church. 'God the Infinite Being is composed of three powers – the Father or Existence, the Son or Action, and the Spirit or Intelligence produced from the power of the Father and the Son.' It became a belief in a single Artificer or Architect of the World. The Temple of the human body could house a spark of the divine Intelligence. The individual could communicate directly with God without the church as an intermediary. And the duty of the human Temple was charity and love.

Many of the elements of this creed were Eastern or Celtic in origin and resulted in charges of heresy, particularly the direct approach to God. At their trials, the Templars were accused in devilish terms of the veneration of the serpent of wisdom and the skull or severed head, the ancient symbol of fertility and the cornucopia of the Grail. But these were only symbols of more profound beliefs. The Templar emphasis on God as a sovereign Intelligence and Creator and on the duty of charity were to devolve to the later Masons. Only the tradition of the martyrdom of the Biblical Hiram cannot be traced directly to Templar origins. Its roots lay elsewhere, in the ancient idea of blood sacrifice.

The Meaning of the Martyr

A fighting faith demands a martyr. In Norse belief, the Lord of the gods Odin achieved wisdom by learning the lore of the runes after a ritual self-sacrifice, stabbing himself and hanging from the tree that kept up Heaven from earth. As the *Elder Edda* recorded in 'The Words of the High One':

> Wounded and hanging on a windy gallows
>> For nine long nights,
> Pierced by a spear, offered to myself, I
>> Gave me to me.

Such self-sacrifice to win wisdom in the Norse pantheon was matched by the death of the virtuous Baldur from a dart of mistletoe flung by his blind brother – the martyrdom of mischance. From these Nordic myths, the Vikings derived some of the fatalism behind their berserker behaviour – death in battle was destined. Such fatalism and self-sacrifice were matched by the warriors of Islam in their *jihads* or holy wars. The Sufis and the Assassins had martyrs in their faith and believed that their killing by the enemy was an ascent to Paradise. In preaching the Crusades, the Catholic Church also extolled the militant as well as the martyred Christ to the Military Orders, which were created to spread the message of Christianity with the sword.

From these three sources, the Templars inherited their creed of self-immolation. Odin and Baldur, Christ and the murdered Ali, Muhammad's cousin venerated by the Shi'ites, were among Templar martyrs. Many of the Knights of the Order were Viking and Norman in origin, all were Christian and exposed to Muslim and Eastern beliefs. Their organization and doctrine were similar to those of the sect of the Assassins. One historian of the Templars interprets their war banner and battle-cry *Beauséant* as a corruption of the Celtic word meaning Paradise, so that they rode into battle with the same aim as the Sufis and the Assassins. Certainly, their reckless and berserker courage, which led to the elimination of nearly all the knights in several charges in the Holy Land, proved their will to die in order to reach heaven.

As the knights of the sword and the trowel, the Templars as builders inherited another ancient legacy of blood sacrifice. From time immemorial and in the Old Testament, religious ceremonies

and temples were blessed by the ritual killing of beasts and sometimes of humans. The Druids were accused by the Romans of being
sacred murderers, and the Romans themselves purified their holy
places by the slaughter of animals. In Homeric times, human
sacrifice might buy fair winds to Troy or divine favour on Greek
cities. Later, in classical and Near Eastern building practices, the
butchery of a lamb or a cock and the burial of its bones under the
cornerstone was normal usage. An act of blood was the foundation
of the structure.

The Masonic legend of the death of Hiram, the architect of the
Temple of Solomon, has these ancient roots, some of them brought
back by the Crusaders from the Near East. A Rabbinic legend even
stated that all the workmen of the Temple of Solomon were killed
'that they should not build another Temple devoted to idolatry,
Hiram himself being translated to heaven like Enoch.' Cabbalistic
literature preserved the legend of martyrdom in the building of the
Temple of Solomon, and it probably reached the medieval guilds
through returning Crusaders. Yet in its final form as an examination
in the Third Degree, the legend of Hiram demonstrated Celtic and
Christian, cabbalistic and Muslim influences – all of which were part
of the heritage of the Templars. 'The Knights of the Cross,' one
Masonic historian confirmed, 'were enthusiastic builders: the remains of their churches dot the Holy Land to this day. The
European builders must, in the nature of things, have acquired
large numbers of native workmen to assist them, and among these
the Temple legend, if it existed, would certainly be known. The
builders on their return would have brought the legend with them,
and it would have been adopted all the more readily as it was in
perfect accord with the traditions, even the practices, of that age in
England.'

In his confession about the mysteries of masonry to the Portu-
guese Inquisition in 1743, John Coustos divulged the ritual of
Hiram the Martyr, who was given by King Solomon the hidden
Sign of the Craft:

Some of the Officers or Apprentices perceiving this, and desiring to learn the secret sign which he had, three of the said Officers arranged amongst themselves that, upon the first occasion on which he next came to the Temple to give the customary orders, they would compel him to reveal the said Sign, guarding for this purpose the three doors of the said Temple which faced the East, the West, and the South; and when the said Master was come, he was first asked by the Officer at one of the doors for the said Sign, to which he replied that he could not divulge it since he was forbidden to do so; and that they, having already been a long time in the service, would in due course attain and discover that position they desired; whereupon the Officer struck him upon the head with a wooden cudgel; and the Master seeking to escape by the remaining doors, the others likewise gave him other blows, one with a wooden crowbar, and the other with a hammer, also of wood; so that with the last blow he fell dead.

Once the murder was done, the three masons buried Hiram. But King Solomon instituted a search, ordering fifteen other masons to divest themselves of metal and wear aprons and gloves. They found the corpse. While trying to remove the body from the earth, three hand signals were used:

Making first the Sign of the Apprentices, which is to lay hold of the joint of the finger next to the thumb, it became severed due to its rottenness; and making the second Sign, which is to lay hold of the joint of the principal finger, seeking thus to raise up the body, it also became detached in the same manner, whereby they saw clearly that it was necessary to lay hold of the wrist, and thus raising him upright, the first word which he who raised him uttered was in fact 'Mag Binach' which means in our language that 'it did stink'; and so it came to pass that from that time onwards the sign of the Master was this last action of laying hold of the wrist, and the said words; and for this reason they still today observe the same insignias, ceremonies and signs as have already been stated above.

And they took the body of the Master to the King, who ordered it to be buried, being accompanied by the Officers and Apprentices with the same insignias as stated earlier: and upon his sepulchre there was ordered to be engraved the following – Here lies Hiram, Grand Master Architect of the Freemasons.

The instruments of the murder of Hiram were specifically designated as a 24-inch gauge, a square and a gavel or setting maul. All these symbols are to be found on the Georgian Masonic tombs that still lie cheek by jowl with broken Templar gravestones in the old properties of the Order in East Scotland near the Firth of Forth, at Balantrodoch or Temple and Pentland, at Currie and Westkirk, where the very Templar stones bear the insignia of the gauge and square and maul and compasses alongside Crusaders' swords. The subsequent execution of the three murderers of Hiram was further enshrined in Masonic ceremony, one of them being dispatched after falling on his left knee, the second after falling on his right knee, and the third on both knees.

The origins of the legend of Hiram have also been seen in the Biblical account of Noah, uncovered by his three sons. Analogies have also been drawn with the killing of Thomas à Becket by the three knights and the denunciation by three renegade Templars and subsequent death of Jacques de Molay himself, the last Grand Master of the Order of the Temple of Jerusalem. But the most direct reference in the Middle Ages is the legend of the Apprentice, murdered with a setting maul by his Master for making the spiral pillar in Rosslyn Chapel, so rich in Templar and Masonic insignia. A head with a gash on its forehead, that of the Apprentice or perhaps of Hiram, is still carved in the chapel. 'There can be but little doubt that this legend referred to that of the Third Degree', an *Encyclopaedia of Freemasonry* recently stated, 'which is thus shown to have existed, at least substantially, at that early period'.

The legend of Hiram was also related to the Fall of Man. The Temple of Solomon was his Garden of Eden. The three conspirators were the angels with the fiery sword who drove him out to mortality. Lectures on *The Meaning of Masonry* took their text from St Paul: 'Know ye not that *ye* are the Temple of God?' The three great Master Builders – King Solomon; Hiram, King of Tyre; and Hiram Abiff – foreshadowed the Trinity of Christianity and also of Gnosticism. Yet in himself, Hiram Abiff represented the Architect 'by whom all things are made', as well as the action taken by the Son of Man and the Intelligence of the Holy Spirit. 'The tragedy of Hiram Abiff, then, is not the record of any vulgar, brutal murder of an individual man. It is a parable of cosmic and universal loss; an allegory of the breakdown of the divine scheme.' It is also the living proof of how the doctrines of the Near East came to influence the most powerful workmen's organizations of the West, particularly in their early homes in Scotland.

The Judgement of Solomon

In an early examination for a Mason's admission to the Third Degree, the inquiry ran:

Question: *What's the name of your Lodge?*
Answer: The Lodge of Kilwinning.
Question: *How stands your Lodge?*
Answer: East and West, as the Temple of Jerusalem.
Question: *Where was the first Lodge?*
Answer: In the porch of Solomon's Temple.
Question: *Are there lights in your Lodge?*
Answer: Three, the North east, the South west, and the Eastern passage. The one Denotes the Master Mason, the other the Words and the Third the fellow-craft . . .
Question: *Which is the Kye of your Lodge?*

Answer: A well-hung tongue.

Question: *Where lies the Kye of your Lodge?*

Answer: In the Bone Box . . .

Question: *How many Points of fellowship are there?*

Answer: Five. First, Foot to Foot. Secondly, Knee to Knee.
Thirdly, Heart to Heart. Fourthly, Hand to Hand.
Fifthly, Ear to Ear. There are the Signs of fellowship; and Shaking Hands, you will be acknowledged a very Mason.

Question: *Where are the Words to be found?*

Answer: In 1 Kings, Chapter 7, Verse 21 and 2 Chronicles,
Chapter 3, Last Verse.

The secret words of masonry were Jachin and Boaz, the twin pillars
of the Temple of Solomon. This catechism from the 'Mother
Kilwinning', held to be the oldest Lodge in Scotland, re-affirmed
the close links between the Masons and ancient beliefs in the
Temple of Solomon. Kilwinning Abbey had been built in the
twelfth century at the direction of the de Morville family, who were
Grand Constables of Scotland. They granted lands at Herdmanston
to the Knights Templars and to the St Clairs of Rosslyn and made
them Sheriffs in Lothian. They established the connection between
the St Clairs and Kilwinning, where Masons congregated to build
the abbey. Sir David Brewster, who wrote the first *History of Free
Masonry* in 1859 under the name of William Alexander Laurie, was
adamant on the origins of Scottish Masonry:

> That Free Masonry was introduced into Scotland by those
> architects who built the Abbey of Kilwinning is evident, not
> only from those authentic documents by which the existence
> of the Kilwinning Lodge has been traced back as far as the end
> of the fifteenth century, but by other collateral arguments
> which amount almost to a demonstration. In every country
> where the temporal and spiritual jurisdiction of the Pope was
> acknowledged, there was a continual demand, particularly
> during the twelfth century, for religious structures, and

consequently for operative Masons, proportionate to the piety of inhabitants and the opulence of their ecclesiastical establishment; and there was no kingdom in Europe where the zeal of the inhabitants for Popery was more ardent – the kings and nobles more liberal to the clergy – or the Church more richly endowed than in Scotland. The demand, therefore, for elegant cathedrals and ingenious artists must have been proportionately greater here than in other countries, and that demand could be supplied only from the trading associations on the Continent. When we consider, in addition to these facts, that this Society monopolized the building of all the religious edifices in Christendom, we are authorised to conclude that those numerous and elegant ruins, which still adorn various parts of Scotland, were erected by foreign Masons who introduced into this island the customs of their Order.

The *History of Free Masonry* further stated that during the reign of King James II, the office of Grand Master of the Crafts and Guilds and Orders of Scotland was granted to William St Clair, Earl of Orkney and Baron of Rosslyn. The office was made hereditary and continued until the formation of the Grand Lodge of Scotland three centuries later. The annual courts of the Grand Master for judging disputes between or within the fraternities were held at Kilwinning, the site of the Mother Lodge.

The statement was correct, except that the St Clairs had been made hereditary Grand Masters by Robert the Bruce over a century earlier after the Battle of Bannockburn, when he had reorganized the artisans and Orders of Scotland on Templar principles. He particularly had support in his victory from the workmen of Scotland, who made up the bulk of his infantry, from the refugee Templar Knights and from three members of the St Clair family – one of them, William, was buried as a Grand Master of the Temple, as we know from his tombstone in Rosslyn Chapel.

King Robert set himself up as the Sovereign Master over all the Ancient Scottish Guilds and Orders. Beneath him, he appointed a

Grand Master, as the Templars had. He made the post hereditary and vested it in the St Clair family of Rosslyn, the defenders of Scotland from any English attack from the south-east. The post of Grand Master held the rank of a Prince of the Royal Order of Scotland, which explained the occasional use of a coronet on the St Clair emblems and coats of arms. The job of Grand Master was to sit as the judge of disputes between and in the Guilds and Orders at an annual court at Kilwinning. His decree was final. He stood between the workmen's organizations and his Sovereign Master the King. His judgement was truly the judgement of Solomon.

Any enquiry into the way in which the rites of the Temple of Solomon entered the Masonic movement must acknowledge the fact that the Military Order of the Temple was extremely powerful in Scotland, where it held more than 600 properties; that some of its French knights fled with their fleet and treasure to Scotland; that the Templars and the St Clair family were closely connected and helped to win the Battle of Bannockburn; and that Robert the Bruce did reorganize the government of Scotland after his victory. The excommunicated Templars were made to go underground, although as late as 1405, an enactment by a court in Stirling declared that no 'Templar' should buy or sell goods reserved to members of the Guilds. Necessarily, the Templars were absorbed into the new government of Scotland, either within the Royal Order under their Sovereign Master the King, or into the ancient Scottish Orders and Guilds, under the hereditary jurisdiction of the St Clairs of Rosslyn, the neighbours and supporters of the Templar headquarters at Balantrodoch.

This inclusion of the survivors of the Order of the Temple of Solomon within the Scottish Orders and Guilds would explain the introduction of the rites and legends of the Temple into the Masonic movement. The artisans of Scotland were divided into two symbolic groups: the pillars of the realm as Jachin and Boaz in Solomon's Temple. There were those who worked with hand or rigid materials, such as stone or iron or wood, like the Masons and the Hammermen and the Shipwrights; and those who worked with soft materials, canvas or rope or leather, like the Cordiners, whose surviving medieval regalia still include a gilded human skull with cross leg-bones and a crown – the Templars were accused of worshipping a jewelled head. These groups of workmen now began to be organised into Lodges, each with a Master, who would report any dispute each year to the court at Kilwinning, where a St Clair would exercise his judgement of Solomon.

The earliest Masonic document in existence in Scotland the Kirkwall Teaching Scroll, which is held to date from the fifteenth century, when William, the third Earl of Orkney, was building Rosslyn Chapel. The Scroll began with the Creation of fish and fur and fowl, all things that swim and live and creep upon earth. Below it lay Paradise and the angels. And below them, the Ark of the Covenant was disclosed within the Temple of Solomon. The Temple was held up by the twin pillars of Jachin and Boaz, and one of them showed the spiral shape of Hebrew and Byzantine and Masonic architecture, also the shape of the Apprentice Pillar at Rosslyn.

Certainly, the grandson of Prince Henry St Clair, Earl William of Orkney, was given or had confirmed by the King the post of hereditary Grand Master Mason of Scotland. By the fifteenth century, the Templars and their rites and customs had permeated the Orders and Guilds of Scotland. Their hereditary judge and catalyst, Earl William, was the first to build a whole new town for his masons, who were imported with their beliefs and practices from all over Europe, in order to build his unique chapel. 'Because he thought the massones had not a convenient place to lodge in,' Father Hay wrote, 'near the place where he builded this curious colledge, for the towne then stood half a mile from the place where it now stands . . . therefor he made them to build the towne of Rosline, that now is extant, and gave every one of them a house, and lands answerable thereunto; so that this towne, all that time, by reason of the great concourse of people that had recourse unto the Prince . . . became very populous, and had in it an abundance of victualls, so that it was thought to be the chiefest towne in all

Lothian, except Edinburgh and Hadingtone. He rewarded the massones according to their degree, as to the master massone he gave forty pounds yearly, and to every one of the rest ten pounds, and accordingly did he reward the others, as the smiths and the carpenters with others.'

Earl William was unique in building a whole Lodge for his masons, who did not have to live in huts, but in houses with land. In fact, Roslin was soon confirmed as a royal borough. The wandering bands of masons came to rest under the patronage of their hereditary judge:

> Therfor, to the end he might not seem altogither unthankfull to God for the benefices he received from him, it came in his minde to build a house for God's service, of most curious worke, the which, that it might be done with greater glory and splendor, he caused artificers to be brought from other regions and forraigne kingdomes, and caused dayly to be abundance of all kinde of workemen present, as masons, carpenters, smiths, barrowmen, and quarriers, with others; for it is remembered, that for the space of thirty-four years before, he never wanted great numbers of such workmen. The Foundation of this rare worke he caused to be laid in the year of our Lord 1446.

He was building a house for God's service, a Temple of Solomon. He believed in the Temple; he ruled over the masons, he gave the judgement of Solomon.

The Temple of the Masons

Wherever the Templars were in Scotland, Masonic graves can be found in the cemeteries and sometimes representations of the Temple of Solomon. At ruined Dunkeld Cathedral, where two St Clairs were Bishops, an octagonal tower still resurrects memories of sacred architecture, while Green Men cavort in stone about its height, and a fresco of the Judgement of Solomon can still be dimly seen within the lower walls. Masonic tombs abound around the eroding windows of the roofless nave, as they do at Westkirk and at Culross, where the merchant's house of Sir George Bruce is particularly interesting because of another painting of the Temple of Solomon on its timber walls. There, the Guild of Hammermen used to have the meetings of their Lodge, and their symbol of the hammer is set in the garden walls, as it is set on an old Templar gravestone in Westkirk nearby. At St Andrews and Abdie, in the Douglas Chapel and at Currie and Corstorphine, at Melrose and Balantrodoch, in Kilmory and Siddall, wherever we have found broken Templar tombstones, we have seen later Masonic graves bearing similar emblems nearby. The merging of the Templars into the Masons is writ on stone all across Scotland.

It is especially writ in Rosslyn Chapel. There Templar insignia proliferate beside Masonic emblems. Earl William was a most careful designer of all the luxuriant carvings in the holy place, and he was the hereditary Grand Master of all the Orders and Crafts and Guilds of Scotland. 'And to the end the worke might be more rare,' Father Hay wrote of him, 'first, he caused the draughts to be drawn upon Eastland boards, and made the carpenters to carve them according to the draughts thereon, and then gave them for patterns to the massons, that they might thereby cut the like in stone.' He was his own Master of the Works, and he ordered the construction of the spiral Apprentice Pillar with its ornate fellow, Earl's Pillar, the Jachin and Boaz of his new Temple of Solomon.

By the pillar, there is a direct reference to the rebuilding of the Temple in Jerusalem after the destruction of the original one by Nebuchadnezzar and the Persians. It shows King Darius waking from a dream to hear the meaning of a riddle. One of his three guards was Zerubbabel, the original warrior of the sword and the trowel, a model for the later Templars. He told the Persian King these words of his dream, carved in Latin:

WINE IS STRONG
THE KING IS STRONGER
WOMEN ARE STRONGEST
BUT TRUTH CONQUERS ALL.

The King was so pleased with this dictum that he permitted the rebuilding of the Temple at Jerusalem – an act commemorated beside the Apprentice Pillar at Rosslyn.

Opposite the Templar gravestone of Sir William de St Clair, a Templar Knight is carved on a boss, followed by an angel bearing the Cross. In the retro-chapel, there is the sign of the bound Lucifer, falling down from Heaven – and other angels making the hand signals of the Templars and the Masons, those used in the Hiram myth and initiation ceremonies. On the south wall, there is a carving of two hands drawing aside a curtain to reveal the Lamb of God, the Agnus Dei – still blazoned on the rod of office of the Grand Prior of the present Scottish Templars. Outside the chapel, there is a head, miscalled the devil Baphomet, a corruption of Muhammad, and the representation of a dromedary in memory of eastern crusades. The most frequent of the mason's marks on the stone blocks of the walls is the eight-pointed Templar cross. Also in the crypt, a carving of an eagle with two heads signifies the Emperors of the East and West – the symbol of a Mason of the highest degree, which the founder of the chapel, Earl William, most certainly was.

The emblem of the rose covers sections of the roof and appears in many other places in the chapel. It signified both the Rose of Sharon in the Song of Solomon and the Virgin Mary, the mystical union between Bride and Bridegroom, between Mary and Christ and the Church. Dozens of small Temples of Solomon encrust the bosses and architraves with the Gardens of the Temple springing from the two or three pillars holding up their domed roofs. In a sense, the whole chapel celebrates the rebuilding of that Temple in a new Jerusalem at Rosslyn, and in that chapel, the heirs of the Military Orders and the Masons may discover a wealth of references to their inherited rites.

The building of this Collegiate Church of St Matthew with stipends for a provost, six prebendaries and two choristers was also an act of belief. Its purpose was worship and the teaching of the faith. Earl William also bestowed religious treasures and rare vestments on the priests, as he did to other religious institutions. Rosslyn Chapel became a treasury not only in symbols and architectural detail, but also in a wealth of holy relics. Since the first St Clair had come to Scotland as the cup-bearer of Queen and St Margaret, the family had been the guardians of sacred things. And in the fall of the family, they would remain the keepers of that golden trust.

13

The Fall of the Sancto Claros

Power and Glory

THE EARLS OF ORKNEY from Rosslyn became the victims of their own power and glory. The second Earl Henry inherited a position of wealth and ambiguity. He was the guardian of the Crown Prince of Scotland and imprisoned with his royal master by the English. But he equally owed allegiance to the Kings of Norway for his jurisdiction over Orkney and the Shetlands – strategic islands that the Stewart Kings wished to acquire from Norway as they had the Western Isles. In the two decades of his power before his death from the plague in 1420, Earl Henry never renewed his links with the Norwegian Crown, relying on his actual possession of the Orcadian Islands. He was, after all, Admiral of Scotland with large land-holdings in Midlothian and Fife and Aberdeenshire. His Scottish commitments precluded his Norse duty.

'He was a valiant Prince,' Father Hay wrote, 'well-proportioned, of middle stature, broad bodied, fair in face, hasty and sterne.' He had 'all his victualls brought by sea from the north in great abundance, for his house was free for all men, so that there was no indigent that were his friends but received food and rayment, no tennants sore oppressed, but had sufficient to maintain them, and, in a word, he was a pattern of piety to all his posterity.' He gifted the Abbey of Holyrood with lands that could feed 7,000 sheep. 'As for the rich vestures that he gave for the service of God att that time . . . they were of gold and silver, and silkes.' His wife Egidia Douglas was even more famous for her generosity and nature. 'She was of stature somewhat above ordinarie, but the excellency of her minde, the candor of her soule, and the holynes of her life made her incomparably more pleasant.'

From their position to the north of England, the Scottish nobles found themselves embroiled in the Hundred Years War. Their French allies called on them to harry the Borders, if the English pressed forward in France, or even to cross the sea to Flanders and help to resist invasion. Earl Henry of Orkney was unfortunate in his encounters with the old enemy, although his brother John took the Scottish St Clairs back to the land from which they had sprung before the Norman Conquest. He was to found a dynasty there, and many St Clairs were to serve in the Scottish Royal Guard.

At the Battle of Homildon Hill, Earl Henry was taken prisoner. No sooner was he released than he was captured again with the Crown Prince on a sea voyage to France and held in an English prison for several years, although allowed two safe-conducts to proceed north and settle family business during his captivity. He also went with his brother John and his brother-in-law Lord Douglas to fight for the Dauphin before the disaster at Agincourt. He had to return to defend Scotland against furious English counterattacks, which ended in the burning of Penrith. Between the politics of Scandinavia and France, the St Clairs were best placed in the defence of their homeland.

When his father died of disease in 1420, the new Lord of Rosslyn, William, could not claim the title of Earl of Orkney. He was a minor, and also had to act as a hostage in England against the unpaid ransom for King James of Scotland. King Erik of Norway took the opportunity to assert his sovereignty over the Northern Isles. Sir David Menzies of Weem was the brother-in-law of the previous Earl of Orkney and held the castle of Kirkwall, establishing a reign of terror there. Other members of the St Clair family, now spelt Sinclair, possessed lands and rights and jockeyed for power and privilege. The King of Norway gave royal authority to various claimants at different times, in order to assert his own mastery – to David Menzies and to John Sinclair and to Thomas Sinclair and even to Thomas Tulloch, the Bishop of Orkney, at last reconciled with the Norwegian Crown and briefly granted 'all the Orkneys with all royal rights'. The Bishop, however, helped to write one of the more important documents of the history of the islands, the *Genealogy* or *Deduction of the Earls of Orkney*. It showed how the claim of the young William, the third St Clair Earl of Orkney, was legitimate and descended from Rögnvald of Møre, first granted the title by the ancient Kings of Norway. Not until 1434, under strong pressure from the Scottish Crown, did King Erik formally grant the earldom to William St Clair according to the oaths and promises used at his grandfather's installation. It was the opening move in a strategy of the Stewarts to gain the Northern Isles for their country.

For fifty years, Earl William exercised his power in the north. 'He was a very fair man, of great stature, broad bodied, yellow haired, straight, well proportioned, humble, courteous, and given to policy, as building of Castles, Palaces, and Churches, the planting and haining of forrests, as also the parking and hedging in of trees.' He lived in great state and was royally served in gold and silver vessels with Lord Dirleton as Master of his Household and Lord Borthwick as his cup-bearer and Lord Fleming as his Carver. 'He had his halls and his chambers richly hung with embroidered hangings: he builded the church walls of Rosline haveing rounds with faire chambers, and galleries theron. He builded also the foreworke that looks to the northeast: he builded the bridge under the castle and sundrie office houses.' And he built the supreme chapel and the new town of Roslin especially for his masons and had it made into a royal borough.

Earl William maintained his first wife and cousin, Elizabeth Douglas, in an extravagant style. 'She was holden in great reverence, both for her birth and for the estate she was in; for she had serving her seventy-five gentlewomen, of which fifty-three were daughters to noblemen, all cloathed in velvets and silks, with their chains of gold, and other pertinents; togither with two hundred rideing gentlemen, who accompanied her in all her journeys. She had carried before her when she went to Edinburgh, if it was darke, eighty lighted torches . . . None matched her in all the countrey, save the Queen's Majesty.'

Such royal state caused some jealousy and envy in the Court of Scotland; but Earl William's service was too valuable for his dismissal. He was made Admiral of Scotland and sent to France with the King's sister to marry her to the Dauphin, taking with him a hundred gentlemen, 'twinty in white and black velvet, signifieing his armes, which is a ragged cross in a silver field; twinty cloathed with gold and blew coloured velvet, which signified the armes of Orknay, which is a ship of gold with a double tressure, and flower de luces goeing round about it in a blew field.' After the disaster of the Battle of Neville's Cross in 1446, he pushed back another English invasion two years later and was ordered on diplomatic missions to London to secure peace at the end of the Hundred Years War. He supported King James II in a struggle with the Douglas family and was made Lord Chancellor of the kingdom. Yet in 1456, he fell out with the King, perhaps because the governor of Iceland and his treasure were seized while sheltering from a storm in Orkney – an incident that sabotaged the efforts of the Stewarts to come to good terms with the King of Norway. Ten years later, Earl William's eldest son was to throw Bishop William Tulloch into prison in another effort to break Scottish-Norse relationships and end talk of a marriage between the two royal families, by which Orkney and the Shetlands would go to the young King James III, who had Earl William as his Regent during his minority. In fact, the King's marriage with the daughter of King Christian of Denmark was concluded, and the Northern Isles were handed over to Scotland as a pledge for the payment of the princess's dowry of 60,000 gold florins.

This pledge was followed by the removal of the title of Earl of Orkney from William St Clair. He was also required to exchange

Kirkwall Castle for Ravenscraig Castle, built to withstand artillery attacks and admirable for defending his lands in Fife. In exchange for his lands in Nithsdale, he had already been made Earl of Caithness. And as his Scottish properties were now far more valuable than the royal domains he controlled in Orkney and the Shetlands, he was pleased to resolve the problem of his dual allegiance to two Crowns in favour of Scotland.

He had retained, however, considerable estates in the Northern Isles, those he had acquired by conquest or purchase or donation. There were so many of these that the retention of them led to a civil war between Earl William's grandsons, Lord Henry Sinclair and Sir William of Warsetter, and eventually to a battle at Summerdale, from which all that returned to the mainland was the severed head of the Earl. By the sixteenth century, there was a confusion of Sinclair families in Orkney and the Shetlands, not only at Warsetter, but at Aith, Brecks Brough, Eday, Essingquoy, Evie, Havera, Houss, Hunto, Isbister, Ness, Quendale, St Ninian's, Strome, Sumburgh, Tuquoy, Ustaness and Voster. Divided among themselves over the remnants of the great St Clair empire on the Northern Isles, the family never ruled again.

Lord Henry, however, did restore something of Earl William's prestige during his own life and was known as a great patron of the arts. He asked his relative Gavin Douglas, Bishop of Dunkeld, to turn the *Aeneid* into a Scottish version. The prologue stated:

> At the request of ane lorde of renowne,
> Of ancestry most nobill, and illustir baroun,
> Fader of bukis, protector to science and lair,
> My special gude lord, Henry lord Sinclare,
> Quhilk with great instance, diverse tymes, sere
> Prayit me translate Virgil or Homere . . .

He served the King as 'Master of all our Machines and Artyllerie' and sold to James IV 'eight of the machines called serpentynis for a hundred pounds', paid to his widow after both of their deaths at Flodden.

Earl William had also maintained his own power in the second half of the fifteenth century with his remaining properties in Orkney and the Shetlands, in Caithness and Aberdeenshire, in Fife and Lothian. He was, as Father Hay wrote,

> a man of rare parts, haveing in him a mind of most noble composition, a perceing witt, fitt for managing great affairs, he was famous not only for moral vertue and piety, but also for military discipline, in high favour with his Prince, and raised to the greatest dignitys that in those times a subject had. He was averss from putting criminels to the rack, the tortures whereof make many ane innocent person confess himself guilty, and then with seeming justice be executed, or if he prove so stoute as in torments to deny the fact, yet he comes off with disjoynted bones, and such weakness as rendres himself and his life a burthen ever after. He built the Castle of Roslin, ameniously seated in a most fruitfull countrey on the water of Esk, riseing upon a litle hill, and accessable by a stately arch cut out upon both sides of the rock . . . Earl William built likewise the Chapell or Collegiat Church, amidst the woods, with pillars, which contents the sight by divers aspects, and have had their invention from good perspective, Toscane, Rustick, Dorick, Ionick, Corinthian, and the Compos'd or Italick.

In accordance with the spirit of the Treaty of Northampton, the Black Rood had been restored to Scotland. The Stone of Destiny, thought to be the real one, was not restored. According to the chronicles, the citizens of London would not allow it to be removed. They revered the sacred character of the relic, ignorant that it was not the actual stone, which had always remained at Scone in Scotland. It had been substituted for another boulder. A rock is a rock is a rock, and the English could not tell one from another. That is why Robert the Bruce had not asked for its return, only for holy relics with a better provenance.

Although the Black Rood was again seized after Neville's Cross and stood 'with Mary and John made of silver, being as yt were smoked all over' on a pillar by St Cuthbert's shrine in Durham Cathedral, the return of these relics to Scotland was arranged by Earl William during his diplomatic missions to the south. The Black Rood had been carried by the first St Clair in Scotland, the cup-bearer to Queen Margaret Atheling, while the 'Mary and John made of silver' was a donation to Newbattle Abbey by his father. Thus the St Clairs of Rosslyn resumed one of their hereditary duties as the guardians of the holy things of their country. But this time they intended to keep them in security against any English incursion. Earl William built a treasury for the safe-keeping of these sacred pieces in any time of danger.

The rebuilding of the castle and the chapel as well as the new borough of Roslin ruined the considerable resources of the St Clairs. The castle had already been destroyed by fire. During a hunt, a blind rat with a straw in its mouth had been seen as a sign of ill omen, and four days later, a lady of the chamber set fire to a bedspread with a candle while trying to rescue a puppy. The fire spread to the destruction of most of the castle, but a chaplain managed to save four great trunks of charters and papers, which were restored to the Earl. 'Yet all this stayed him not from the building of the Colledge, neither his liberality to the poor; but was more liberall to them than before – applying the safety of his Charters and Writings to God's particular Providence.'

He was known as 'the Prodigious', but he was also prodigal. He left few resources to help his heirs on his divided estate, for at his death, the King of Scotland required the dismemberment of the properties of so over-mighty a subject. The Earl's lands in Orkney and the Shetlands were disputed by quarrelling grandsons. His eldest son, Lord Sinclair, known as William 'the Waster' because of a court decision that he was *incompos mentis et fatuus* and 'a waster of his lands and goods', dissipated some of the family possessions, while others were taken by his bastard brother, Sir David Sinclair. The Earldom of Caithness and the Fife and Lothian lands went to two sons of Earl William's second marriage to Marjory Sutherland, a descendant of Robert the Bruce. The new Earl of Caithness fell foul of King James IV of Scotland, but redeemed himself by arriving with the whole clan wearing green to die with their royal master at Flodden Field. Since then, green has hardly been worn by a Sinclair.

Also killed at Flodden was Sir John Sinclair of Dryden near Roslin. He was called by the poet Dunbar the Queen's Knight.

> Sir John Sinclair begouth to dance,
> For he was new come out of France:
> For any thing that he do micht,
> The ane foot gaed aye unricht,
>   And to the tother wald not gree.
> Quoth ane. Tak up the Queen's knicht:
> A merrier dance micht na man see.

The new master of Roslin, Sir Oliver Sinclair, completed the building of the chapel, although not of the whole cruciform church that his father had designed. His many sons further split control of the Sinclair estates in Lothian and Fife, although his heir Oliver retained Roslin and Pentland and became the favourite of King James V and commander of the Scottish army. Father Hay called him 'the great minion' and told of his rout at Solway Moss, which signalled the impending downfall of Scottish independence and of the Sinclair family.

Oliver thought time to shew his glory, and so incontinent was displayed the King's banner, and he holden up by two spears lift up upon men's shoulders, there, with sound of trumpet, was declared Generall Lieutenant, and all men commanded to obey him as the King's person, under the highest pains, so soon a great noise and confusion was heard. The enimie, perceaveing the disordre, rushed on, the Scots fled, some passed the water, but escaping that danger, not well acquainted with the ground, fell into the slimy mosse; happy was he that might get a taker. Stout Oliver was without stroke taken, flying full manfully, and so was his glory suddenly turn'd to confusion and shame.

The Fall of the Sancto Claros

'Oh fled Oliver!' King James V of Scotland cried when he heard that his favourite, Oliver Sinclair, had lost the battle of Solway Moss. 'Is Oliver tane? Fie fled Oliver! All is lost!' Soon afterwards he took to his death-bed at the age of thirty, and when he heard the news that his wife, Marie of Guise, had borne him a daughter, he said of his kingdom, 'Adieu, farewell, it came with a lass, it will pass with a lass.' The independent kingdom had come to the Stewarts through their marriage with a Bruce princess, and it would pass with James's child, Mary, Queen of Scots. Although the Stewarts would inherit the English throne as well as that of Scotland, the twinning of the Crowns would mean the lessening of Scottish liberty and the fall of the Sinclairs of Rosslyn from power in their country.

The Sinclairs were a devout Catholic family, bound to the Crown of Scotland. Father Hay accused Oliver Sinclair and 'other minions who were pensioners to priests' of blinding James V to the Reformation, so that 'he made a solemn vow to spare none that was suspected of heresie, although it were his own sone.' Proof lies in an extraordinary Bond and Obligation signed by Marie of Guise on 3 June 1546, when she had become Regent of Scotland in the four years after the death of her husband. The Bond was given to 'Sir William Sinclar of Roslin for his personal service', and it reads:

Be it kend to all men . . . Forasmeikle as the said Sir William is Bounden and obligit to us in Speciale Service and Manrent for all the days of his life to gang and Ryde with us, and tak our sauld part with his kyn, servandis and freyndis . . . Herfor we bind and oblige us to the said Sir William. In Likewise that we sall be Leal and trew Maistres to him, his Counsill *and Secret shewn to us we sall keep Secret* – and in all mattres gif to him the best and trewest Counsell we can as we sall be requirit therto, and sall not with his Skath nor Damage but we sall stop it att our power and sall [be] Reddy att all tymes to maintain and defend him . . .

A royal pension of 300 marks a year for life was granted, and Sir William Sinclair was also made the Lord Justice General of Scotland. It was a time of trouble with Calvinist radicals wishing to force a Reformation on the Catholic Church in Scotland in alliance with Protestant English forces, which had sacked Edinburgh and Melrose and Holyrood Abbey and Rosslyn Castle itself two years before. They wished to conquer Scotland before it became a Catholic threat backed by the Guise family and France. Although the tombs of the Kings and Queens of Scotland were desecrated, and an eagle lectern and a solid brass font given by the Bishop of Dunkeld were stolen from Holyrood Abbey, the English raiders failed to seize the religious regalia and treasure there.

The reason was that William Sinclair, whose family had endowed the Abbey, had removed the holy reliquaries and rich chalices, and he refused to restore them. For the Sinclairs of Rosslyn had been great benefactors to the Monastic Orders. Henry, the Earl of Orkney, had given the Abbey of Holyrood sufficient land to graze 7,000 sheep, vestments of gold and silver, and 'a number of rich, embroidered cups' or chalices 'for the more honourable celebration of divine worship'. The charters of the Cistercian abbey of Newbattle – also sacked during the English invasion – further praised his generosity, including the gift of missals and a silver cross worth £50, flanked by the figures of the Virgin Mary and temporarily stolen by the English after the Battle of Neville's Cross. Many of the treasures of the Scottish Church before the Reformation were the donation of the Sinclairs of Rosslyn, who felt it their duty to keep these safe.

In March 1545, the Lords in Council ordered William Sinclair to return all jewels, vestments and ornaments of 'the abbay and place of Holyrudhouse . . . put and reservit within his place'. But he would not yield them. They were part of the blessed hoard hidden in the vaults of Rosslyn Chapel beside the shrine, the *Secret shewn to us* in the Bond of Marie of Guise, *we sall keep secret*. Most probably, these also included the piece of the True Cross in its reliquary of silver and gold and jewels, the Holy or Black Rood of Scotland, which had been guarded by St Margaret's cup-bearer and the St Clair family for five centuries as Scotland's most precious holy relic. The Reformation in England had already destroyed almost all the shrines and precious relics of the old Catholic faith, and Holyrood Abbey would be defaced forever. Scotland would become even more zealous in extirpating the holy treasures of the Middle Ages.

It was as well that these sacred relics were not returned from Rosslyn. After another Scottish defeat at Pinkie Cleugh, Holyrood was again sacked. This time, the English invaders found only lead to carry away, stripping the roof of that last base metal. The destruction was so complete that the most ornate church in Scotland became a stone quarry for looters after the Reformation. Yet the guardian of the religious treasures, Sir William Sinclair, was also trusted to accompany the child Mary, Queen of Scots, to France, where she would be betrothed to the Dauphin, while her Guise mother tried to rule unruly Scotland in her daughter's absence. There were already attacks being made on high Catholic officials. John Knox, a future leader of the Reformation, had seen the hand of God in the previous defeat at Solway Moss by the English, while he had described the putting of the Regent's Crown on the head of Marie of Guise as putting 'a saddle upon the back of an unruly cow'. In the same month as she signed her Bond to William Sinclair, a band of Fife lords broke into St Andrews Castle and tortured Cardinal Beaton to death for condemning a leading Protestant preacher to be burned at the stake. John Knox himself joined the rebel lairds and preached from the pulpit of St Andrews parish, before he was sent to the galleys by a French expedition, which retook the castle for Marie of Guise. By a Right of Passage in 1556, the Regent had to send her trusted William Sinclair again to France to ask for more support. During his year's absence, he was excused from his judicial duties, and Marie of Guise swore to defend the hidden treasures at Rosslyn.

The religious wars in Scotland intensified with the death in 1558 of the childless Catholic Queen of England, Mary Tudor, and the accession to the throne of her Protestant half-sister Elizabeth. By this time, Mary, Queen of Scots, was married to the Dauphin, and his father, King Henry II of France, immediately had her proclaimed Queen of England and Ireland as well as Scotland. The poet Ronsard wrote that Jupiter had decreed that she should govern England for three months, Scotland for three and France for half the year. The French and Catholic menace appeared so imminent that Scottish Protestant insurgents attacked the Border regions and temporarily took Edinburgh. Another urgent summons to 'our chosen son', William Sinclair of Rosslyn, was signed by Marie of Guise a year before her death in 1560 on behalf of Francis and Mary, *deo gratia Rex et Regina Scotorum*. It ordered him to counterattack the Border rebels, to capture and apprehend them of whatever quality and quantity they were, to destroy their fortified houses, and to punish their homicide and arson. He himself was given immunity from any criminal action he might have to take.

Known supporters of the Stewart and Catholic cause, the Sinclairs of Rosslyn were doomed by the Reformation, which came to pass the following year with the Scottish Parliament instituting a Protestant confession of faith, abolishing the jurisdiction of the Pope and prohibiting the celebration of the Mass under sentence of death for the third offence. These acts should have received the assent of Mary, Queen of Scots, but they never did. Yet they ensured that the Reformation would succeed in Scotland, and that the Lords of Rosslyn would be condemned for their faith and their loyalty to the Crown. With the fall of Mary, Queen of Scots, and her capture by the English seven years after her mother's death, William Sinclair was arrested and the future of his estates put in jeopardy, although they were eventually restored to him.

Mob attacks from Edinburgh were to devastate Rosslyn Chapel in 1592, although the hundred images of the Virgin Mary and the apostles and the saints had already been removed from their niches and hidden in the vaults with the shrine and the sacred treasures of the Catholic faith. The four altars dedicated to the Virgin Mary and to the Saints Matthew and Andrew and Peter were pulled down. Yet for two reasons, the ornate chapel, so full of idols and Green Men, was not wholly destroyed. The first was that the Sinclairs remained the hereditary Grand Masters of the Crafts and Guilds and Masons of Scotland, even though many of these trade organizations were leaving the Catholic faith and becoming Protestant. The second reason was the *Secret shewn* to Marie de Guise, which she did *keep secret* – the location of the shrine below the altar and other Catholic religious treasures and relics, some from Holyrood Abbey or from the downfall of the Templars, all in the safe-keeping of the Sinclairs or Sancto Claros. The knowledge that Rosslyn Chapel was a holy place, which was revered by Masons as well as Catholics, stayed the hammers and axes of the religious radicals.

In the last years of the sixteenth century, when King James VI of Scotland was preparing to become King James I of England upon the death of Queen Elizabeth, the Sinclairs of Rosslyn were recognised as loyal subjects in allegiance to their Sovereign, although they kept their hidden Catholic treasures below their chapel. This is an explanation for the extraordinary Schaw petition of 1600. It was signed by William Schaw, the Master of the King's Work and the leading Mason in all Scotland, as John Morow had been the century before. The other signatures are from chief figures among the building trades. The document is authentic and seminal in the records of Scottish Masonry. It asks the Sinclairs of Roslin to resume their role as hereditary Grand Masters of the Crafts and the Guilds and the Orders of Scotland because there have been great disorders in the past decade, when the function of the Sinclairs was in abeyance. The opening of the petition absolutely acknowledges the authority of the Barons of Roslin during the preceding centuries:

> We deacons, masters and free men of the Masons within the realm of Scotland with express consent and assent of William Schaw, Master of Work to our Sovereign Lord the King – for so mickle as *from age to age* it has been observit among us that the Lairds of Roslin has ever been patrons and protectors of us and our privileges – like as our predecessors has obeyit and acknowledgit them as patrons and protectors . . .

The traditional judicial position of the Lords of Roslin had been suspended because of religious conflict and suspicion that they still supported the Catholic cause as well as the Stewart line. But the fact that Queen Elizabeth was dying and that King James VI would soon be moving with his Court to London made intolerable the prospect of more turmoils among the trade organizations with their only judge in distant Westminster. The Sinclairs were traditionally royalist, and their old role was essential in Scotland. This is confirmed by another petition to them thirty years later, again signed by all the leading Scottish Masons. By this time, a second Stewart was on the Scottish and English throne, King Charles I, and his support of the authority of bishops against congregational power once more threatened a religious conflict that was to end in the Civil War. The Barons of Roslin represented a past stability in an uncertain future. As the document pledged:

> We for ourselves and in the name of our hail bretheren and craftsmen agree and consent that William St Clair now of Roslin for himself and his heirs purchase and obtain at ye hands of our Sovereign Lord liberty freedom and jurisdiction upon us and our successors *in all times coming* as patrons and judges to us and the hail professors of our craft within this realm.

Yet in 1615, William Sinclair was condemned to death for harbouring a Jesuit priest and holding a Mass at Rosslyn. In the event, only the priest was hanged, while the Lord of Rosslyn was reprieved by King James VI, mindful of the long service of the family to the dynasty. He was forced into exile in Ireland. As Father Hay wrote, 'the cause of his retreat was rather occasioned by the Presbyterians, who vexed him sadly because of his religion, being Roman Catholic.' Nine years later, however, the Rosslyn Charters were publicly proclaimed by trumpet and a reading at the Market Place in Edinburgh on behalf of the King.

This ceremony was to be repeated in 1648, when King Charles I had already lost the Civil War. Two years later, following the disaster of the Battle of Dunbar, the significance of Rosslyn Chapel was revealed by the strange mercy of vengeful English Puritans. True as always to the Stewarts, another Sir William Sinclair fought the English attack from the south. His body was brought back to the chapel and interred in full armour in the vaults on the day of the defeat at Dunbar, where his son and heir John was fighting. Father Hay was to see his corpse when the vaults were opened for the last time in the seventeenth century before being filled with sand and rubble and then sealed by stone masons with ashlar blocks, as we found when we tried to discover the secret shrine and buried religious treasures there.

> His corps seemed to be intire att the opening of the cave, but when they came to touch his body it fell into dust; he was laying in his armour, with a red velvet cap on his head on a flat stone: nothing was spoiled except a piece of the white furring that went round the cap, and answered to the hinder part of the head. All his predecessors were buried in the same manner in their armour. Late Roslin, my good father, was the first to be buried in a coffin, against the sentiments of King James the Seventh, who was then in Scotland, and severall other persons well versed in antiquity . . .

When General Monk arrived with his troopers after the victory at Dunbar, he reduced most of Rosslyn Castle to ruin, although it was valiantly defended by Sir William's son John, who was taken prisoner and sent to England. General Monk had his horses stabled in the chapel. But he again did not purify its idolatry by fire and hammer, nor did he try to break into the vaults. The most convincing reason is that the Lord Protector himself, Oliver Cromwell, had studied at the Temple in London, was a Master Mason in England, and knew that the Sinclairs were the hereditary Grand Master Masons of Scotland and had built the chapel as another Temple of Solomon to house Masonic mysteries.

The Lords of Rosslyn remained loyal to the Stewart and Catholic cause. The new Master, James Sinclair, followed the ways of his ancestors. 'He was mutch taken up with building, and addicted to the priests,' Father Hay noted of his stepfather, 'those two inclinations spoiled his fortunes. He died a good age, and with the reputation of ane honest man, yet . . . he was too easie.' And also, he was too loyal. His son was killed fighting for King James at the Battle of the Boyne, while the 'Glorious Revolution' and the accession to the throne of the Protestant Prince William of Orange led to another mob attack on chapel and castle. Father Hay chiefly mourned the sack of the famous library with its collection of medieval Catholic missals, many of them collected in the sixteenth century after they 'had been taken by the rabble out of our monasterys in the time of the reformation.' Hay himself lost 'several books of note, and amongst others, the original manuscript of Adam Abel,' who was a Grey Friar from Jedburgh Monastery, the composer of the *Rota Temporum*, a history of Scotland from early to Tudor times. After this final attack, the chapel was left to nature with only its solid stone roof and sealed vaults protecting the mysteries within. 'But as nothing is done to keep it together,' Dorothy Wordsworth was to note on a visit, 'it must in the end fall.'

The last expedition of the Sinclairs to the Baltic had also ended in their downfall. In the Kalmar War of 1612, Denmark and Norway had fought Sweden, which had recruited troops in Scotland. A detachment of 400 men landed at Romsdalfjord in Norway near the ancient lands of the Møre ancestors of the Sinclairs and marched east towards Sweden. They lived off the land by looting, but in a mountain pass at Kringen, they were ambushed by the local farmers. Warned by a horn blown by a village girl, Prillarguri, the Norwegians began a rockslide and charged and massacred the Scottish contingent, including one of its captains, George Sinclair. A ballad of the disaster is still sung in the schools of Norway, a monument to Jorgen Sinkler marks the bloody spot, and the place is called Sinclair's Pass.

The St Clairs fell in Orkney as well because of their loyalty to the Stewart cause and the Catholic faith. The Castle of Kirkwall had already been dismantled when John, Master of St Clair, fled there after his share in the Jacobite rebellion of 1715. His memoirs are poignant about his suffering for his fidelity. As he wrote of the long St Clair attachment to the Scottish royal family:

> . . . Without anie other thanks, having brought upon us considerable losses, and among others that of our all in Cromwell's time; and left in that condition, without the least relief, except what we found in our own virtue. My father was the only man of the Scots nation who had courage enough to protest in parliament against King William's title to the throne, which was lost, God knows how; and this at a time when the losses in the cause of the royall familie, and their usual gratitude, had scarce left him bread to maintain a numerous familie of eleven children, who had soon after sprung up to him, in spite of all which he had honourably persisted in his principle. I say, these things considered, and after being treated as I was, and in that unluckie state, when objects appear to men in their true light, as at the hour of death, could I be blamed for making some bitter reflections to myself, and laughing at the extravagance and unaccountable humour of men, and the singularetie of my own case (an exile for the case of the Stewart family), when I ought to have known that the greatest crime I or my familie could have committed, was persevering, to my own destruction, in serving the royal familie faithfully though obstinately, after

so great a share of depression, and after they had been pleased
to doom me and my familie to starve?

Although the Caithness and the Fife branches of the Sinclair family
sometimes flourished, the power of the Roslin branch declined. By
the end of the eighteenth century, the ownership of the castle and
the chapel had passed with a lass, married to an Erskine and a
Wedderburn who became Lord Loughborough, then Lord Chancellor, then the First Earl of Rosslyn. The last of the long line of
male Sancto Claros, which had ruled at Roslin for seven centuries
and had preserved the mysteries of the Templars and the Masons
and the faith of the Middle Ages, was still named William St Clair or
Sinclair. A member of the Royal Company of Archers, the King's
bodyguard for Scotland, he was admired by Sir Walter Scott, who
wrote of him:

> The last Roslin was a man considerably above six feet, with
> dark grey locks, a form upright, but gracefully so, thin-flanked
> and broad-shouldered, built, it would seem, for the business of
> war or chase, a noble eye of chastened pride and undoubted
> authority, and features handsome and striking in their general
> effect, though somewhat harsh and exaggerated when con-
> sidered in detail. His complexion was dark and grizzled, and as
> we schoolboys, who crowded to see him perform feats of
> strength and skill in the old Scottish games of Golf and
> Archery, used to think and say amongst ourselves, the whole
> figure resembled the famous founder of the Douglas race . . .
> In all the manly sports which require strength and dexterity,
> Roslin was unrivalled; but his particular delight was in
> Archery.

Of course, 'the famous founder of the Douglas race' was the giant
who had died five centuries before in Spain with the Heart of Bruce
and Sir William de St Clair, whose Templar tombstone still lies in
Rosslyn Chapel. But this 'last Roslin' surrendered his family's
hereditary role as Grand Master of the Crafts and Guilds and Orders

of Scotland in order to become the first elected Grand Master of the Grand Lodge of his country. The document yielding his inherited rights confirmed their existence:

> I, William St Clair of Rossline, Esquire, taking to my consideration that the Masons in Scotland did, by several deeds, constitute and appoint William and Sir William St Clairs of Rossline, my ancestors, and their heirs to be their patrons, protectors, judges, or masters; and that my holding or claiming any such jurisdiction, right, or privilege, might be prejudicial to the Craft and vocation of Massonrie, whereof I am a member, and I being desirous to advance and promote the good and utility of the said Craft of Massonrie to the outmost of my power, doe therefore hereby, for me and my heirs, renounce, quit, claim, over-give, and discharge all right, claim, or pretence that I, or my heirs had, have or any ways may have, pretend to, or claim, to be patron, protector, judge or master of the Massons in Scotland, in virtue of any deed or deeds made and granted by the said Massons, or any grant or charter made by any of the Kings of Scotland . . .

This renunciation by the 'last Roslin' of the great role he had inherited was the final proof that the St Clairs were the bridges between ancient aristocracy and democracy. If there was a direct bloodline in any family that translated the arcane knowledge of medieval times to the modern age, the St Clairs of Rosslyn might claim that role. For more than five centuries, they were the hereditary Grand Masters of the Crafts and Guilds and Orders and finally the Masons of Scotland. By their connection with the Templars, they introduced ancient Eastern rites into Masonic practice. For many centuries, they were the guardians of the Crown Prince of Scotland as well as leaders in the defence of the kingdom against any English attack. Through them, Orkney and the Shetland Isles were brought under the Scottish Crown. They were Crusaders, who also went on the quest for the New World and for the Grail, which was housed in symbol in the luxuriant chapel built from their curious knowledge. Much of their learning is lost, except for what they wrote in stone. But if this book illuminates something of that strange Sancto Claro family of the Holy Light, then one small ray pierces the darkness of that wise past.

Legends of the Secrets and the Treasure

In the twelfth century, Joachim of Fiore elaborated a vision of the world as divided into several epochs, which would culminate in a New Age. The German revival of the faith of the Templars and of the Rosy Cross in the eighteenth century saw the sixth age as beginning with the death of the last Grand Master of the Order of the Temple of Solomon, Jacques de Molay. He had received the secrets of the Cabbala and of the Essenes, and he was first given the Masonic name of Hiram, the martyred architect of the Temple. He was the possessor not only of secret wisdom, but of huge amounts of sacred treasure, which was kept in the two pillars of the Temple in Paris. This included the Crown of the Kingdom of Jerusalem, the seven-branched candlestick of the original Temple, and the four golden evangelists from the Church of the Holy Sepulchre at Jerusalem.

This was the treasure said to have been carried by the refugee Templar fleet to Scotland by the self-styled George Frederick Johnson, 'Provost-General of the Templar Order of Scottish Lords'. An influential German Templar, Baron von Hund und Altengrotkare, claimed to have been recruited to the Order by Prince Charles Edward Stewart himself, the Young Pretender. He in his turn recruited twelve German reigning Princes to Templar high office, although their belief was more in the mystical treasure of the Holy Grail of *Parzifal* than in the actual hoard of the Temple of Paris.

In the early nineteenth century, the French followed the Germans by discovering a charter, said to date from 1324, in which a

Jean-Mark Larmenius had been appointed Grand Master of the Order by de Molay before his death and had passed on the succession to a Thomas Theobald of Alexandria. The refugee Templars in Scotland were condemned as deserters, and the rift between the Templars of France and Scotland continues to this day. The sword of Jacques de Molay was also thought to have been rediscovered and became a potent symbol. Those against Free-masonry in France saw in the revival of the Templars a long conspiracy that ran forward from the heretic Gnostics through the Essenes and the Assassins and the Cathars and the Templars and the Masons to modern times, an enduring subversion against Pope and King, a form of revolutionary anarchism.

As the St Clairs of Rosslyn had been guardians and donors of holy relics, and as they had a long association with the Templars, it is not surprising that the Templar treasure was thought to be hidden in Rosslyn. Actually, they had concealed their country's most sacred objects, such as the Black Rood, containing a piece of the True Cross, as well as other religious pieces. The *Theatrum Scotiae* of 1693 stated:

> A great treasure, we are told, amounting to some millions, lies buried in one of the vaults. It is under the guardianship of a lady of the ancient house of St Clair, who, not very faithful to her trust, has been long in a dormant state. Awakened, however, by the sound of a trumpet, which must be heard in one of the lower apartments, she is to make her appearance, and to point out the spot where the treasure lies.

Certainly, the huge wealth of the St Clairs after the arrival of the refugee Templars in Scotland for the next two centuries would lead to beliefs that their treasure was still buried at Rosslyn. The evidence of documents and oil exploration techniques, of radar and radio pulses, and even of dowsers and psychic researchers, all find metal or treasure in the vaults below. But we cannot reach down there, as yet.

A most enduring myth has been that a Holy Grail of precious metal lies within the Apprentice Pillar. Its propagator was Walter Stein, an Arthurian scholar, who claimed that the Templars took the Grail from a spiral pillar near Cintra in Portugal to its sister at Rosslyn and had it incarcerated there. Their pilgrim route had been followed by Basilius Valentinus, the author of *The Triumphant Chariot of Antimony*, an enigmatic key to the mysteries of alchemy. Stein was approached by Hitler through Rudolf Hess to help find the Grail, which fascinated the secret societies of the Nazi movement, imbued with Wagner and the crusade of the Teutonic Knights towards the East – Hitler fully restored their headquarters at Marienburg. A belief that the Grail was, indeed, in Scotland may have been another inducement for the deluded Hess to fly there during the Second World War – like the Templar deserters. An intimate of Hess and member of the secret Nazi Thule society, Hans Fuchs, visited Rosslyn Chapel in May 1930, and signed the visitors' book and told members of the Edinburgh Theosophical Society that Hess identified with Parsifal – his nickname in Nazi circles – and believed Rosslyn was a Grail chapel or the Grail chapel.

These legends and resonances at Rosslyn have some groundings. The St Clairs were keepers of the nation's treasures, the chapel was built as a Temple of Solomon and of the Holy Grail, and Templar and Masonic insignia are carved within it. The stained-glass windows of Victorian times not only depict the Grail in a Last Supper, but also concentrate on the four warrior Saints, George and Maurice and Michael and Longinus, all armed with sword or lance. And the investiture of present-day Templars from Nova Scotia in Rosslyn Chapel suggests an abiding tradition, which may be allied to the fact that King Charles I designated a court in Edinburgh Castle as a part of the territory of Nova Scotia and created Barons of that country there, including members of the St Clair family.

The fact is that the treasure at Rosslyn is the chapel itself in its luxuriance and singular curiosity. On one pillar, the Three Magi set out their three gifts or Grails on a trestle table in front of the Virgin

Mary and Child. There are also cut in stone the medieval allegories of the Seven Acts of Mercy, and the Seven Deadly Sins and an elaborate Dance of Death. In its ornaments, the chapel is the richest in the world, lavish in symbol, extravagant in meaning, prodigal in shapes. Its fabric creates its secrets. It is its own hoard of tradition. Its history is the stuff of legends, but its glory is itself.

Epilogue, 2002

RESEARCH NEVER ENDS. As in detective stories, new evidence always turns up to unsettle previous inquiries. When *The Sword and the Grail* was first published in 1993, it did for Rosslyn Chapel, rather more historically, what *The Holy Blood and the Holy Grail* had done for Rennes-le-Château. Many books followed my pioneer discoveries about Rosslyn and Prince Henry St Clair and the Templar Grail stones and the Masons. Most of these works were somewhat fantastic, but some new and valuable insights were provided with convincing proofs. The culmination of this research was at a Sinclair Symposium held in 1997 at Kirkwall in Orkney. There the quest for the hidden secrets of the St Clairs and the Templars and the Masons appeared to reach some conclusions, later described in my film and book culminating in an interpretation of the Kirkwall Scroll.

Fresh findings in the Zeno Voyage emphasized the importance of the Northern Commonwealth at the end of the fourteenth century with its Viking trading empire stretching from the Baltic to Newfoundland and beyond. With its loss of trade in the Near East under the rising power of the Turkish sultans, who would capture Constantinople itself in 1453, the Venetians looked to increase their commerce to the north and the west. For two centuries, however, the Hanseatic League had controlled the overland routes from the Baltic to the Mediterranean and had even made themselves dominant in the North Sea. From their six major counters –

in Lübeck, Wisby in Gotland, Bergen, Novgorod, Bruges and London at the Steelyard – the Hanseatic cities dominated the major river mouths and the sounds, straits and channels of northern Europe from Russia to Britain.

Few goods passed from east to west or north to south, except at a German price. Salt and fish had made the original fortunes of Lübeck; to these were added Scandinavian and Atlantic timber and iron, rope and pitch, sailcloth and brimstone for gunpowder and furs. Backed by the Teutonic Knights, the Hansa like the Templars became a state within every northern state. Only Scottish ships and merchants competed seriously with the Hansa, until the arrival of Venetian fleets in convoys twice a year to Flanders for the wool trade. These foragers speculated on outflanking the German traders by themselves establishing mercantile posts and privileges in Scotland and Scandinavia. If the English Channel was closed against them, they could use the Templar escape route round Ireland to the Western Isles and Orkney, the entrepôt of the whole rich North Atlantic trade.

Such a strategy was part of young Henry St Clair's mission for his country, when he left Roslin in 1363 as a diplomat bound for Copenhagen. There he would meet the following year the Venetian ambassador Carlo Zeno, the explorer Paul Knutson and the Greenland traveller Ivar Bardsson with their knowledge of transatlantic routes. King Waldemar of Denmark had seized Gotland two years previously and had defeated King Magnus of Sweden at Helsingsborg despite the aid of a large Hanseatic fleet. He would be followed by King Haakon VI of Norway, who was to marry the Danish princess, Margaret, so closing the vital German counter at Bergen. The League was under serious threat.

The opportunity could hardly be more favourable. The Black Death had winnowed the population of Norway, perhaps killing two-thirds of its sailors and shipwrights. The area extending over all the lands near the Arctic as far as North America, called 'Norveca' on early medieval maps, was slipping from the grasp of the Norse royal house, and the colonies as far as Greenland were under threat by plague and pirate attack. So enfeebled was Norway that when Queen Margaret shifted the centre of Scandinavian power to Denmark, the whole of the area of Norse sovereignty would be called the Danish province of Greenland, *Gronlandia Provincia*. This created the chance to found a Northern Commonwealth.

The Hanseatic League had struck back with a vengeance against Denmark and Norway, where Queen Margaret wrote to her husband from Akershus Castle in 1368 of a German blockade: 'My servants are in great want of food and drink, neither they nor I receive what we need.' The following year, Bergen was burned and sacked by a Hansa fleet; this was followed by the capture of Copenhagen; within another three years, Denmark and Norway had restored even greater privileges to the German merchants.

Queen Margaret did not dare to assault the Hansa as her father had; but she invaded and defeated Sweden, so becoming the ruler of all Scandinavia. Thus her childhood friend, Henry St Clair, now her vassal as the Earl of Orkney, became a powerful ally in her dream of establishing a Northern Commonwealth of trade, which would extend from Scandinavia through the Orcadian Isles on to the Norse colonies and bishoprics in Iceland and Greenland, and to outposts in North America. His absence during the important signing of the historic Treaty of Kalmar in 1397 was another proof of his engagement in other voyages across the Atlantic.

The worst threat to trade in the Baltic and the North Sea now derived from pirates, known as the Vitalien Brethren. Chased out of Wisby by the Teutonic Knights, they attacked Bergen and seized ports in southern Norway. Queen Margaret's need to use the Earl of Orkney's fleet and his access to shipbuilding materials against the Vitalien pirates was another factor in her continuing support for his enterprises. In the National Library in Copenhagen are state documents showing the St Clair seal, second in precedence to the Queen. In 1389, indeed, when Erik of Pomerania was declared her heir to the thrones of Denmark and Norway, Henry St Clair's signature followed immediately on that of Archbishop Vinoldus of Nidaros, now Trondheim. Queen Margaret had put her trust in the power of her Earl of Orkney, and he once used a safe-conduct from King Richard II of England to bring three ships from London to her aid.

Such was the historical scene set at the opening of the *Zeno Narrative*. As stated before, Carlo Zeno, the saviour of Venice, had two sailor brothers, Nicolò and Antonio. When Marco Barbaro, another Venetian patrician, wrote his account of the noble families of Venice, his entry under the Zeno name, dated 1536, recorded Nicolò as 'the rich man' and the captain of a galley in the Chioggia battle against Genoa, won by his brother Carlo. In his *Libro di nozze* Barbaro further stated that Nicolò then went on to explore the northern seas, followed by his brother Antonio. They wrote together 'the voyages among the islands under the Arctic Pole and the discoveries of 1390 – by order of Zicno, King of Frislanda, he [Antonio] took himself to the continent of Estotilanda in Northern America. He dwelt fourteen yeas in Frislanda, four with his brother Nicolò, and ten alone.'

Barbaro's assertion did not coincide with the later publication of the *Zeno Narrative*, which was based on mangled evidence; but it did correspond to the biographical details of the two brothers, as they emerged in my later research. Nicolò Zeno was captain and commander of the Venetian biennial fleet to London and Flanders between the spring of 1383, when he had been ambassador to Hungary, and the June of 1388, when he was transferred to Adriatic duties. In that period and in pursuit of the Venetian push to the north, he had every opportunity to sail to Orkney and the Shetlands to assist Zicno or Prince Henry St Clair in his campaigns to assert control over those islands and destroy the domination of the Hansa in the northern Atlantic.

There was also no record of Nicolò Zeno in the archives between 1396 and August, 1400, when he made a will in Venice. He had been banned from office and sent into exile on charges of corruption while serving as procurator in various Venetian colonies. If he had taken his brother Antonio with him from the Flanders convoy on his first expedition to Orkney and left him, as Barbaro wrote, with Zicno as a hostage for fourteen years, he could then have gone to rejoin him, having heard of his northern campaigns and exploits in the correspondence that came back to Canareggio. That would have allowed one or both of the Zeno brothers to survey Greenland and to navigate the northern expedition to Estotilanda between 1398 and 1400, which was the basis of the *Zeno Narrative*. The fact that there was no record kept in Venice of Antonio Zeno between 1380 and his death there just before 1403 made still more plausible Barbaro's claim of his long stay in Orkney and later voyage to North America.

The chief interest of the *Zeno Map* was its placing of two cities in North America, appearing to confirm a colonizing expedition there after 1390, the previous date given for the Zeno voyage by Marco Barbaro. Yet there had also been significant other cartographical evidence for North American colonization by knights, who knew how to build fortifications and wore a Templar or Engrailed Cross. The earliest version of a map called the *Rudimentium Novitorium* was published in the Hansa centre of Lübeck about 1475 and clearly showed 'Winland' as an island with a fortified church to the far north-west – a location similar to that of Estotilanda on the *Zeno Map*. Another version of that German map derived from Augsburg five years later and marked the stronghold on a promontory as 'Vinland' – the Viking name for New England. These two maps were to bolster me greatly in my later researches into the mysterious Newport Tower on Rhode Island, for they suggested a pre-Columbian structure there.

In his extensive researches over decades, James Whittall confirmed all I thought I had discovered at the Newport Tower. The structure was pre-planned and based on sacred geometry, particularly on the round Templar churches and tower at Charroux in the south-west of France and Llanleff in Brittany. 'The tower was aligned to the East, and each of the eight pillars was similarly aligned on the cardinal points known to the Knights Templars.' The tool marks matched fourteenth-century chisels; the single and double splay windows resembled those of the Bishop's Palace in Kirkwall;

the lintel design and triangular keystone feature of the arches were found in Orkney and Greenland churches; the plinths and pillars had no parallels in English colonial building, but they did in medieval Kirkwall Cathedral.

Furthermore, the fireplace of the Newport Tower with its double flues was out of date by the fifteenth century and copied from Scottish and Scandinavian round churches – eighteen of these also had fireplaces on the first floor, which was reached by an outside ladder. 'The Newport Tower was built and served as a church, observatory, lighthouse.' Its most likely builder was Earl Henry St Clair, who was familiar with the sacred geometry of Templar round towers.

After this brilliant exposition of the origins of the Newport Tower, I was allowed to inspect the Kirkwall Scroll in the local Lodge, and I was given pieces of it for radio-carbon dating. Investigated in the Oxford laboratory which pronounced the Turin Holy Shroud a medieval forgery, the centre section of the Kirkwall Scroll proved to date from the middle of the fifteenth century, providing the missing link through the St Clair Earl of Orkney with Rosslyn Chapel, built by the mystic Third Earl William, who had passed the Gnostic and hermetic knowledge of the crusading Knights Templars on to the Ancient Scottish Masonic Rite.

The many esoteric symbols on the long cloth, particularly the Ancient Ark Mariners Degree and the Garden of Eden with its hermaphrodite Eve, coincided with late medieval knowledge and the early science of alchemy. The commissioner and possessor of the best library in Scotland of the time, Earl William would appear to have had the Scroll first painted for the early Masons attached to Rosslyn where so many of the symbols are still carved on the chapel walls.

There was still a final discovery to be made, if any discovery is ever final. There was no known picture of Prince Henry St Clair, certainly not from the Canadian Indian point of view. And then the Smithsonian Museum in Washington put out a Viking travelling show to emphasize the Norse contribution to the early voyages to

America. In the exhibition was a small wooden doll, an Innuit carving from South Baffin Island, which was on the Norse trading route from the doomed Western Settlement in Greenland making for Newfoundland. The doll was evidently that of a knight of the Military Orders, and was radio-carbon dated to the fourteenth century. The only known Templar expedition to the New World was that of Prince Henry St Clair. There the case must rest, if it will ever let me rest.

APPENDIX

The Zeno Narrative

THIS NEW TRANSLATION of the *Zeno Narrative* is based on the original and on the translation made by Richard Henry Major for the Hakluyt Society in 1873. My notes on the text derive chiefly from Major's excellent notes and the work of Frederick J. Pohl in his *Prince Henry Sinclair: His Expedition to the New World in 1398* (New York, 1974).

The Discovery of the Islands of FRISLANDA, ESLANDA,
ENGRONELANDA, ESTOTILANDA, and ICARIA:
made by two Brothers of the Zeno Family,
SIR NICOLÒ, the Chevalier, and SIR ANTONIO
With a Map of these Islands

In the year of our Lord 1200, there was in the city of Venice a very famous gentleman named Sir Marino Zeno. For his great virtue and wisdom, he was elected president over some of the republics of Italy. While governing them, he was such a discreet manager that his name was beloved and held in great respect, even by those who had never known him personally. Among his honourable actions, he set at rest some very serious civil disturbances which arose among the citizens of Verona. A war might have been provoked, if he had not been extremely active and given good advice.

This gentleman had a son named Sir Pietro, who was the father of the Doge Rinieri, who died without issue and left his property to

Sir Andrea, the son of his brother Sir Marco. This Sir Andrea was Captain-General and Procurator, and he was held in the highest reputation for his many rare qualities. His son, Sir Rinieri, was an illustrious Senator and several times Member of the Council. His son was Sir Pietro, Captain-General of the Christian Confederation against the Turks. He was given the name of Dragone because he bore a Dragon on his shield, instead of a Manfrone, which he had borne previously. He was father of the great Sir Carlo, the famous Procurator and Captain-General against the Genoese in those perilous wars in which nearly all the leading princes of Europe attacked our liberty and empire. By his great prowess, as Furius Camillus had delivered Rome, so he delivered his country from falling into the hands of the enemy. On this account he was given the name of the Lion, which he had painted on his shield as an enduring memorial of his deeds of valour. Sir Carlo had two brothers, Sir Nicolò the Chevalier and Sir Antonio, the father of Sir Dragone, who was the father of Sir Caterino, the father of Sir Pietro. His son was another Caterino, who died last year and was the father of Nicolò, now living and the compiler of this book.

Now Nicolò the Chevalier was a man of great courage. After the Genoese war of Chioggia, which gave our ancestors so much to do, he had a very great desire to see the world and to travel and make himself acquainted with the different customs and languages of mankind. Then he would on occasion be better able to serve his country and gain reputation and honour. So he had a vessel made and equipped from his own resources, for he was a rich man. And he sailed out of our seas and passed the Strait of Gibraltar, steering always to the north with the object of seeing England and Flanders.[1] Being, however, caught in those seas by a terrible storm, he was so tossed about for many days by the sea and the wind that he did not know where he was. When he discovered land at last as he was not able to beat against the violence of the storm, he was cast on the Island of Frislanda.[2] The crew, however, were saved, and most of the goods that were in the ship. This was in the year 1380.[3] The people of the island came running in great numbers with weapons to attack Sir Nicolò and his men, who were exhausted with their struggles against the storm and did not know in what part of the world they were. They were not able to make any resistance at all, much less defend themselves with the vigour necessary in such danger. And they would doubtless have been very badly treated if a certain chieftain had not fortunately happened to be near the spot with an armed retinue. When he heard that a large vessel had just been wrecked upon the island, he hurried in the direction of the noise and outcries from the attack on our poor sailors. He drove away the natives, addressed our people in Latin and asked them who they were and where they came from. And when he learned that they came from Italy and that they were men of that country, he was exceedingly pleased. Promising them all that they would not be made captive, and assuring them that they had come into a place where they would be well treated and very welcome, he took them under his protection and gave his word of honour that they were safe. He was a great lord and possessed certain islands called Portlanda, lying not far from Frislanda to the south; these were the richest and most populous of all those places.[4] His name was Zichmni.[5] Besides being the lord of these small islands, he was Duke of Sorano, which lay over against Scotland.[6]

I thought it good to draw a copy of these northern lands from the sailing chart which I find that I have still among our family heirlooms. Although it is rotten with age, I have succeeded with it tolerably well. To those who take pleasure in such things, it will serve to throw light on what would be hard to understand without it. As well as Zichmni being the man I have described, he was warlike and valiant and especially famous in naval exploits. The year before he had gained a victory over the King of Norway, who was lord of the island. Anxious to win more renown by deeds of arms, he had come with his men to attempt the conquest of Frislanda, which is an island rather larger than Ireland. Seeing that Sir Nicolò was a man of judgement and very experienced in naval and military matters, he gave him permission to go on board his fleet with all his men. The [Scottish] captain was ordered to pay him all respect and to take advantage of his advice and experience in everything.

This fleet of Zichmni consisted of thirteen vessels. Two only were rowed with oars, the rest were small barks and one was a ship. With these they sailed to the west. With little trouble, they gained possession of Ledovo and Ilofe and other small islands in a gulf called Sudero, where they captured some small barks laden with salt fish in the harbour of the country called Sanestol.[7] Here they found Zichmni, who came by land with his army, conquering all the country as he went. They stayed here a little while. Making their course still westwards, they came to the far cape of the gulf, where they turned again and fell on certain islands and lands which they captured in the name of Zichmni. This sea through which they sailed was full of shoals and rocks, so that if Sir Nicolò and the Venetian seamen had not been their pilots, the whole fleet would have been lost in the opinion of all that were on it. Zichmni's men were so inexperienced in comparison with ours, who had been born, trained up, and grown old in the art of navigation.

Now the captain of the fleet took the advice of Sir Nicolò and determined to go ashore at a place called Bondendon, to learn what success Zichmni had had in his wars.[8] There they were satisfied to hear that he had fought a great battle and put to flight the army of the enemy. After this victory, ambassadors were sent from all parts of the island to yield the country into his hands, and their ensigns were taken down in every town and village.

So the seamen decided to stay where they were and wait for his coming, taking it for granted that he would be there very shortly. On his arrival there were great demonstrations of joy for the victory by land and by sea. For that, the Venetians received from all such great honour and praise that there was no talk but of them and of the great courage of Sir Nicolò. Then the chieftain, who loved valiant men, especially those who were skilled seamen, had Sir Nicolò brought before him. He honoured him with praise and complimented his great zeal and skill, and he acknowledged that he himself had received a very great benefit from the preservation of his fleet and the winning of so many places without any trouble. So he conferred on him the honour of knighthood and rewarded his men with very handsome presents. Leaving there, they went in triumph towards Frislanda, the chief city of the south-east of that island.[9] It lay inside a bay in which there is such great quantity of fish that many ships stow it to supply Flanders, Brittany, England, Scotland, Norway and Denmark. By this trade they gather great wealth.

So far my account is taken from a letter sent by Sir Nicolò to Sir Antonio, his brother, asking him to find some vessel to bring him out to him. Since Antonio had as great a desire as his brother to see the world and its various nations, and to make himself a great name, he bought a ship and directed his course that way. After a long voyage full of many dangers, he joined Sir Nicolò in safety and was received by him with great gladness, as his brother not only by blood, but also in courage.

Sir Antonio remained in Frislanda and lived there fourteen years, four years with Sir Nicolò, and ten years alone.[10] Here they won such grace and favour with the prince that, to gratify Sir Nicolò, and still more because he knew very well his value, he made him captain of his navy. With much warlike preparation they went out to attack Estlanda, which lies off the coast between Frislanda and Norway.[11] Here they did much damage, but hearing that the King of Norway was coming against them with a great fleet to draw them off from this attack, they left under such a terrible gale of wind, that they were driven upon certain shoals and a good many of their ships were wrecked. The remainder took shelter in Grislanda, a large island but uninhabited.[12] The King of Norway's fleet was caught in the same storm and utterly wrecked and lost in those seas.

When Zichmni heard the news of this from one of the enemy's ships that was driven by chance on Grislanda, he prepared his fleet. Knowing that the Islande lay not far off to the north, he determined to make an attack upon Islanda, which was subject to the King of Norway together with the rest.[13] Here, however, he found the country so well fortified and defended that he had to give up that enterprise since his fleet was small and badly equipped with weapons and men. He changed his attack to the other islands in those channels which are called Islande; they are seven in number, Talas, Broas, Iscant, Trans, Mimant, Dambere, and Bres.[14] After taking them all he built a fort in Bres, where he left Sir Nicolò with some small vessels and men and stores. Thinking that he had done enough for the present, he returned with those few ships that remained safely to Frislanda.

As Sir Nicolò was left behind in Bres, he resolved the next season to make an expedition with the view of discovering more land. He fitted out three small barks in the month of July and sailed towards the North and arrived in Engroneland.[15] Here he found a monastery of the Order of the Preaching Friars and a church dedicated to St Thomas by a hill which vomited fire like Vesuvius and Etna.[16] There is a spring of hot water there which is used to heat both the church of the monastery and the chambers of the Friars. The water comes up into the kitchen so boiling hot that they use no other fire to cook their food. They also put their bread into brass pots without any water, and it is baked as if it were in a hot oven. They also have small gardens covered over in the winter time, which are watered with this water and protected against the snow and the cold, very severe in those parts under the pole. By this method, they produce flowers and fruits and herbs of different kinds, just as in temperate countries in their seasons. Seeing these supernatural effects, the simple and savage local people take those Friars for Gods and bring them many presents of chickens and meat and other things, holding them as Lords in the greatest reverence and respect.

When the frost and snow are very great, the friars heat their houses in the same manner. By letting in the hot water or opening the windows, they can in an instant temper the heat and cold of a chamber at their pleasure. In the buildings of the monastery they use only the material which is supplied to them by the fire. For they take the burning stones cast out like cinders from the fiery mouth of the hill, and when these are at their hottest, they throw water on them and dissolve them into an excellent white lime, which is extremely tenacious and never decays when used in building. These cold clinkers are very serviceable in place of stones for making walls and arches; once chilled, they will never yield or break unless they are cut with some iron tool; and the arches built from them are so light that they need no strong support and last for ever in their beauty and consistency. These great advantages allow these good Friars to construct so many buildings and walls that it is curious to witness.

The roofs of their houses are usually made in the following manner: first, they raise up the wall to its full height; then they make it incline inwards, little by little, in the form of an arch, so that it forms an excellent passage for the rain in the middle. But they are not much threatened with rain, because the pole, as I have said, is extremely cold. When the first snow is fallen, it does not thaw again for nine months, the duration of their winter. They live on wild fowl and fish; for where the warm water falls into the sea, there is a large and wide harbour, which never freezes all the winter because of the heat. The result is that there is such an attraction for sea-fowl and fish that they are caught in unlimited quantity and support a large amount of people in the neighbourhood, who are employed in building, in catching birds and fish, and in a thousand other necessary occupations about the monastery.

Their houses are built about the hill on every side. They are round in form and twenty-five feet broad and they become narrower and narrower towards the top. At the summit there is a little hole, through which the air and light come into the house, and the ground below is so warm that those inside feel no cold at all. In summer time, many vessels come from the near islands and from the Cape above Norway and from Treadon.[17] They bring the Friars all sorts of comforts and take in exchange fish, which they dry in the sun or freeze, and skins of different kinds of animals. So the Friars obtain wood for burning and admirably carved timber and corn and cloth for clothes.

All the countries round about them are only too glad to trade with them for fish and furs; and so, without any trouble or expense, they have all that they want. To this monastery Friars resort from

Norway, Sweden, and other countries, but the greater part come from the Islande.[18] A number of vessels are detained continually in the harbour by the frozen sea; they have to wait for the next season and for the ice to melt.

The fishermen's boats are made like a weaver's shuttle. They take the skins of fish and stitch them with the bones of the same fish. Sewn together and doubled over, they become so sound and substantial that it is wonderful to see how the fishermen will shut themselves close inside in bad weather and expose themselves to the sea and the wind without the slightest fear of coming to grief. If they happen to be driven on any rocks, they can stand a good many bumps without receiving any injury. In the bottom of the boats they have a kind of sleeve, which is tied fast in the middle. When any water comes into the boat, they put it into one half of the sleeve, then close it above with two pieces of wood and open the band underneath, and so they drive the water out. They do this as often as they must, without any trouble or danger.

Moreover, as the water of the monastery contains sulphur, it is carried into the chambers of the principal Friars in vessels of brass or tin or stone. It is so hot that it heats the place like a stove without giving out any stench or offensive odour.

Besides, they have another method of conveying hot water by a conduit under the ground so that it should not freeze. It is taken into the middle of the court, where it falls into a large vessel of brass that stands in the middle of a boiling fountain. This heats their water for drinking and for watering their gardens. So they derive from the hill every comfort that can be wanted. These good Friars devote the greatest attention to the cultivation of their gardens and to the construction of handsome and spacious buildings. They are not short of ingenious and painstaking workmen for this purpose; for they are very liberal in their payments, and their generosity is unlimited to those who bring them fruits and seeds. Therefore, workmen and masters in different crafts resort there in plenty, attracted by the handsome pay and good living.

Most of them speak the Latin language, especially the superiors and principals of the monastery. This is all that is known of Engroneland as described by Sir Nicolò, who also gives a special description of a river that he discovered, as may be seen in the map that I have drawn. At length, Sir Nicolò, not being used to such severe cold, fell ill. After a while, he returned to Frislanda, where he died. [*In fact, he died in Venice*]

Sir Antonio succeeded him in his wealth and honours. Although he tried hard in various ways and begged and prayed most earnestly, he could never obtain permission to return to his own country. For as Zichmni was a man of great enterprise and daring, he had determined to make himself master of the sea. So he proposed to use the services of Sir Antonio by sending him out with a few small vessels to the west, because some of his fishermen had discovered certain very rich and populous islands in that direction. This discovery Sir Antonio relates in a letter to his brother Sir Carlo in detail in the following manner, except we have changed some of the old words and the antiquated style, but we have left the substance entirely as it was.

Twenty-six years ago four fishing boats put out to sea and encountered a heavy storm. They were driven over the sea utterly helpless for many days. When the tempest died at last, they discovered an island called Estotilanda lying to the west over one thousand miles from Frislanda.[19] One of the boats was wrecked, and the six men in it were taken by the inhabitants and brought to a fair and populous city, where the king of the place sent for many interpreters. None could be found that understood the language of the fishermen, except one that spoke Latin, who had also been cast by chance on the same island. Speaking for the king he asked them who they were and where they came from; and when he relayed their answer, the king wanted them to remain in the country. As they could not do otherwise, they obeyed his command and stayed five years on the island and learned the language. One of them in particular visited different parts of the island

and reported that it was a very rich country, abundant in all good things. It is a little smaller than Islanda, but more fertile.[20] In the middle of it is a very high mountain, from which rise four rivers which water the whole country.

The inhabitants are very intelligent people and possess all the arts as we do. It is believed that in time past they have had dealings with our people, for he said that he saw in the king's library Latin books, which they do not now understand. They have their own language and letters. They have all kinds of metals, but especially they are rich in gold. Their foreign connections are with Engroneland, to which they export furs, sulphur and pitch.[21] He says that towards the south there is a great and populous country, very rich in gold. They sow corn and make beer, which is a kind of drink that northern people take as we do wine. They have woods of immense extent. They make their buildings with walls, and there are many towns and villages. They make small boats and sail them, but they have not the lodestone, and they do not know the north by compass bearing.

For this reason these fishermen were highly valued, and the king sent them with twelve boats to the south to a country which they called Drogio.[22] On their voyage they met contrary winds and were in fear for their lives. Although they escaped one cruel death, they fell into another even crueller. For they were taken and most of them eaten by savages, who were cannibals and considered human flesh as very savoury meat.

Yet as our fisherman and his remaining companions could show them how to catch fish with nets, their lives were saved. Every day he would go fishing in the sea and in the fresh water and catch a great amount of fish, which he gave to the chiefs. So he grew into favour and he was very much liked and held in great consideration by everybody.

As this man's fame spread through the surrounding tribes, a neighbouring chief became very anxious to have him and see how he practised his wonderful art of catching fish. Therefore he made war on the chief who had the fisherman, and as he was more

powerful and a better warrior, he overcame him in the end. So the
fisherman was sent over to him with the rest of his company.
During the thirteen years he lived in those parts, he says that he was
sent to more than twenty-five chiefs. They were continually
fighting among themselves, this chief with that and only with
the purpose of having the fisherman to live with them. Forced to
wander up and down the country without any fixed home, he
became acquainted with almost all that land.

He says that it is a very great country and, as it were, *a new world*.
The people are very simple and uncultivated, for they all go naked
and suffer cruelly from the cold. They do not have the sense to
clothe themselves with the skins of the animals which they take in
hunting. They have no kind of metal. They live by the chase and
carry lances of wood, sharpened at the point. They have bows, the
strings of which are made of beasts' skins. They are very fierce and
have deadly fights among themselves and eat one another's flesh.
They have chieftains and certain laws, but these differ from tribe to
tribe. The farther you go south-west, however, the more refinement you meet, because the climate is more temperate. There they
have cities and temples dedicated to their idols, in which they
sacrifice men and afterwards eat them. In those parts they have some
knowledge and use of gold and silver.

After having lived so many years in these parts, this fisherman
made up his mind, if possible, to return home to his own
country. His companions were in despair of ever going home
again, but they bade him Godspeed and stayed where they
were. He said farewell and made his escape through the woods
in the direction of Drogio, where he was welcome and
acceptable to its chief, who knew him and was a great enemy
of the neighbouring chieftain. Again passing through the
hands of the same chiefs, after a long time and with much
hardship, he at last reached Drogio, where he spent three
years. Here by good luck he heard from the natives that some
boats had arrived off the coast. Full of hope at being able to

make his escape, he went down to the seaside and was delighted to find that they had come from Estotilanda. He asked them to take him with them, which they did very willingly. And as he knew the language of the country, which none of them could speak, they employed him as their interpreter.

Afterwards he traded in their company so well that he became very rich and fitted out a vessel of his own and returned to Frislanda. Then he gave an account of the rich countries he had seen to this nobleman [St Clair]. His sailors had had much experience in hearing strange tales and fully believed what they heard. This nobleman is now determined to send me out with a fleet towards those parts. There are so many that want to join in the expedition on account of the novelty and strangeness of the thing, that I think we shall be very well equipped, without any public expense at all.

Such is the tenor of the letter I referred to, which I have set out here in detail in order to throw light upon another voyage which was made by Sir Antonio. He set sail with many vessels and men, but he was not the commander, as he had expected to be. For Zichmni went himself. And I have a letter describing that enterprise, which reads:

Our great preparations for the voyage to Estotilanda began unluckily. For exactly three days before our departure, our fisherman and our guide died. Yet Zichmni would not give up the enterprise, but instead of the deceased fisherman, he took some sailors that had come out with him from the island. Steering west, we discovered some islands subject to Frislanda, and passing by certain shoals, we came to Ledovo, where we stayed seven days to rest and restock the fleet.[23]

After leaving there we arrived on the first of July at the Island of Ilofe, and as the wind was fair, we pushed on.[24] Not long after, when we were on the open sea, so great a storm arose that we were continuously working for eight days and driven we knew not where, while many of the boats were lost. At length, when the storm abated, we gathered the scattered boats and sailed with a prosperous wind to discover land to the west. Steering straight for it, we reached a quiet and safe harbour, but there we saw an infinite number of armed people, who came running furiously down to the waterside to defend the island.

Zichmni now caused his men to make signs of peace to them, and they sent ten men to us who could speak ten languages, but we could understand none of them except one that was from Islanda.[25] This interpreter was brought before our prince and asked what was the name of the island and what people inhabited it and who was the governor. He answered that the island was called Icaria, and that all the kings who reigned there were called Icari, after the first king, who was the son of Daedalus, King of Scotland.[26] When he had conquered that island, he had left his son there as king and had given them those laws that they still keep. After this on a further voyage, he was drowned in a great tempest. In memory of his death, that sea was yet called the Icarian Sea and the kings of the island were called Icari. They were contented with the state which God had given them, and they would neither alter their laws nor admit any stranger.

Therefore they asked our prince not to attempt to interfere with their laws, which they had received from that king of noble memory and had observed up to the present time. The attempt would lead to his own destruction, for they were all prepared to die rather than relax in any way the use of those laws. Yet they did not wish us to think that they altogether refused to meet other men. They ended up saying that they would willingly take in one of our people and give him an honourable position among them, if only for the sake of learning our language and finding out about our customs. They had already received people from ten different countries, who had come into their island.

To all this our prince made no reply beyond enquiring where there was a good harbour and making signs that he wanted to depart. Sailing round the island, he sent all his fleet in full sail into a harbour which he found on the eastern side. The sailors went on shore to take in wood and water, which they did as quickly as they could, for fear they might be attacked by the islanders. And indeed, the inhabitants did make signals to their neighbours with fire and smoke, and took to their arms with more coming to their aid. They all came running down to the seaside to attack our men with bows and arrows, so that many were slain and several wounded. Although we made signs of peace to them, it was no use. Their fury increased more and more, as though they were fighting for their very existence.

Forced to depart, we sailed in a great circle round the island, always followed on the hill tops and along the sea coasts by an infinite number of armed men. Doubling the north cape of the island, we came upon many shoals, among which we spent ten days in continual danger of losing our whole fleet; but fortunately the weather kept very fine. All the way until we came to the east cape, we saw the islanders still on the hill tops and by the sea coast, keeping up with us and howling and shooting at us from a distance to show their hatred of us. So we resolved to put into some safe harbour and see if we might once again speak with the interpreter, but we failed in our object. For the people were more like beasts than men and stood always prepared to beat us back if we should attempt to come on land.

When Zichmni saw that he could do nothing, he realized the fleet would fall short of provisions if he were to persevere in his attempt. So he took a fair wind and sailed six days to the west; but when the wind shifted to the south-west and the sea became rough, we sailed four days with the wind aft. Then at last we discovered land. As the sea ran high and we did not know what country it was, we were afraid at first to approach it. But by God's blessing, the wind lulled, and then a great calm came on. Some of the crew then pulled ashore and soon returned with the joyful news that they had found an excellent country and a still better harbour. So we brought our barks and our boats in to land, and we entered an excellent harbour, and we saw in the distance a great mountain that poured out smoke. This gave us hope that we should find some inhabitants in the island. Although it was a great way off, Zichmni would not rest without sending a hundred soldiers to explore the country, and bring an account of what sort of people the inhabitants were.

Meanwhile, we took on a store of wood and water and caught a considerable quantity of fish and sea-fowl. We also found such a quantity of birds' eggs that our men, who were famished, ate of them until they were stuffed full. While we were at anchor here, the month of June came in, and the air in the island was mild and pleasant beyond description. Yet as we saw nobody, we began to suspect that this pleasant place was uninhabited. We gave the name of Trin to the harbour and the headland which stretched out into the sea we called Capo di Trin.[27] After eight days the hundred soldiers returned and told us that they had been through the island and up to the mountain. The smoke naturally came from a great fire in the bottom of the hill, and there was a spring giving out a certain matter like pitch which ran into the sea, and there were great multitudes of people, half-wild and living in caves.[28] These were very small of stature and very timid; for as soon as they saw our people, they fled into their holes. Our men also reported that there was a large river nearby and a very good and safe harbour.[29]

When Zichmni heard this and noticed that the place had a wholesome and pure atmosphere, a fertile soil and good rivers and so many other attractions, he conceived the idea of staying there and founding a city. But his people had passed through a voyage so full of hardship that they began to murmur, saying that they wished to return to their own homes. The winter was not far off, and if they allowed it to set in, they would not be able to get away before the following summer. He therefore kept only the rowboats and those people who were willing to stay with him, and he sent all the rest away in the ships. He appointed me against my will to be their captain. I had no choice, and so I departed and sailed twenty days to the east without sighting any land. Then I turned my course towards the south-east and reached land in five days and found myself on the island of Neome.[30] Knowing the country, I saw I was past Islanda, and as the inhabitants were subject to Zichmni, I took in fresh stores and sailed with a fair wind in three days to Frislanda.[31] The people there thought they had lost their prince because of his long absence on the voyage we had made. So they gave us a hearty welcome.

What happened afterwards I do not know beyond what I gather from a piece of another letter, which maintains that Zichmni settled down in the harbour of his newly discovered island and explored the whole of the country thoroughly as well as the coasts on both sides of Greenland. I know this because of the particular details on the sea charts; but the description is lost. The beginning of the letter runs like this:

Those things you want to know from me about the people and their habits, the animals and the countries nearby, I have written in a separate book, which, please God, I shall bring with me. In it I have described the country, the monstrous fishes, the customs and laws of Frislanda, of Islanda, of Estlanda, of the Kingdom of Norway, of Estotilanda and Drogio. Lastly I have written the life of our brother, Nicolò the Chevalier, with the discovery he made and all about Engroneland. I have also written the life and exploits of Zichmni, a prince who deserves immortal memory as much as any man that ever lived for his great bravery and remarkable goodness. In it I have described the survey of Greenland on both sides and the city that he founded. But I will say no more of this in this letter. I hope to be with you very shortly and to satisfy your curiosity on other things by word of mouth.

All these letters were written by Sir Antonio to Sir Carlo his brother. I am sorry that the book and much else on these subjects have, I don't know how, been destroyed. For I was only a child when they fell into my hands, and as I did not know what they were, I tore them in pieces, as children will do, and ruined them. It is something which I cannot now recall without the greatest sorrow. Nevertheless, in order that such an important memoir should not be lost, I have put it all in order as well as I could in this Narrative. More than its predecessors, the present age may derive pleasure from the great discoveries made in those parts where they were least expected. For our age takes a great interest in new narratives and in the discoveries, made in countries unknown before, by the high courage and great energy of our ancestors.

Notes

1. Twice a year, two Venetian ships sailed to Flanders to trade.
2. Possibly Fer of Fair Isle between Orkney and the Shetland Isles, although Frislanda on the *Zeno Map* refers to the Faroe Islands.
3. The *Zeno Narrative* and *Map* both gave the date of Nicolò Zen's voyage as ten years too early. Marco Barbaro, however, who wrote of this voyage twenty-two years before the publication of the *Zeno Narrative*, gave the correct date of 1390, as did the globe world map of 1697 in the Corror Museum.
4. Portlanda refers to Pentland, which is called Podanda on the *Zeno Map*.
5. Zichmni is St Clair. Marco Barbaro previously called the Scottish prince Zieno, much closer phonetically to a chieftain who spoke his name in Latin, SANCTO CLARO, spelt it as SAN CLO, and would have pronounced it as ZINCLO. Although the spelling in the *Zeno Narrative* is inaccurate, the Scottish Prince can only be Henry St Clair, First Earl of Orkney and Prince of Norway.
6. Sorano refers to Caithness.
7. Lille Dimon and Skuoe and Sudero Fjord and Sandoe in the Faroe Isles.
8. Bondendon refers to the harbour of Norderdahl.
9. Thorshaven. In the Middle Ages, the capital of an island was often given the name of that island or group of islands.
10. The Zen brothers would have lived on the Orkneys, for Prince Henry St Clair did not succeed in holding the Faroes for long.
11. Estlanda is Shetland.
12. Grislanda is Grossey in the Orkneys. The enemy fleet was not that of the King of Norway, but of Baltic raiders of the Hanseatic League.
13. Islande and Islanda are again the Shetlands and Shetland.
14. The seven islands are now called Yell, Barras, Unst, Fetlar, Mousa, Whalsay and Bressay, where the sea-fortress was built.
15. Greenland.
16. St Thomas refers to St Olavus (St Olaf) on Gael Hamke Bay.
17. Treadon is Trondheim.

18. Islande are the Shetlands.
19. Estotilanda refers to Nova Scotia in Canada.
20. Islanda is Shetland or Iceland.
21. Engroneland is Greenland. There was certainly trade as far as the Norse colony at L'Anse aux Meadows in Newfoundland at this time, and to Markland in Labrador or Nova Scotia.
22. By its description, Drogio probably refers to the Caribbean Islands and the Aztec empire in Mexico.
23. Ledovo refers to Lille Dimon in the Faroes.
24. Ilofe refers to Skuoe in the Faroes.
25. Islanda is Shetland.
26. The mythical Icaria in the *Zeno Narrative* and *Map* is a reason to doubt the veracity of both. But Richard Henry Major gives a most convincing explanation, that the author Nicolò Zeno mixed up two letters home from his ancestor Antonio, the first of which described an earlier reconnaissance expedition to St Kilda or Kerry in Ireland. The characteristics and customs of the people there at that time correspond with the descriptions given of them, while the myth of Daedalus, King of Scotland, was current in Celtic medieval legend. Even the chief opponent of the truth of the *Zeno Narrative*, F.W. Lucas, admitted that Icaria referred to St Kilda, formerly called Hirta or Irte, a contraction of the Gaelic *h-Iartir*.
27. Pohl gives convincing reasons that the harbour and cape were called Trin because the expedition reached the New World on Trinity Sunday. Our researches and the discovery of the Venetian cannon and spring and circular fortress base at Louisburg on Cape Breton Island make us identify it as Trin Harbour.
28. Cape Smokey is evidently the smoking mountain, while coal seams exuding pitchy and oily substances run into the sea for thirty miles north of Louisburg towards Cape Smokey. There are Indian sacred caves near the coast, and there are still four Micmac Indian reservations round Lake Bras d'Or.
29. St Peter's was the other harbour where a Venetian cannon like that at Louisburg was discovered, but destroyed. Micmac legend tells of white settlers before the French, who also chose Louisburg and St Peter's as the sites of their first two settlements.
30. Neome is possibly Westray in the Orkneys, subject to Prince Henry St Clair.
31. The Faroes and Thorshaven.

Notes

1. A Quest

I AM DEEPLY indebted for my interpretation of Rosslyn Chapel to its curator, Judith Fisken. I am also most grateful to Robert Brydon, the expert on the Templars in Scotland, for his wise insights. Professor Jeffrey Barrow, a leader in medieval studies, literally went down on his knees to verify that the Lombard lettering and the hilt of a sword on a stone dated from the first part of the fourteenth century: the dating of the hilt was corroborated by the Armoury of the Tower of London. On the architecture and restoration of Rosslyn Chapel, James Simpson and Edwina Proudfoot were useful. But I am most indebted in every way to Niven Sinclair, who always believed in the Templar connection to the St Clairs, and whose support and good advice have been unflagging, and who commissioned Marianna Lines, the expert at cloth impressions who brought out the Grail on the stone.

Dr W.W. Wescott in his *Miscellanea Latomorum, xxviii*, no. 5, 1944, gives the excerpt about the Shamir from an 'old ritual' of the Masons: the tradition certainly existed in the 'Old York ritual'. Alexander Horne, a Thirty-third Degree Mason of the Ancient and Accepted Scottish Rite, writes well on the Shamir legend in his *King Solomon's Temple in the Masonic Tradition* (London, 1972), pp. 165–7. There is mention of the stone-splitting worm Shamir as early as the fourteenth century in the *Polychronicon* of Ranulf Higden, manuscript in Huntingdon Library, Pasadena, California.

In the Orphic gnostic tradition, naked members of the cult worshipped a sacred winged serpent. A bowl depicting the rite is recorded in Emma Jung, *The Grail Legend* (Boston, 1968). As Hippolytus says in his *Elenchos*: 'Now no one can be saved and rise up again without the Son, who is the serpent.' Through Arabic sources, Gnostic cult objects reached Spain and the South of France. *Coffrets gnostiques*, boxes portraying naked initiates, were prevalent in Provence in the twelfth and thirteenth centuries, when the *cathari*, the pure ones, preached their faith.

2. Venice and the Zens

All enquiries into the Crusaders still begin and end with Sir Stephen Runciman's *A History of the Crusades* (3 vols., Cambridge, 1951–1954). Generally useful on the subject are Zoé Oldenburg, *The Crusades* (London, 1966); Richard Barber, *The Knight and Chivalry* (London, 1970); and Amin Maalouf, *The Crusades Through Arab Eyes* (London, 1984). The reference to the Norse Crusade of 1152 from the Orkneys is taken from Riant, *Expeditions et Pélérinages des Scandinaves en Terre Sainte* (Paris, 1865), pp. 248–50.

According to the German historian Wilcke, the other six Templar founding knights were Roral, Gundemar, Godfrey Birol, Payens de Montidier, Archibald de St Aman and Andrew de Montbar. The unreliable William de Tyre gives 1118 as the date of the founding of the Templars. However, Michael Baigent, Richard Leigh and Henry Lincoln, in *The Holy Blood and the Holy Grail* (London, 1982), pp. 56–9, make a convincing case for an earlier and secret date for its founding by Hugh de Payens, the first Grand Master of the Order, and for the recruitment of many new Templars, certainly the Count of Champagne, before the successful European tour of de Payens in 1128, which enabled him to return to Jerusalem 2 years later with 300 knights. The swift expansion of the Templars in men and resources would have been difficult without an earlier beginning. The letter to the Master of the Temple in France of 1267 is quoted in Stephen W.R. Howarth, *The Knights Templar* (London, 1982), pp. 223–4.

For the early history of the Zen family, I am indebted to Philip M. Giraldi, *The Zen Family (1500–1550): Patrician Office Holding in Renaissance Venice* (PhD Thesis, London Univ., 1975). His bibliography is essential. The Zen family once had an extensive archive, but little of its material survives. What does is preserved in the *Archivio Zen* of the library of the Museo Correr. In *Venezia e la sua laguna* (vol. I, Venice, 1847), pp. 60–1, the archive of Count Pietro Zen is described, but few of these manuscripts can now be traced. There is a list of young patricians serving on the Great Council – the *Barbarelli* – in the *Arogadori da Comun, Ballo d'Oro*, from 1414 to 1544, also recorded in the *Raccolta dei Consegi* in the library of the Museo Marciana. Also useful on the later Zen family is the *Libro d'Oro*, the proof of nobility, kept from 1506 in *Archivio di Stato*. Marco Barbaro, in his *Libro di nozze, 1380–1568*, relates in 64 manuscripts the history of Venetian noble families of the sixteenth century. His account of the Zen family is in the Marciana Library, Mss Italiani, Cl. 7, No. 928, Coll. 8597, under entry 1216. Frank J. Swetz, *Capitalism and Arithmetic* (La Salle, Illinois, 1987) is essential reading on the importance of Treviso in Venetian northern trade, and contains a full translation of the *Treviso Arithmetic* of 1478.

Admiral Gottardo, the head of the Museo Storico Navale in Venice, confirmed to the author that the *petriera* was used by Carlo Zen at the battle of Chioggia and was manufactured between 1370 and 1400, after which it became obsolete. The effigy of the crowned knight is on one of Vavassatore's engravings of 1558, taken from Caspar Vopell of Cologne's world map of 1545 (the only surviving copy is in the Houghton Library at Harvard University). Nicolò Zeno published *Dello Scoprimento dell' Isole FRISLANDA, ESLANDA, ENGRONELANDA, ESTOTILANDA, & ICARIA, fatto per due fratelli ZENI, M. Nicolò il Cavaliere, & M. Antonio. Libro Uno, col disegno di dette Isole* in Venice in 1558, the same year as the Vavassatore engravings of the Vopell map. It was republished for the Hakluyt Society in a bilingual version in 1873, edited with an introduction and end matter by Richard H. Major, who was convinced of the arguments for its authenticity apart from the author's obvious invention of Icaria. The important work on the relationship of Venice with Constantinople is Donald W. Nicol's *Byzantium and Venice: A Study in Diplomatic and Cultural Relations* (Cambridge, 1988).

Nothing makes the long connection of the Zen family with the Military Knights more clear than the later career of Pietro Zen, a Venetian ambassador to Damascus in the early sixteenth century. At that time, the Turks had taken Constantinople, the Mamelukes controlled Egypt, the Sofi of Persia threatened the Levant, while Rhodes was still held by the Hospitallers and Venice retained only Cyprus and Crete and some of the Greek islands. Pietro Zen secretly corresponded with the Grand Master of the Order in Rhodes, telling him of rich fleets sailing from Alexandria to Beirut and Constantinople. Acting on this information, the Knights of St John attacked the Muslim ships and destroyed them. As a result, Pietro Zen was put in chains in Cairo and nearly executed, although he denied plotting with the knights and the Sofi of Persia, who was his cousin and wanted Venetian artillery. An embassy from Venice secured his release, but he was sent on another mission to Constantinople, after the Turkish Sultan had captured Rhodes and expelled the last surviving Hospitallers.

As with all envoys, Pietro Zen was sent abroad to lie and inform. He kept the Senate in Venice posted on all movements by Turkish armies and fleets. On his return to Venice, he served in the Council of Ten and constructed a new family palace near the church in the parish of Crosichieri. He kept in contact with the Hospitallers, who had taken over the Templar presbytery by San Georgio di Schiavoni: it is still in the possession of the Knights of St John or Malta. Pietro Zen continued to be sent on missions to the Near East until the age of eighty and to supply the Hospitallers, now established in Malta, with news of Muslim shipping, which they attacked repeatedly, thus contesting Muslim domination of the eastern Mediterranean.

3. The Knights of the Sword, the Trowel and the Grail

Arnold of Villanova wrote about the Circle and the Stone of the Philosophers. L. J. Ringbom, *Graltempel und Paradies* (Stockholm, 1951), is invaluable on the connections of the Grail Castle with oriental thought and architecture. Some of its theories were first put forward in L.E. Iselin, *Der morgenländische Ursprung der Graalslegende* (Halle, 1909). See also the stimulating work of P. Ponsoye, *L'Islam et le Graal* (Paris, 1957).

The sanctuary of Sacred Fire at Shîz was rebuilt under the Muslim rule of the successors of Genghis Khan, and is still venerated by the Parsees. One of these successors, Abaka Kahan, took the title of 'Priest-king John' or Prester John, the reputed son of the Grail King's daughter in *Parzifal* and final guardian of the Grail. *The Young Titurel* also stresses the legend of Prester John.

The Arab commentators on the sack of Jerusalem were Ibn al-Athār and Ibn-al Qalānisi. Both are quoted in an admirable counterview by Amin Maalouf, *The Crusades Through Arab Eyes* (London, 1984). The most accessible collection of texts is edited and translated by Francesco Gabrieli, *Arab Historians of the Crusades* (London, 1969).

O. Rahn, *Kreuzzug gegen den Graal* (Fribourg, 1933), tries to prove that the Grail was a cult object of the Cathars, whose beliefs inspired all the Grail romances. The connection of Montségur and Provence with the Grail and the secret dynasty of the Priory of Zion is alleged forcefully in Baigent, Leigh and Lincoln, *The Holy Blood and the Holy Grail*, (London, 1982), where there is a confusion between the *Sangreal*, the Holy Grail, and the *Sang Real*, or Royal Blood. There is no real connection, particularly not to a bloodline supposed to descend through the House of Anjou back to the offspring of a union between Jesus Christ and Mary Magdalene.

4. The Blood of the Holy Light

The two indispensable sources on the early history of the St Clair family are Father Richard Augustine Hay, *Genealogie of the Sainteclaires of Rosslyn* (Edinburgh, 1835), and Roland William Saint-Clair, *The Saint-Clairs of the Isles* (Auckland, 1898). Hay is the source of the quotations on the early St Clairs. T.M. Gilbert, in his *Hunting and Hunting Reserves in Medieval Scotland* (Edinburgh, 1979), speaks of the Bruce grants in Contentin and the St Clair grants near Cérisy. L.-A. de Saint Clair, *Histoire Généalogique de la Famille de Saint Clair et de ses Alliances (France-Ecosse)* (Paris, 1869), is vital on the early history of the family. The marriage of Walderne de St Clair to Helena, a daughter of Richard III, the Fifth Duke of Normandy, is asserted by J. Van Bassan in his unreliable account of the early St Clair family, reprinted by Hay and R.W. Saint-Clair.

Gordon Donaldson, in 'The Contemporary Scene', the excellent introductory essay to the magisterial *St. Magnus Cathedral and Orkney's Twelfth Century Renaissance* (Barbara E. Crawford, ed., Aberdeen, 1988), rightly identifies King Malcolm's first wife Ingibjorg as Thorfinn's daughter, not his widow. The quotation about the curative powers of St Katherine's balm well comes from Bishop Lesley, *History of Scotland* (Edinburgh, 1578). I am again indebted to Robert Brydon, the Scottish Templar archivist, for his researches into the early history of the St Clair family in Scotland.

5. The Fall of the Templars

The testimony of John de Châlons is quoted in Heinrich Finke, *Papsttum und Untergang des Templerordens* (2 vols., Münster, 1907), vol. 2, p. 339. On pages 74–5 of his second volume, Finke prints the list of escaped Templar Knights, given in documents in the Bibliothèque Nationale, Cod. Lat. 10919, fol. 84 and 236. It states that Gerard de Villiers fled with forty knights, but twelve others escaped, notably Hugh de Châlons and Imbert Blanc, who was in England. The best assessment of the Templar escape to Scotland is to be found in Michael Baigent and Richard Leigh, *The Temple and the Lodge* (London, 1989). They discovered the Templar graves in Argyll and at Athlit, but they ignore the probable arrival of part of the Templar fleet in the Firth of Forth near their estates and the Seton and St Clair lands. A. Bothwell-Gosse, a Mason of the Eighteenth Grade, published the invaluable *The Knights Templar* (London, 1912). The Scottish Templars still exist, and some of their lodges admit women. The author is expert in her knowledge of Masonic tradition in Scotland and Templar symbolism and vocabulary. I am indebted to Richard Barber, *The Knight and Chivalry* (London, 1970), for his excellent descriptions of the Teutonic Knights and the Knights of Calatrava.

Invaluable on the fall of the Templars is Baigent, Leigh and Lincoln, *The Holy Blood and the Holy Grail* (London, 1982). Also useful are Gérard Serbanesco, *Histoire de l'Ordre des Templiers* (Paris, 1970); and Stephen W.R. Howarth, *The Knights Templar* (London, 1912). The episode of the punishment for the outbreak of sodomy is told in the copy of the Rule reprinted in Henri de Curzon, *La Règle du Temple* (Paris, 1886).

6. The Search for the Stones

The *Chronicle of Melrose*, which runs from 1175 to 1275 approximately, is preserved in the British Library. A copy is on display in the Commendator's House at Melrose Abbey. Mr T. White wrote to *The Gentleman's Magazine*, 1789, vol. I, pp. 337–8, of the exhumation of the Templar Knight at Danbury. I am indebted to Andrew Collins for showing me the church of St John the Baptist at Danbury and writing *The Knights of Danbury* (Wickford, Essex, 1985). W.E. Aytoun's poem 'The Heart of Bruce' was based on the account of the death of the Scottish knights after the battle of Theba in Spain in 1328, given in Balfour's *Annals*. The ballad of 'Help and Hold' was written by G.J. Whyte-Melville and is reproduced in the invaluable R.W. Saint-Clair, *The Saint-Clairs of the Isles* (Auckland, 1898). The excavations at Soutra are being conducted under the supervision of Dr Brian Moffat, whose organization of 700 experts works under the acronym of SHARP, 36 Hawthornvale, Edinburgh EH6 4JN. The two gravestones at Old Pentland were drawn in 1879 and reported by Thomas Arnold to the Society of Antiquarians in Scotland in their *Proceedings*, 8 December 1879.

Sir Gilbert Hay's translations of *The Buke of the Law of Armys* and *The Buke of the Ordre of Knychthude* and *The Buke of the Governance of Princes* are in manuscript in the National Library of Scotland, taken over from the old Advocates Library. In the Midlothian County Library are copies of the *Registrum Ecclesie Collegiae of Midlothian* and the *Registrum S. Marie de Neubotle, Abbacie Cisterciensis, 1140–1528* (Edinburgh, 1849), which attest to the close connections between the St Clairs of Roslin, the Cistercian monks and the Templars. They are confirmed from the same source by the *Munimenta de Melros*, the documents from Melrose Abbey between the twelfth and sixteenth centuries.

7. Finding the Grail

For an interpretation of the Grail, I am much indebted to the remarkable work of Emma Jung, completed by Marie-Louise von Franz, *The Grail Legend* (Boston, 1986), from which I quote about the *Queste del Saint Graal*, p. 103. Most useful is the introduction by Ruth Harwood Cline to her translation of *Perceval* by Chrétien de Troyes (Athens, Georgia, 1985).

Eleanor of Aquitaine may have also inspired an earlier, lost Grail romance by the troubadour Rigaut de Barbezieux, who wrote before 1160: 'Just as Perceval, when he was alive, was lost in wonder at the sight, so that he could never ask what purpose the lance and grail served, so I likewise, *Mielhs de Domna* (arguably Eleanor of Aquitaine), for I forget all when I gaze on you.' See Rita Lejeune, 'The Troubadours', *Arthurian Literature in the Middle Ages* (R.S. Loomis, ed., Oxford, 1969).

In his illustrated *The Grail: Quest for the Eternal* (London, 1981), John Matthews is searching on the religious tolerance expressed in *Parzifal*, although he omits to mention its occasional anti-Semitism. As he points out, Feirefis married the daughter of the Grail King, and their son was Prester John, the fabled Christian King of Africa, who ruled over his subjects with a sceptre of emerald and became another legendary guardian of the Grail.

It is possible that the author of the original *Perceval*, Chrétien de Troyes, may have visited England, because Henry de Blois, the uncle of his patron Count Henry of Champagne, also became Abbot of Glastonbury and Bishop of Winchester as well as being a notable patron of the arts. An early knightly romance by Chrétien, *Cligès*, does show a great deal of geographical knowledge about England, including the location of London, Oxford, Dover, Southampton, Windsor, Canterbury and Winchester. Of course, the Norman royal family of England had many French connections.

A Scottish Templar pamphlet by James E. Craik, *The Templars and the Holy Shroud* (Stirling, 1987), is useful on the Mandylion at Temple Combe. When the Holy Lance of Longinus was discovered during the First Crusade, the Byzantines incorporated it also into their liturgy in memory of St John Chrysostom. The priest struck the host with the Holy Lance, and quoted St John's Gospel, 'One of the soldiers pierced His side with a spear, and at once there came out blood and water.' The Victorian author of *The Rosicrucians: Their Rites and Mysteries* was Hargrave Jennings, who published his scattershot of revelations in two volumes in London in 1887.

The royal succession by blood royal or of those anointed on Jacob's Pillar or the Stone of Destiny was held to derive from Jacob and to include the following:

Ten Chieftains of the Tribe of Judah
Judah, Phares, Hezron, Aram, Aminadab, Naashon, Salmon, Boaz, Obed, Jesse.

Two Kings of Israel
David, Solomon.

Nineteen Kings of Judah
Rehoboam, Abijah, Asa, Jehoshaphat, Jehoram, Ahaziah, Joash, Amaziah, Uzziah, Jotham, Ahaz, Hezekiah, Manasseh, Amon, Josiah, Jehoahaz, Jehoiakim, Jehoia-chin, Zedekiah, whose daughter Tamar Tephi married.

Fifty-six Ardaths or High Kings of Ireland
Eochaidh the First, Irial Faidh, Eithriall, Follain, Tighernmas, Eanbotha, Smiorguil, Fiachadh Labhruine, Aongus Oilbhuagach, Maoin, Rotheachta, Dein, Siorna Saoghalach, Oiliolla Olchaoin, Giallchadh, Nuadha Fionn Fail, Simon Breac, Muriadhach Bolgrach, Fiachadh Tolgrach, Duach Laighrach, Eochaidh Buillaig, Ugaine More the Great, Cobhthach Caolbreag, Meilage, Jaran Gleofathach, Conla Cruaich, Cealgach, Oiliolla Caisfhiaclach, Eochaid Foltleathan, Aongus Tuirimheach, Eanda Aighnach, Labhra Luire, Blathachta, Eamhna, Easamhuin Eamhna, Roighneim Ruadh, Finlogha, Finn, Eochaidh Feidhlioch, Bias Fineamhnas, Lughaidh Riebdearg, Criomhthan Niadhnar, Fioraidhach Fionfachtnach, Fiachadh Fionchudh, Tuathal Teachtman, Feidh-limhioh Reachtmar, Conn Ceadchadhach, Art Aonfhir, Cormac Ulfhada, Cairbre Liffeachaire, Fiachadh Streabhthuine, Muirreadhach Tireach, Eochaidh Moihmeodhain, Niall of the Nine Hostages, Eogan, Mureadhach (who married Earca).

Fourteen Kings of Argyll
Fergus More, Dongard, Conran, Constantine the First, Aidan, Eugene the Third, Donald, Dongard the Second, Eugene the Fourth, Findan, Eugene the Fifth, Ethafind, Achaias, Alpin.

These Sovereigns were followed by 38 kings and queens of Scotland, from Kenneth MacAlpin to Mary, Queen of Scots, and 16 kings and queens of Great Britain, from James VI of Scotland and I of England to Elizabeth the II. Edward VIII was omitted because he refused consecration and coronation on the sacred stone at Westminster.

In 'Notes on the Library of the Sinclairs of Rosslyn', 14 February 1898, Professor

H.J. Lawlor testifies to the St Clair manuscripts in my text. I am indebted to the Scottish Templar Archivist Robert Bryden for his analysis of the binding on the Rosslyn-Hay Manuscript, also for the copy of the extract from *Orcades Seu Rerum Orcadensium* regarding the testimony of Thomas, Bishop of Orkney and Zetland, to Eric, King of Norway, in 1446. The biographer of the St Clair family is R.W. Saint-Clair in *The Saint-Clair of the Isles* (Auckland, 1898).

Michael Davidson is the American Master Mason who visited Rosslyn Chapel in 1991. Elaine Pagels, *Adam, Eve and the Serpent* (New York, 1988), is an authority on Gnostic teaching and provides the quotation from the early Christian *Testimony of Truth*. The old Masonic ritual is quoted in W.W. Westcott, *Miscellanea Latomorum*, *xxviii*, no. 5, 1944; and in Alexander Horne, *King Solomon's Temple in the Masonic Tradition* (London, 1972). The arms of Prince Henry St Clair are taken from the *Armorial de Gelre, 1369–1388*, an early work of heraldry in the Bibliothèque Royale, Brussels. My translation of *Parzifal* derives from that of Jessie L. Weston, published in London in 1894.

On the Grail at Rosslyn, see Walter Johannes Stein, *The Death of Merlin* (New York, 1989), and Trevor Ravenscroft and T. Wallace-Murphy, *The Mark of the Beast* (London, 1990). See also the Scottish *Daily Express* of 13 and 14 June 1962.

8. Green Men and Medicine

William T. Stearn, *Botanical Latin: History, Grammar, Syntax, Terminology and Vocabulary* (3rd rev. ed., London, 1983), sums up the language of the garden. Arturo Castiglioni, *A History of Medicine* (2nd rev. ed., New York, 1947), is authoritative on early medical practice; Howard W. Haggard *Devils, Drugs, and Doctors* (London, 1929), is stimulating and contentious: he gives the quotations from Hippocrates. Donald Campbell, *Arabian Medicine and Its Influence on the Middle Ages* (2 vols., London, 1926), rightly stresses the importance of Islamic medicine in the period between classical Greece and early modern Europe.

J.C. Squire, *Medieval Gardens* (2 vols., London, 1924), is essential on its subject. It contains the full list of the plants in Charlemagne's *Capitulare de Villis* and in other medieval writings, as well as the quotations from Walafridus Strabo and Alexander Neckham. *Sharp Practice*, 1 & 2 & 3 (Edinburgh, 1986–90), report on the important work being done during the excavations at Soutra, which are revealing medieval medical techniques. Marie Luise Gothein, *A History of Garden Art* (2 vols., London, 1928), contains the plans of St Gall and Westminster and the Botanic Garden at Oxford. For the references to Andrew Marvell on Eden and the introductory poem to the catalogue of plants in the Oxford Botanic Gardens, I am grateful to John Prest, *The Garden of Eden: The Botanic Garden and the Re-Creation of Paradise* (New Haven, Connecticut, 1981).

Elizabeth B. Moynihan, *Paradise as a Garden: In Persia and Mughal India* (London, 1980), broke important new ground. William L. Hanaway, Jr, identified 'The Vegetation of the Earthly Garden' in his paper to the Fourth Dumbarton Oaks

Colloquium in *The Islamic Garden* in 1976. Lise Manniche, *An Ancient Egyptian Herbal* (London, 1989), revealed the latest research into the botany of the Pharaohs. The four rivers that flowed from Eden were identified in biblical commentary as the Euphrates and the Tigris or Hiddekel, the Phison and the Gihon: the last two were later thought to be the Nile and the Ganges. John Prest, *The Garden of Eden* (New Haven, Connecticut, 1981), is essential reading on the subject.

The quotation on the enclosed biblical garden comes from Teresa McLean, *Medieval English Gardens* (London, 1981), an important study. Eleanour Sinclair Rohde has made a study of *Garden-Craft in the Bible* (London, 1927). For the section on the medieval significance of the rose, I am indebted to Allen Paterson, *The History of the Rose* (London, 1983); and to Eithne Wilkins, whose book *The Rose Garden Game* (London, 1969) is a pioneering work on the meaning of the rose in the cult of the Virgin Mary.

It is interesting that on his copy of *Extracta E Chronices Scotie* (Edinburgh Advocates Library MS. 356.13), Sir William Sinclair of Rosslyn wrote in his own hand in 1569 about Robin Hood as a historical character. See Bishop Latimer, *Sermons* (London, 1906), and Philip Stubbes, *Diaries* (Furnivall, ed., 2 vols., 1877–79), vol. I, p. 149. J.C. Holt, *Robin Hood* (rev. ed., London, 1989), is authoritative on the subject, although Holt will not recognize the connection with Robin of the Woods. Nathaniel Johnston's drawing of Hood's tombstone is to be found in Richard Gough, *Sepulchral Monuments of Great Britain* (London, 1786), while the verse from the Robin Hood play and the lines from Andrew de Wyntoun are quoted by Holt.

9. Sailing to the West

The only example of the *Gemma Frisius-Mercator* globe of 1537 is in the Schlossmuseum at Zerbst in Germany, while the only example of the Vopell-Vavassatore map in good condition is in the Houghton Library at Harvard. It was drawn from English, French, Spanish and Portuguese voyages of discovery in the previous decades. Michael Bradley and Deanna Theilmann-Bean, in *Holy Grail Across the Atlantic* (Ontario, 1988), have some insights into the presence of the Templars on Prince Henry St Clair's expedition to Canada. They have also carried out investigations of Oak Island and of other rubble-stone foundations in Nova Scotia. Their general conclusions, however, about the Grail and a conspiracy of the descendants of the Holy Blood to colonize America are most speculative.

Mercator's map of 1569 was published at Duisberg. I am grateful for details of the use of the *Zeno Map* to *A Book of Old Maps* (comp. and ed. by E.D. Fite & A. Freeman, Cambridge, Massachusetts, 1926). Most important on the accuracy of the *Zeno Map* is Miller Christy, *The Silver Map of the World* (London, 1890). The text on the 1693 globe in the Correr Museum reads in the original:

NUOVA FRANCIA

ESTOTILANDIA

THE NEW BRETAIGNE

TIERRA DE LABRADOR *scoperta Ser Antonio Zen Patrizio Veneto nel 1390 primo gli altri Paesi dell' America Fossero conosciuti.*

See Rodney W. Shirley, *The Early Mapping of the World: Early Printed World Maps 1472–1700* (vol. 9, London, 1984); and W.F. Ganong, *Crucial Maps in the Early Cartography and Place – Nomenclature of the Atlantic Coast of Canada* (Toronto, 1933). Also see Leo Bagrow, *Giovanni Andreas di Vavassore: A Descriptive List of His Maps* (Jenkintown, 1939).

Johann Reinhold Forster first suggested that Icaria was Kerry in the eighteenth century, and many other early supporters of the veracity of the *Zeno Narrative* and *Map* have agreed with him, including Humboldt, *Examen critique de l'Histoire de la Géographie* (Paris, 1837–9), vol. II, p. 122; Joachim Lelewel, *Géographie du Moyen Age* (Brussels, 1852–7), vol. II, pp. 84, 169; Count Miniscalchi Erizzo, *Le Scoperte Antiche* (Venice, 1855); Gravier, *Découverte de l'Amerique par les Normands au X Siècle* (Paris, 1874); Cornelio Desimoni, *I Viaggi e la Carta dei Fratelli Zeno Veneziana, 1390–1405* (Florence, 1878), and Adolf Erik Baron von Nordenskiöld (Stockholm, 1883), who proves conclusively how far in advance was the *Zeno Map* of all preceding maps of the northern seas, even that of Olafus Magnus.

Nicolò Zeno's other writing included the *Storia della guerra Veneto – Turca del 1537 in 4 libri*, see BMV, Ms. It. Cl. VII 2053 (7920). Other published works were *Dell Origine de Venetia et Antiquissime memorie de i Barbari che distrussero l'imperio de Roma* (Venice, 1558); and *Trattato dell'Origine et costumi de gli Arabi* (Venice, 1582). The Hakluyt Society republished the Ramusio Version of the *Zeno Narrative* and *Map* (op. cit), and of Caterino Zeno's *Travels in Persia* (London, 1873).

Professor William Herbert Hobbs, 'Zeno and the Cartography of Greenland', was published in *Imago Mundi*; his 'The Fourteenth-Century Discovery of America by Antonio Zeno' appeared in *Scientific Monthly*, vol. 72, 1951. He substantiated the accuracy of Nicolò Zen's first report from Greenland, as did Professor E.G.R. Taylor and Sigurd Amundsen, 'Zeno Truth Obscured by Smoke', in *The Geographical Magazine*, vol. 49, 1977. The most important supporters of the accuracy of the *Zeno Map* are Captain A. H. Mallory, *Lost America* (Columbus, 1954), and Charles H. Hapgood, *Map of the Ancient Sea Kings* (New York, 1966). Lauge Koch, D. McL. Johnson and Helga Larsen have corroborated the evidence of medieval Viking ecclesiastical settlements in eastern Greenland.

I am deeply grateful to Michael Richey for showing me 'The Navigational Background to 1492', a chapter of his unfinished seminal work on medieval navigation. See also E.G.R. Taylor, *The Haven Finding Art* (London, 1956), and T. Campbell, 'Portolan Charts from the Late Thirteenth Century to 1500', *The History of Cartography* (J. Harley and D. Woodward, eds., Chicago, 1987). The research on the myth of Atlantis and Arcadia derives from my own *The Naked Savage* (London, 1991), and from Lewis Spence, *The History of Atlantis* (New York, 1968).

10. Earl and Prince of Orkney

The claims of Henry St Clair to the Earldom of Orkney are fully documented in the 'Deduction concerning the genealogies of the Ancient Counts of Orkney, from their First Creation to the Fifteenth Century. Drawn up from the most authentic Records by Thomas, Bishop of Orkney, with the assistance of his Clergy and others', June 1446, at Kirkwall. The full text of the Deed of Investiture of 2 August 1379, is printed in Latin in Thormodus Torfaeus, *Orcades, seu rerum Orcadensium historiae* (Hauniae, 1697), and translated into English in Thomas Sinclair, *Caithness Events* (Wick, 1899). It reads as follows:

To all who shall see or hear the present letters Henry, Earl of the Orkneys, Lord of Roslin, wishes salvation in the Lord. Because the very serene prince in Christ, my most clement lord, Haquin, by the grace of God the king of the kingdoms of Norway and Sweden, has set us by his favour over the Orcadian lands and islands, and has raised us into the rank of jarl over the beforesaid lands and islands, and since this is required by the dignity, we make well known to all, as well to posterity as to contemporaries, that we have made homage of fidelity to our lord the king himself, at the kiss of his hand and mouth, and have given him a true and due oath of fidelity, as far as counsels and aids to our same lord the king, his heirs and successors, and to his kingdom of Norway, must be observed. And so, let it be open to all that we and our friends, whose names are expressed lower, have firmly promised in faith and with our honour to our same lord the king, and to his men and councillors, that we must faithfully fulfil all arrangements, conditions, promises, and articles which are contained in the present letters to our beforesaid lord the king, his heirs and successors, and to his kingdom of Norway.

In the first place, therefore, we firmly oblige us to serve our lord the king outside the lands and islands of the Orkneys, with one hundred good men or more, equipped in complete arms, for the conveniences and use of our same lord the king, whenever we shall have been sufficiently requisitioned by his messengers or his letters, and forewarned within Orkney three months. But when the men shall have arrived in the presence of our lord the king, from that time he will provide about victuals for us and ours.

Again, if any may wish to attack or hostilely to invade, in any manner whatsoever, the lands and islands of the Orkneys, or the land of Zetland, then we promise and oblige us to defend the lands named, with men whom we may be able to collect in good condition for this solely, from the lands and islands themselves, yea, with all the force of relatives, friends, and servants.

Also, if it shall be necessary that our lord the king attack any lands or any kingdoms, by right or from any other reason or necessity, then we shall be to him in help and service with all our force.

Moreover, we promise in good faith that we must not build or construct castles or any fortifications within the lands and islands beforesaid, unless we shall have obtained the favour, good-pleasure, and consent of our same lord the king.

We also shall be bound to hold and to cherish the said lands and islands of the Orkneys, and all their inhabitants, clergymen and laity, rich and poor in their rights.

Further we promise in good faith that we must not at any time sell or alienate that beforesaid county and that lordship, whether lands or islands, belonging to the earldom, or our right which we obtain now to the earldom, the lands, and islands by the grace of God and of the king our lord, from our lord the king himself, or his heirs, and successors, or from the kingdom, nor to deliver these or any of these for surety and for pledge to any one or to expose them otherwise, against the will and good-pleasure of him and his successors.

In addition, if it happen that our lord the king, his heirs, or successors wish to approach those lands and islands for their defence, or from other reasonable cause, or to direct thither his councillors or men, then we shall be held to be for help to our same lord the king, and his heirs, to his councillors and men, with all our force, and to minister our lord the king, and his heirs, his men and councillors, those things of which they may be in need for their due expenses, and as necessity then requires, at least to ordain so from the lands and islands.

Moreover, we promise that we must begin or rouse no war, law suit, or discussion with any strangers or natives, by reason of which war, law suit, or discussion the king my lord, his heirs, or successors, or their kingdoms of Norway, or the beforesaid lands and islands, may receive any damage.

Again, if it happen, but may this be absent, that we notably and unjustly do wrong against any within the beforesaid lands and islands, or inflict some notable injury upon any one, as the loss of life, or mutilation of limbs, or depredation of goods, then we shall answer to the pursuer of a cause of that kind in the presence of our lord the king himself and his councillors, and satisfy for the wrongs according to the laws of the kingdom.

Also, whensoever our lord the king shall have summoned us, on account of any good causes, to his presence, where and when he shall have wished to hold his general assembly, then we are bound to go to him, to give him advice and assistance.

Further, we promise that we shall not break the truces and security of the same lord the king, nor his peace, which he shall have made or confirmed with foreigners or natives, or with whomsoever others, in any manner whatever, to violate them, nay, defend them all as far as our strength, and hold those as federated to us whom the king of Norway himself, our lord, may wish to treat as his favourers and friends.

We promise also that we must make no league with the Orcadian bishop, nor enter into or establish any friendship with him, unless from the good-pleasure and consent of our lord the king himself; but we must be for help to him against that bishop, until he shall have done to him what is of right, or shall be bound to do so for that special reason, upon those things in which my lord the king may wish or be able reasonably to accuse that bishop.

Besides, when God may have willed to call us from life, then that earldom and that lordship, with the lands and islands, and with all the jurisdiction, must return to our lord the king, his heirs and successors freely; and if we shall have children after us, procreated from our body, male, one or more, then he of them who shall claim the above said earldom and lordship must demand, with regard to this, the favour, good pleasure, and consent of our lord the king himself, his heirs, and successors.

Further, we promise in good faith that we shall be bound to pay our abovesaid lord the king, or to his official at Tunisberg, on the next festival of St. Martin the bishop and confessor, a thousand golden pieces, which are called nobles, of English money, in which we acknowledge us to be bound to him by just payment.

Also we promise, because we have been now promoted to the earldom and lordship oftensaid by our lord the king himself, that our cousin Malise Sparre must cease from his claim, and dismiss altogether his right, if it be discernible that he has any, to those lands and islands; so that my lord the king, his heirs and successors shall sustain no vexation or trouble from him or from his heirs.

Again, if we have made any agreement or any understanding with our cousin Alexander Ard, or have wished to enter into any treaty with him, in that case we will do similarly on our part and on the part of the king my lord to whatever was done in precaution about Malise Sparre.

Further, we, Henry, earl abovesaid, and our friends and relatives within written, namely, Simon Rodde, William Daniels, knights, Malise Sparre, William Chrichton, David Chrichton, Adam Byketon, Thomas Bennine, and Andrew Haldaniston, armsbearers, conjunctly promise in good faith to our oftensaid lord the king, Haquin, and to his first-born lord the king, Olaf, and to his councillors and men within-written, namely to the lords Siguard, Haffthorsen, Ogmund Findersen, Eric Ketelsen, Narvo Ingualdisen, John Oddosen, Ulpho Johnsen, Ginther de Vedhonsen; John Danisen, Haquin Evidassen, knights of the same lord the king; Haquin Jonssen, Alver Hardlssen, Hantho Ericsen, Erlend Philippsen and Otho Remer, armsbearers; and for this, under preservation of our honour, we bind ourselves and each of us in a body to the aforesaid lords, that we must truly and firmly fulfil all the agreements and conditions and articles which are expressed above to our lord the king, within the above-written feast of St. Martin the bishop and confessor, so far as one particular business was declared by itself above.

That all these things now promised may have the greater strength for this, and may be fulfilled the sooner, we, the aforesaid Henry, Earl of the Orkneys, place and leave behind us our cousins and friends Lord William Daniels, knight, Malise Sparre, David Chrichton, and the lawful son of the said Simon, by name Lord Alexander, here in the kingdom hostages. Upon their faith they oblige and promise themselves to this that from our lord the king of Norway, or from that place in which he shall have wished to have them within his kingdom of Norway, they in nowise may go away, publicly or secretly, before all the abovesaid things be totally fulfilled with entire integrity to our lord the king; and particularly and specially, the conditions and articles for whose observation the within-written reverend fathers, bishops, and prelates of the churches of the kingdom of Scotland, and the other nobles within-written of the same kingdom, Lord William, Bishop of St. Andrews; Lord Walter, bishop of Glasgow; Lord William, Earl of Douglas; Lord George, Earl of March; Lord Patrick Hepburn, Lord Alexander Haliburton, Lord George Abernethy, Lord William Ramsay, knights, must promise in good faith, and upon this remit their open letters to our same king the lord, with their true seals, in the before-noted time, as in our other letters written upon this is declared more fully.

Also, we promise in good faith that we must assume in no direction to us the lands of our lord the king, or any other rights of his which his progenitors and the king our lord are known to have reserved to themselves; and concerning those lands or jurisdictions not to intromit in any manner whatsoever. They have reserved those laws indeed, and those pleas within the Orcadian earldom, as is before said, and the lands and pleas of that kind will remain in all cases safe for them; but if, upon this, we shall have his special letters, then we ought to be specially bound thereafter to our same lord the king.

Besides, but may it be absent, if all those abovesaid things shall not have been brought to conclusion, and totally fulfilled to the same my lord the king as it has been expressed above, or if we should have attempted anything in the contrary of any of the premises, then the promotion and favour which we have experienced from the king our lord, and of his grace, ought to be of no strength; yea, the promotion and favour of that kind done to us must be broken down altogether, and in their forces be totally empty and inane, so that we and our heirs for the rest shall have no right of speaking for the beforesaid county or for the lands or beforesaid islands, or we of acting about those lands and islands in any way whatsoever, that it may be manifest to all that the promotion and grace of this kind was given by no force of law or justice.

And so we append our seal, together with the seals of our said friends, to present letters, in testimony and the firmer evidence of all the premises.

These things were done at Marstrand, in the year of the Lord 1379, the 2nd day of August.

The quotations from Father Hay came from his *Genealogie of the Sainteclaires of Rosslyn* (Edinburgh, 1835). The biography of Carlo Zen by Bishop Giacomo of Padua is preserved in the Marciana Library at Venice, see Muratori, *RIS*, vol. 19. Although Carlo's meeting with the Scottish Prince is ascribed to a later period in his life, the chronology of the biography is accurate and based on stories told by the heroic grandfather without reference to due date. *The Register of the Great Seal of Scotland,* AD 1306–1424 was edited in a new edition by John Maitland Thomson and printed in Edinburgh in 1984. King Robert of Scotland's Resignation of Orkney is quoted in Alexander Nisbet, *A System of Heraldry* (Edinburgh, 1816); Nisbet further claimed that Prince Henry St Clair was Duke of Oldenburg because of his first marriage to a Danish princess, as well as 'knight of the Thistle, knight of the Cockle, and knight of the Golden Fleece.' Frederick J. Pohl quoted the besieger of the Kirkwall Castle in *Prince Henry Sinclair: His Expedition to the New World in 1398* (New York, 1974). *The Icelandic Annals* tell us of the death of Bishop William of Orkney, 'killed or burnt by his flock'. The *Diplomatarium Norvegicum*, vol. 2, no. 515 (Oslo, 1852), tells of Prince Henry St Clair's commitment to the Shetlands. Barbara E. Crawford is the authority on the situation in medieval Orkney; her article 'William Sinclair, Earl of Orkney, and His Family: A Study in the Politics of Survival (privately printed), has informed the writing of this chapter, and the quotation comes from her article.

11. The Zen Voyage

Nicolò Zeno's frank admission that he had destroyed his ancestors' book and letters and worked from a sailing chart 'rotten with age' has been held by his two leading enemies as a clever stratagem to excuse the discrepancies in his published *Narrative* and *Map*. Although his account was generally believed and used by distinguished cartographers and explorers until the nineteenth century, it was attacked by Admiral Zahrtmann in 1836 in the fifth volume of the *Journal of the Royal Geographical Society*, and by Frederick W. Lucas in *The Annals of the Voyages of the Brothers Nicolò and Antonio Zeno in the North Atlantic About the End of the Fourteenth Century, and the Claim Founded Thereon to a Venetian Discovery of America, a Criticism and an Indictment* (London, 1898). The first attack was ably refuted by Richard Henry Major in his introduction to his edition of the *Zeno Narrative* and *Map* for the Hakluyt Society in London in 1873, while many defenders of the general veracity of Nicolò Zeno have replied to Lucas's assault, beginning with Miller Christy in his erudite *The Silver Map of the World* (London, 1900). Other defenders are quoted in my text or notes, while identifications of proper place names are contained in my notes on my retranslation of the *Zeno Narrative* in the appendix. It is regretful that Samuel Eliot Morrison, in his influential *The European Discovery of America: The Northern Voyages,* AD 500–1600 (Oxford, 1971), chose to believe F.W. Lucas and did not do any primary research on Venetian sources nor conduct any archaeological research in Nova Scotia.

For the equation of Estotilanda with Markland, I am indebted to Professor E.G.R. Taylor, 'A Fourteenth-Century Riddle – and Its Solution', *The Geographical Review*, vol. 54, 1964. As she also stated in 'The Fisherman's Story, 1354', *The Geographical Magazine*, vol. 37, 1964, 'The authenticity of the account has been challenged but on very flimsy grounds. It appears to the present writer to be quite out of the question that any author would invent a story which in its every detail reflects facts of which it is impossible that he would have been aware. Such is the story of Markland which Antonio Zen, then in the Faroes, related in a letter to his brother Carlo in Venice . . .'

In his *Prince Henry Sinclair* (New York, 1974), Frederick J. Pohl used the discovery by the geologist William H. Hobbs of asphalt flowing into the sea in the Stellarton area of Nova Scotia to identify Prince Henry St Clair's harbours at Pictou and Guysborough. Michael Bradley with Deanna Theilmann-Bean in *Holy Grail across the Atlantic*, (Ontario, 1988), made much of the rubble-stone remains at The Cross and Oak Island, Nova Scotia. I am grateful to James P. Whittall, Jr. of the Early Sites Research Society for showing me Malcolm Pearson's photograph of the pre-Columbian cannon at Louisburg, and to Christine Kavanagh for introducing me to Alex Storm. The Victorian who described the second ringed cannon at St Peter's was R.G. Haliburton in *Popular Science Monthly*, May, 1885. For research on the Westford Knight and the Newport Tower I am again indebted to James P. Whittall, Jr. In a stimulating paper, David Trubey writes about the two camps that appeared in Westford on the subject of the authenticity of the knight on the rock. The correspondence between Frank Glynn and T.C. Lethbridge is preserved in the helpful Westford Library.

A.H. Mallory, C.E. Gardner and J. Howieson made a special interim report to the Council of the City of Newport on 20 October 1955, stating that the Tower was not a colonial windmill or the summer house of Governor Benedict Arnold. It may have been a Viking tower or a Christian church, but undoubtedly was the oldest European building standing on the mainland of America.

Edward Adams Richardson's study of the Newport Tower, *Journal of the Surveying and Mapping Division, Proceedings of the American Society of Civil Engineers*, February, 1960, comments on the fourteenth century fireplace on the first floor of the tower and on the engineering as unsuitable for a windmill. To him it was a signals station for ships entering the bay. The report of 1632 that mentions a 'rownd stone towre' in the Public Records Office is *The Commodities of the Island Called Manate or Long Isle Within the Continent of Virginia*. It also refers to New England and is reproduced in *Collections of the New York Historical Society for 1869*, vol. II, pp. 217–8. E.A. Richardson, C.S. Peirce, Frederick J. Pohl and H.R. Holand have all confirmed that the design measurements are those of the Scottish ell or Rhineland-Norse yard, two of which make up a fathom. (Its exact length is 0.31374 metres, or 37.063 inches.)

The William Wood map is contained in *A Book of Old Maps* (Emerson D. Fite and Archibald Freeman, eds., Cambridge, Massachusetts, 1926). The weight in stone of the tower is over 200 tons, requiring a sizable colony to construct it. Philip Mears, *The Newport Tower* (Newport, 1942), further destroyed the validity of the case that Governor Benedict Arnold built the tower as a windmill. William S. Godfrey's dig of the surrounds of the tower, reported in *Archaeology*, Summer, 1950, discovered only artifacts nearby, but did not invalidate an earlier origin of the tower.

The director of the National Museum of Denmark is Dr Johannes Brøndsted, and his remarks on the Newport Tower were published in *Aarbog før Nordisk Oldkyndighed og Historie*, 1950. Charles M. Boland, *They All Discovered America*, claims that aerial survey pictures taken by the Commodity Stabilisation Service in 1951 revealed evidence of a nave attached to the Newport Tower. Other archaeological digs are planned, which may soon resolve the dating of this structure. Eric Fernie wrote the article 'The Church of St. Magnus, Egilsay', in the admirable collection of essays, *St. Magnus Cathedral and Orkney's Twelfth Century Renaissance* (Barbara E. Crawford, ed., Aberdeen Univ., 1988). The *Orkneyinga Saga* tells of the martyrdom of St Magnus. The armorial experts who have identified the period of the sword hilt of the Westford Knight include those from the Armory of the Tower of London.

Frederick J. Pohl, *Prince Henry Sinclair* (New York, 1974), particularly emphasises the correspondences between Prince Henry and the Glooscap legends. My enquiries with present Micmac scholars make me certain that the Glooscap legend antedated the arrival of Prince Henry's expedition to Cape Breton Island. However much he added to the myth, it is clear that he did not exploit the Indians as Columbus would do. His good behaviour left a remembrance of a superior and wise being. The quotations are taken from the Reverend Silas Rand, *Legends of the Micmacs* (New York, 1894); and C.G. Leland and J.D. Prince, *Kulo' skap the Master and Other Algonkin Poems* (New York, 1902). The quotations about the death of Prince Henry St Clair come from Father Hay's *Genealogie of the Saintclaires of Rosslyn* (Edinburgh, 1835), and the 1446 Diploma of the Bishop of Orkney, also cited.

12. The Templars and the Masons

Parentalia, or Memoirs of the Family of the Wrens; but Chiefly of Sir Christopher Wren was compiled by his son Christopher and published in London in 1750. The leading researcher on *King Solomon's Temple in the Masonic Tradition* (London, 1972) is Alexander Horne, a Thirty-third Degree Mason. I am deeply indebted to his scholarly enquiry and have quoted from him. The Question and Answer of the Masonic catechism are taken from *Jachin and Boaz*, a London Lodge catechism of 1762. The creed of the Templars from the *Léviticon* is quoted in the significant book by A. Bothwell-Gosse, *The Knights Templar* (London, 1910). J.N. Casavis, *The Greek Origin of Freemasonry* (New York, 1955), tells of Dionysian roots. The poem on the Four Crowned Martyrs is the medieval *Ars Quatuor Coronatorum*. D. Knoop, G.P. Jones and D. Hamer edited the *Cooke MS* in *The Two Earliest Masonic MSS* (Manchester, 1938). They also edited *The Early Masonic Catechisms* (Manchester, 1943), which included the *Chetwode Crawley MS* of about AD 1700, relating to the original Lodge of Kilwinning. A Grand Commander of the American Temple, Albert Pike, in *Morals and Dogma of the Ancient and Accepted Scottish Rite* (Washington, DC, 1871), asserted the theory of the dual beliefs of the

Templars ending in 'Occult, Hermetic, or Scottish Masonry'.

The quotation from Cyril of Alexandria derives from his *Contra Julianum*. Michael Mifsud, a senior modern Templar, sees *Beauséant* as a battle-cry for Paradise. The reference to Hiram's being translated to Heaven like Enoch in Rabbinic legend is taken from Joseph Fort Newton's interesting *The Builders: A Story & Study of Masonry* (London, 1918), while the quotation comes from the *Jewish Encyclopedia* (New York, 1901). The Templar connection with bringing back the legend of Hiram from the Holy Land is quoted from G.W. Speth, *Builders' Rites and Ceremonies: The Folk Lore of Masonry* (Ars Quatuor Coronatorum Pamphlet, London, 1951). The confession of the Hiram legend and Masonic hand signals comes from S. Vatcher, 'John Coustos and the Portuguese Inquisition', *Ars Quatuor Coronatorum*, vol. 81, 1968. The quotation on the association of Hiram and the Apprentice Pillar legends is to be found in Albert G. Mackey, *Encyclopedia of Freemasonry* (2 vols., revised edn, Chicago, 1946). I also quote from W.L. Wilmsherst, *The Meaning of Masonry* (London, 1922).

The Kilwinning Catechism is taken from the *Chetwode Crawley MS* of about 1700, reproduced in D. Knoop, G.P. Jones and D. Hamer, *The Early Masonic Catechisms* (Manchester, 1943). Kilwinning always believed that it was the first Scottish Lodge and that this was founded in the Middle Ages. Later, on the foundation of the Grand Lodge of Scotland in 1736, Masonic historians of the Hanoverian and Protestant persuasion denigrated the claims of the Jacobite and Catholic St Clair family and Kilwinning to the hereditary Grand Mastership and priority among lodges. They preferred to play down the 1600 Schaw petition of the Scottish Masons, which acknowledged the hereditary Grand Mastership of the Lords of Rosslyn: 'From age to age . . . ever . . . patrons and protectors of us and our privileges.' The Lodge at Kirkwall still keeps a copy of the medieval original Teaching Scroll.

13. The Fall of the Sancto Claros

Essential reading on the St Clair Earls of Orkney are two articles by Barbara E. Crawford: 'The Fifteenth-Century 'Genealogy of the Earls of Orkney' and Its Reflection on the Contemporary Political and Cultural Situation in the Earldom,' *Medieval Scandinavia*, vol. 10, 1976; and 'William Sinclair, Earl of Orkney, and His Family: A Study in the Politics of Survival'.

Gavin Douglas called Lord Henry Sinclair 'Fader of bukis . . .' Father Hay is always indispensable on the history of the St Clair family. Thomas Sinclair, in his *Caithness Events* (Wick, 1899), is most entertaining on the Sinclair family. Some idea of the riches of the Sinclair family in the fifteenth century can be found in the Inventory of the Goods of Alexander Southerland, MCCCCLVI, reprinted by Father Hay, in which he gives a Chalice to the new College Church of Roslin. The Black Rood and the Newbattle Silver Cross were variously described in Durham Cathedral in *Antiquities of the Abbey and Cathedral Church of Durham* and in *Rites of Durham* by the Surtees Society.

An article in the *Dundee Courier*, 11 April 1991, pointed out that the Stone of Scone remains in Scotland. It was exhibited in 1990 at the People's Palace in Glasgow and seen by more than half a million visitors. The Knights Templars of Scotland intend to house the Stone in the former church of the village of Dull near Aberfeldy.

In the National Library of Scotland are preserved the Bond of Mary of Guise of 3 June 1546; the Acts of the Lords in Council on Public Affairs of 21 March 1545; the Right of Passage from Marie de Guise to Sir William St Clair of 14 June 1556; her Commission to him of 20 January 1559; and the arrest warrant of William and Oliver Sinclair of 1 September 1567. The account of the benefactions of Henry, Earl of Orkney, is taken from R.W. Saint-Clair, *The Saint-Clairs of the Isles* (Auckland, 1898), p. 109, and from Thomas Hearne, *The Antiquities of Great Britain* (London, 1735). The Schaw petition of 1600 and the Masonic petition of 1630 and the St Clair renunciation of 1736 are reprinted and analysed in David Murray Lyon, *History of the Lodge of Edinburgh* (Edinburgh, 1873), and in Robert Freke Gould, *The History of Freemasonry* (2 vols., London, 1885). Although both historians admit the authenticity of all the documents, they are somewhat hostile to the St Clair claims to the hereditary Grand Mastership, owing to a Protestant belief in the Hanoverian Succession, which was opposed to the St Clair covert support of the Stewarts and Catholicism.

The earlier and seminal book by William Alexander Laurie, *The History of Free Masonry and the Grand Lodge of Scotland* (Edinburgh, 1850), fully supports the St Clair position as hereditary Grand Masters for five centuries.

The final mob attack on Rosslyn Chapel and Castle was on 11 December 1688, and was recorded by Father Hay in his cited history of the St Clairs of Rosslyn; Dorothy Wordsworth visited the ruined chapel with the poet William Wordsworth on 17 September 1803, and wrote of its melancholy and exquisite beauty in her diary.

Peter Partner, *The Murdered Magicians: The Templars and Their Myth* (Oxford, 1982), shows that the rebirth of Templarism took place in Germany, where egalitarian Freemasonry was resisted by an elitist society, and there was a demand for a version of the Masonic craft acceptable to conservative taste. A man claiming to be a Scottish Templar, who went under the name of George Frederick Johnson, asserted the legend of the Templar treasure surrendered by Jacques de Molay. Charles Gotthelf, Baron von Hund and Alten-grotkare, was also influential in recruiting aristocratic Templars, including twelve German reigning princes: they were much influenced by *Parzifal* and *Titurel* and the myths of the Holy Grail. See Robert Bryden, 'The Germanic Tradition, the Scottish Knights and the Mystery of the Holy Grail', *The Scottish Knights Templar*, Winter 1984/85. I am also indebted to Robert Bryden for information on the relationship of Rudolf Hess with Rosslyn Chapel in a letter of 8 May 1991. The conspiracy theory of the Templars is stressed in Josef von Hammer-Purgstall, *Le Mystère de Baphomet Revélé* (Paris, 1818). The downfall of the St Clairs because of their loyalty to the Stewarts is described in the Memoirs of John, Master of St Clair; these are quoted in Charles Mackie, *Historical Description of the Chapel and Castle of Roslin and the Caverns of Hawthornden* (Edinburgh, 1830).

Epilogue, 2002

Most of the important findings on Rosslyn and the Zeno Voyage in the last decade have been the result of a lifetime's work on the Newport Tower by the late James P. Whittall Jr of the Early Sites Research Center, and by Niven Sinclair, under whose generous auspices a Sinclair Symposium was held in Kirkwall, Orkney, in the summer of 1997. At the conference, I was able to present my further Venetian and medieval architectural researches, also to view and record the fifteenth-century Templar and Masonic Scroll hanging in Lodge Kirkwall Kilwinning No. 38.[2] These discoveries are fully documented in my book, *The Secret Scroll* (London, 2001), and my film for the History Channel, *The Holy Grail and the Secret Scroll*, first broadcast at Easter 2002.

The likely dating of the voyages of Antonio and Nicolò Zeno with their Scottish prince to Orkney and the Shetlands, Greenland and the New World, has been the subject of much controversy. An article by A. de Mosto of 1933, 'I navigatori Nicolò e Antonio Zeno', published in Florence in *Ad Alessandro Luzio, Miscellanea di studi storici*, questioned the dating of the Zeno brothers' voyage to the northern seas, given the dates of Nicolò's other engagements as attested in the Venetian archives. His article was followed by Brian Cuthbertson, 'Voyages to North America Before John Cabot: Separating Fact from Fiction', a paper read before the Royal Nova Scotia Historical Society on 15 November 1994. He was unaware of the brilliant refutation of Mosta by Giorgio Padoan in *Quaderni Veneti* (Ravenna, 1989). His researches and my own inquiries in the Libreria Marciana confirmed the dates for Antonio and Nicolò Zeno given in this text, which even Cuthbertson had to admit were borne out by the Venetian records. This revised dating of Venice's push to the north allows for the long sojourn of the Zen brothers in the Orcadian Isles.

The *Rudimentium Novitorium* and the De Virga map of Venetian trade of 1414 were brought to my attention by Gunnar Thompson in his remarkable *The Friar's Map of Ancient America, 1360* AD (Seattle, Washington, 1996). Niven Sinclair has particularly emphasized the importance of the Northern Commonwealth, and with James Whittall, the many emerging proofs of European colonization of North America in the Middle Ages. Their pamphlets on Prince Henry Sinclair are invaluable.

Index

Note: Names beginning with 'St' are indexed as spelt, but Christian saints are indexed under their name. At some time the St Clair family began to be known as Sinclair. Anything relating to the families in general is indexed under St Clair, but individuals usually referred to as Sinclair in the text are indexed under that name. The abbreviation '*fl.*' (flourished) with a date has in a few cases been used to distinguish people of the same name.